Singing the Congregation

Singing the Congregation

*How Contemporary Worship Music
Forms Evangelical Community*

Monique M. Ingalls

OXFORD
UNIVERSITY PRESS

OXFORD
UNIVERSITY PRESS

Oxford University Press is a department of the University of Oxford. It furthers
the University's objective of excellence in research, scholarship, and education
by publishing worldwide. Oxford is a registered trade mark of Oxford University
Press in the UK and certain other countries.

Published in the United States of America by Oxford University Press
198 Madison Avenue, New York, NY 10016, United States of America.

Library of Congress Cataloging-in-Publication Data
Names: Ingalls, Monique Marie, author.
Title: Singing the congregation : how contemporary worship music forms
evangelical community / Monique M. Ingalls.
Description: New York, NY : Oxford University Press, 2018. |
Includes bibliographical references and index.
Identifiers: LCCN 2018008017 | ISBN 9780190499631 (hardcover) |
ISBN 9780190499648 (pbk.) | ISBN 9780190499679 (oxford scholarly online).
Subjects: LCSH: Contemporary Christian music—History and criticism. |
Evangelicalism—Social aspects—United States.
Classification: LCC ML3187.5 .I65 2018 | DDC 264/.2—dc23
LC record available at https://lccn.loc.gov/2018008017

For Jason, Georgia, and Jennie

CONTENTS

ILLUSTRATIONS

FIGURES

TABLES

ACKNOWLEDGMENTS

I owe a great debt of gratitude to the many professional colleagues, community contacts, and friends who have encouraged, inspired, pushed, prodded, funded, or otherwise supported the writing of this monograph.

I wish to thank my mentors and colleagues at the University of Pennsylvania, where the idea for this project was birthed during Ph.D. work. Deepest thanks to Timothy Rommen, who encouraged my interest in this topic and has been a perpetual source of inspiration and advice long after the dissertation was complete. I am grateful for faculty colleagues and fellow academic visitors at the University of Cambridge, particularly Nicholas Cook, Juniper Hill, Lisa Margulis, Joel Cabrita, and the members of the Digital Humanities Forum and Locating Religion Research Group for their comments on my work, their insights on the publishing process, and their feedback when I was applying for the various research grants that funded ethnographic work for this project. And I'm thankful to my Cambridge graduate research assistant Melissa Wong for her help transcribing and coding interviews. The Yale Institute of Sacred Music provided a semester of research leave, which allowed me to focus on shaping this book manuscript and afforded me several opportunities to present and refine my work. I'm grateful to Martin Jean, Teresa Berger, Maggi Dawn, Markus Rathey, and the ISM graduate student cohort for many stimulating conversations and for engaging closely with my work during my time at Yale. And I continue to deeply appreciate the support and encouragement of my colleagues at Baylor University. A summer sabbatical grant and a course release helped provide the time and resources I needed to complete the book's final chapters. Randall Bradley, David Music, and Timothy McKinney have been supportive and encouraging of my work on this project and have worked diligently—and sometimes sacrificially—to help me protect my research time during my hectic first few years on the tenure track. Baylor doctoral students in church music, especially Nathan Myrick, Marcell Steuernagel, Maria Monteiro, Sam Eatherton, Joseph Noelliste, and Jacob Sensenig, were critical and constructive conversation partners, engaging deeply with the issues that inform this manuscript, alerting me to new sources across academic disciplines, and providing practical assistance along the way. I'm thankful to the Baylor library staff, particularly Clayton Crenshaw, Ellen Filgo, and Joshua Been, who have provided invaluable resource suggestions along the way. And I am especially grateful to my research assistant Nathan Myrick for his literature suggestions and bibliographic software wizardry.

I consider myself very fortunate to have an engaged network of colleagues invested in the academic study of music and religion who have inspired me to become a better thinker and writer. In particular, I owe a great debt of gratitude to Anna Nekola and Jonathan Dueck, who provided detailed comments on several chapter drafts and whose work has provided me with compelling models of clear thinking and engaging writing. I am thankful, too, for many enlivening conversations with my Christian Congregational Music conference co-organizers and Congregational Music Studies book-series editorial colleagues, including Martyn Percy, Mark Porter, Tom Wagner, Anna Nekola, Andrew Mall, Jeffers Engelhardt, Muriel Swijghuisen Reigersberg, Zoe Sherinian, and Carolyn Landau, who have informed my approach to this material. And I am grateful to these and other colleagues whose work on contemporary worship music, the ethnomusicology of Christianity, or music and religion more broadly continues to inform, challenge, and enrich my own. These include Philip Bohlman, Joshua Busman, Melvin Butler, Byron Dueck, Birgitta Johnson, Alisha Jones, Lim Swee Hong, Bo kyung Blenda Im, Gerardo Marti, Marissa Moore, Suzel Reily, Tanya Riches, Lester Ruth, Jeffrey Summit, Abigail Wood, and so many more.

There are several other individuals who have who have supported or enriched this publication. I'm thankful to Jen Edwards, Logan Craine, and the John Brown University Communications Office for providing a cover photo that is both beautiful and fitting—as it was taken in the very space in which my interest in studying contemporary worship music was first piqued—and to Cameron Akin for his expert Photoshop tweaks. I'm grateful for Suzanne Ryan's enthusiastic support of this project (particularly at those times I felt less enthused with it), and for Leslie Safford's thorough copyediting work. And heartfelt thanks to Joanna Smolko, my writing consultant, coach, and cheerleader, who helped keep me on track during the final months of preparing this manuscript.

My husband, Jason, has worn many hats during my work on this book as sounding board, tech wizard, promoter, therapist, priest, and engaged co-parent. Jason, thank you for encouraging me to persevere through the difficult times, for believing in the importance of this work, for praying for me, for expressing pride in my accomplishments, and for being willing to spend quite a bit of quality time with an infant and a toddler to enable my final push toward the finish line. I'm thankful to my daughter Georgia for being a good sleeper, allowing me productive evening and early morning work time. And I'm grateful to my daughter Jennie, born seven days after I submitted this book's initial draft, for providing me such a compelling motivation to meet the manuscript deadline.

Finally, I want to express my gratitude to the many evangelical individuals and Christian organizations that have provided the ethnographic bedrock of this study, for sharing their perspectives, helping me gain access to events and sources, and ultimately making this study possible. Thank you to the staff, former staff, and congregation members of St. Bartholomew's Church, particularly to Eric Wyse, Dixon Kinser, Jerry Smith, David Madeira, Don Cason, Brea Cox, Susan Houston, Gretchen Abernathy, and other members of St. B's music ministry for their willingness to direct me to helpful resources, for opening their homes to me on follow-up research trips, and for making time for coffee and conversation each time I returned to Nashville. Don Cason has provided key assistance in helping me understand the inner workings of the Christian music industry, in suggesting helpful contacts, and in securing permissions for copyrighted materials. Chuck Fromm has been an invaluable source of contacts in the Christian music and media industry over the years, and I'm grateful for the platform he has given me over the years to share my ideas with evangelical worship leaders. And to the hundreds of conversation partners whom I encountered at conferences, concerts, church services, public events, and online forums whom I am not able to acknowledge here by name, thank you for your openness in sharing your perspectives on music, worship, and community.

Singing the Congregation

INTRODUCTION

☙

Music Making Congregations:
Contemporary Worship Music
and Evangelical Modes
of Congregating

Since the late 1960s, there has been a revolution in the music of evangelical Protestantism: a new musical pop-rock style repertory for congregational singing—known variously as "contemporary worship music," "praise and worship music," or simply "worship music"—has made its way into evangelical churches across denominations and regions. It has become the musical lingua franca for evangelical churches in North America and beyond. Simultaneously a popular music, a vernacular music, and a sacred music, contemporary worship music is distinct from traditional hymns, on the one hand, and Christian pop music for personal listening, on the other. It engages worshipers in a variety of performance spaces that were once distinct, bridging public and private devotional practices, connecting online and offline communities, and bringing competing personal, institutional, and commercial interests into the same domains. As a result, the religious activity that participants understand as "worship" takes on new attributes as it becomes embedded within a range of other activities.

The adoption of this mass-mediated body of song for worship has inaugurated widespread changes not only in the sounds of congregational singing, but also in how evangelicals socially structure their music-making, experience worship, and, ultimately, understand themselves as a religious group. Because of its widespread reach, pervasive influence, and central place within the community's discourse, contemporary worship music can tell us much about the concerns, convictions, and commitments of evangelical congregations at the beginning of the twenty-first century. The contemporary worship music repertory is meaningful and affective because it spills over the bounds of church services, thoroughly pervading evangelical public ritual and the devotional practices of everyday life. The following ethnographic vignettes highlight three of the many social contexts in which this music is collectively performed outside local church worship and suggest the extent to which this music has become a touchstone of evangelical religious life.

October 21, 2007—Chris Tomlin Worship Concert in Nashville, Tennessee

I am standing in the middle of a crowd of three thousand others in the Allen Arena at Lipscomb University, located near the Green Hills neighborhood of southern Nashville. Nearly every seat in the square basketball arena looks down onto a central stage with a six-piece rock band accompanying the headlining artist, Chris Tomlin, a thirty-something guitar-playing singer who has written or popularized many widely known contemporary worship songs. Bright lights of varying colors flash around the arena, illuminating an exuberant, predominantly youthful crowd. Two gigantic screens that flank the stage contain lyrics projected in a font big enough that people from every corner of the arena can see them clearly and sing along with each song. Nearly all participants join in enthusiastically with the worship songs, often raising their hands toward the ceiling as they sway or jump in time to the music. As the final song of the concert begins, the stage lights are brought low and the mood becomes hushed and reverent. Tomlin removes his acoustic guitar and sits at a grand piano at center stage. White spotlights beam down on him as the rest of his band is shrouded in darkness. As Tomlin softly plays the opening chords, I recognize the song as "How Great Is Our God," a slow-tempo worship ballad that is currently a chart-topping hit on Christian radio as well as one of the most frequently sung worship songs in US evangelical churches. In hesitant, breathy tones, Tomlin sings the verse lyrics describing God's splendor and majesty, accompanying himself with sparse piano chords. As the other band instruments begin to fill in the texture, the gathered worshipers join in a loud unison in the song's chorus, which offers simultaneously a collective affirmation and an invitation to come together in song:

> How great is our God
> Sing with me, how great is our God
> And all will see how great, how great is our God

September 11, 2010—The 12th Annual Jesus in the City Parade, Toronto, Canada

On a Saturday afternoon in early September, I stand on a street corner and watch as several thousand evangelical Christians process through Toronto's downtown district. The Jesus in the City Parade is a mass of swirling colors from brightly

hued parade T-shirts, biblically inspired costumes, glittering banners, and hand-made signs. I notice many of the signs contain lyrical hooks from popular contemporary worship songs: "How great is our God!" "Jesus, name above all names!" and "You're the God of this city!" From over a dozen large parade floats, live bands of eight to twenty instrumentalists and singers play and sing upbeat contemporary worship songs. Though a pop-rock style predominates, I hear inflections of gospel, Eastern European pop, and Caribbean soca. Following a large group of participants on foot, the final float in the parade comes into view. White wooden panels that evoke billowing clouds flank its sides, and the front and back are decorated with clusters of white balloons and silhouetted angels blowing trumpets. Across the side of the float, large blue letters proclaim, "Jesus is Coming!" Toward the bottom of the side panels in smaller letters are the names and logos of several sponsoring churches. The church names, which include the Ukrainian Full Gospel Church, River of God Church, and Light of the Gospel Ministries, appear first in a Cyrillic script, with English below. On the top of the trailer bed, as though floating on the clouds, a band of six instrumentalists and eight singers lead a series of worship songs, alternating between English and a Slavic language—what sounds to me like Russian, or perhaps Ukrainian. As the float passes me on the street, the band begins a new song. I cannot understand the lyrics, but I immediately recognize the melody as belonging to the worship song "How Great Is Our God." The Asian, Afro-Caribbean, and white Canadian marchers behind the float take up the song's widely known chorus in English as the band members continue to sing in their native language.

January 22, 2012—Apartment living room, Cambridge, United Kingdom
I sit on the couch in my apartment with my laptop, using Skype's messaging feature to chat with a twenty-something American man I met online. Lucas runs a computer repair shop in Southern California and serves as webmaster for his local nondenominational church. One of his hobbies is creating lyric videos for contemporary worship songs and posting them on his YouTube channel. He is one of several amateur video creators I've spoken with over Skype or instant messaged over the past few weeks. These conversation partners hail from a host of different geographical locations and walks of life, and include a university student from Scotland, a house church pastor from the Chinese mainland, a Hungarian office worker, and a retiree from rural Texas. Each person has created and shared lyric videos for popular contemporary worship songs whose view counts often range into the millions. I ask Lucas specifically about his video for the song "How Great Is Our God," which has amassed over 8 million views since he posted it three years ago. For the video, Lucas has used the audio from Chris Tomlin's original worship album recording and has superimposed some moving background images, song lyrics, and Bible verses. We talk about some of the photos he has chosen, which include dramatic nature scenery, photos of worshipers with hands stretched upward in rapture, and depictions of Jesus from evangelical popular art and films. Lucas tells me that he originally

started making worship videos as an expression of his own personal devotion. He began posting them online both as a tool for reaching out to non-Christians and as a resource for other Christians to use in their own daily worship. Through his YouTube channel, he now regularly receives requests from pastors and church lay leaders to use his videos in a number of public worship settings, including Sunday morning services, Bible study and prayer groups, youth events, funerals, and baptisms.

These three vignettes follow the song "How Great Is Our God" through several performance spaces, illustrating the widespread and varied use of contemporary worship songs. In the first account, a widely known worship leader and songwriter leads a mass gathering of concert participants in singing worship songs. Many are familiar with these songs from singing them in churches, while others know them only from Christian radio or recordings; still others are being introduced to them for the first time in the worship concert setting. In the second vignette, evangelical Christians sing this song as they engage in congregational worship on the streets of their city. Through collective singing and prayer, participants from this group of Slavic immigrant churches foreground their ethnic and linguistic heritage while reaching out to the broader society. In the third narrative, devout individuals bring "How Great Is Our God" into online participatory culture. By adding a visual component, amateur video creators engage in an emerging audiovisual worship practice that connects private devotion from personal small screens with congregational worship facilitated by the large projection screens of churches, camps, and conferences. In sharing the song via social networking sites like YouTube, they ensure the spread of popular commercial worship music recordings to an ever-broadening evangelical audience around the world.

All three examples demonstrate the various intersecting pathways that contemporary worship music travels and speak to its importance as a shared cultural product, musical practice, and site of religious experience for evangelical Christians in North America and beyond. As both a local practice and globally circulating commodity, contemporary worship music reflects and shapes the concerns, convictions, and commitments of evangelical religious community even as it is shaped by the various contexts in which it is practiced. The central aim of this book is to identify how the collective performance of contemporary worship music shapes the activities that evangelicals define as "worship" and how these musically centered performances have brought into being new social constellations. I call these social constellations "congregations" and the activities that form them "modes of congregating." The five modes of congregating examined in the chapters of *Singing the Congregation*—concert, conference, church, public, and online congregations—include but extend far beyond the weekly gatherings of local institutional churches, revealing conflicts over musical authority and carrying broader implications for how evangelical Christianity positions itself relative to other groups in North American society.

The introduction's title "Music Making Congregations" points both to a social process and to its resulting product: it refers to the process whereby participatory musical performances shape evangelical social groupings (music *making* congregations) and to the communities that are formed through participants' embodied musical practices (music-making *congregations*). In exploring both the overlapping elements and the distinctions between these modes of congregating, *Singing the Congregation* demonstrates the extent to which the activity of worship and the social constellation of the congregation are musically constituted within contemporary evangelical Christianity. In doing so, it seeks to reimagine and reinvigorate the analytic categories of "congregation" and "congregational music." Drawing from theoretical models in ethnomusicology and congregational studies, *Singing the Congregation* reconceives the congregation as a fluid, contingent social constellation that is actively performed into being through a set of communal practices—in this case, the practices that comprise the musically structured participatory activity known as "worship"—that are themselves conditioned strongly by ecclesial institutions and commercial media industries. Rather than presuming or prescribing how congregations should function on the basis of a set of normative theological or sociological assumptions, it retools the concept of evangelical congregation by means of the lived experiences of community formation. By extension, "congregational music-making"[1] is reconceived as a participatory religious musical practice capable of weaving together a religious community inside and outside institutional churches. Congregational music-making is not only a means of expressing local concerns and constituting the local religious community; it is also a potent way to identify with far-flung individuals, institutions, and networks that comprise this global religious community.

FROM WORSHIP WARS TO WORLDWIDE OCCUPATION: CONTEMPORARY WORSHIP MUSIC IN NORTH AMERICAN AND GLOBAL PERSPECTIVES

For an understanding of how congregational music-making shapes and reflects the shifting concerns of a large subset of Christian communities in North America, it is first necessary to define two complex and contested designations: "contemporary worship music" and "evangelical." Contemporary worship music (sometimes abbreviated as CWM[2]) is defined here as a global[3] Christian[4] congregational song repertory modeled on mainstream Western popular music styles. Contemporary worship music, whose history spans from the late 1960s to the time of this writing, overlaps but remains distinct from a related repertory known as CCM (Contemporary Christian Music).[5] CCM is a presentationally oriented religious popular music genre intended for performance by solo artists and bands to listening audiences rather than for participatory congregational singing. Until the late 1990s, the commercial music industries that produced contemporary worship music and CCM remained largely separate; however, much contemporary worship music is now produced or circulated by CCM record labels and publishing houses, and many CCM artists have crossed over to become known as "worship leaders" who also write contemporary worship songs for congregational singing. Because contemporary worship music became incorporated increasingly into the CCM recording industry (see Ingalls 2008, 2016), many evangelical leaders and worshippers now understand contemporary worship music to be a subgenre of CCM. (For a detailed examination of the shifting relationship between contemporary worship music and CCM from the 1960s to the late 2000s, see Ingalls, Nekola, and Mall 2013; Ingalls 2008; Nekola 2009).

The term "contemporary" in contemporary worship music implies an opposition, in this case, to the "traditional" hymn repertory and its associated performance style used in congregational singing in the majority of North American evangelical and mainline Protestant congregations in the decades leading up to the 1980s and 1990s. The word "contemporary" invokes a history of a widespread conflict over worship style, a conflict that has become known as the "worship wars."[6] Liturgical historian Lester Ruth describes the worship wars in this way:

> Around 1993, American Protestants declared war on each other. And they did so over worship. Although the weapons used did not inflict physical harm on the combatants, there were wounds nonetheless. Bitter disagreements, angry arguments, and political machinations spilled across the church. Pastors and musicians were fired or sometimes left on their own, shaking the dust off of their feet. Congregants voted with their feet, or their wallets, or with raised hands if the question of which worship style was right was brought to a vote. And thus were the conflicts known as the worship wars. (Ruth 2017b, 3)

Ruth notes that disputes over music in worship often formed the "front line of combat" in worship wars conflicts (3). Musical instruments, ensembles, and media became charged symbols used to represent "traditional" and "contemporary" factions in worship: guitars and drums were pitted against the organ, projection screens against hymnals, and worship bands against choirs. For US evangelical Christians, congregational music was often at the fore of the conflict because it functioned not only as a potent symbol but also as an affective force. Anna Nekola observes that "if evangelicals did not believe music had the power to move people—to affect their character, their emotions, their behaviors—then music could not be dangerous, but neither would it be able to inspire or transform. It is precisely because music has been understood to have such power that it has been a key site of dispute within the church" (2009, 2–3). She notes that disagreements over the meaning of musical styles in worship reveal ideological and political fault lines reflecting long-standing tensions between individual and institutional authority within US evangelical Christianity. In a related vein, Jonathan Dueck has argued for interpreting the worship wars through the lenses of the social relationships that various styles either upheld or challenged. Performing congregational music together provides "an experiential, embodied, practiced, feelingful way of encountering the world" and is deeply grounded in individuals' experiences with others (2017, 3). More than a vehicle for communicating theological or ideological meaning, both traditional and contemporary styles of worship music are also a repository for individual memories and an enabler of the collective activities that hold communities together.

Though disagreements over whether or not to use contemporary worship music continue in some North American congregations, many Christian commentators and liturgical scholars have pronounced an end to the worst ravages of the widespread conflict. As early as 1999, evangelical historian Michael Hamilton pronounced the contemporary faction the "winner" of the worship wars in his article subtitled "How Guitars Beat Out the Organ in the Worship Wars" in the popular evangelical magazine *Christianity Today* (July 12, 25–35). Contemporary worship music, dismissed by some at the beginning of the conflict as a blip on the liturgical screen, became a prominent fixture of congregational worship in the majority of North American evangelical and pentecostal-charismatic churches, as well as in many mainline Protestant congregations. A decade after Hamilton's article heralding the triumph of praise songs, the editor of the same publication introduced a themed issue on worship with an editorial entitled "The End of the Worship Wars" (Galli 2011). Continuing in this vein, Lester Ruth (2017a) has more recently used the metaphor of postwar reconstruction to describe the developments in US Protestant worship in the 2010s, as congregations seek to bind up wounds from years of conflict and explore new solutions that in some cases challenge the presumed binary between traditional and contemporary. Large-scale surveys of US worship practices demonstrate contemporary worship's staying power: according to multi-year comparisons of the National Congregations Study, between 1998 and 2012 the number of US churches using choir and organ in their worship services fell nearly 10 percent each, while the number who used drums increased by 14 percent. Those using electronic projection equipment, frequently used to project song lyrics in contemporary services, increased by nearly a quarter; as of 2012, a full half of US congregations use guitars in worship (NCS Study 2012). And contemporary worship music's influence is by no means limited to North America. As of the second decade of the twenty-first century, it is arguably the most widely sung Christian congregational music repertory in the world. Christian communities world-wide sing English-language versions or translations as a globalized repertory produced and circulated by large transnational megachurches as well as national and international Christian commercial recording industries (Riches and Wagner 2012; Evans 2015; Ingalls 2014; Gladwin 2015). In the year 2015, Sydney-based megachurch Hillsong, one of the best-known global brands producing contemporary worship music, claimed over $15M US in "music and resource" generated revenue and reported that over 900,000 people across all six continents attended one of its live worship events (Hillsong Church 2016). Contemporary worship music has become increasingly localized (Rommen 2007; Magowan 2007, Carl 2015, Webb 2015), particularly within charismatic and Pentecostal churches, which constitute the fastest-growing segment of global Christianity with over 500 million adherents worldwide (Ingalls and Yong 2015).

As a musical repertory with a history dating back to the 1960s in North America and a global reach, contemporary worship music is known by different names, depending on which of its functions or stylistic subgenres is being referenced, and also what Christian denomination, network, or group is doing the naming.[7] There are several synonyms for the repertory that this book calls "contemporary worship music" in current usage within Christian communities, both within and beyond North America. The most widely used alternative designation for this popular music influenced congregational song repertory is "praise and worship music," or simply "praise and worship." This term is commonly used within Pentecostal and charismatic communities worldwide[8] (see Ingalls 2015a; Lim and Ruth 2017) and among African American Christians across denominations (B. Johnson 2008, 2011; Smith Pollard 2013).[9] Praise and worship not only refers to a musical repertoire, but also references a particular ritual structure and philosophy of worship. In *The Spirit of Praise: Music and Worship in Global Pentecostal-Charismatic Christianity* (2015a), I set out the following definition of praise and worship in its global context:

> Within charismatic circles, "worship" came to refer to a twenty- to forty-minute segment during which a worship band leads the congregation in singing a continuous string of songs (the "worship set"). During this time, members of the worshipping community express their praise and devotion through singing combined with other characteristic pentecostal devotional practices, including hand raising, expressive prayer postures, and ecstatic utterances such as tongues speech and prophecy (see Miller 1993; Redman 2002; Liesch 2001). One of the primary goals of pentecostal-charismatic worship is a personal encounter with God, and consequently pentecostal-charismatic worship is not a directionless sing-along. Rather, it is characterized by a goal-oriented progression involving the separate but related actions of "praise" and "worship."

Pentecostal-charismatic theologians often draw from the book of Psalms and other Old Testament passages to explain the differing orientations of praise and worship. They may speak of the progression of worship as a mythic journey from the outer courts of the Jewish tabernacle into the Holy of Holies (Cornwall 1983; Sorge 1987; Liesch 2001). This ritual procession begins with "praise" at the temple gates and then moves to "worship" in the inner sanctum of the temple, where worshippers relate individually and intimately with God. Music plays an important role in facilitating the transition from communal praise to intimate worship. Praise songs, sung at the beginning of the charismatic worship set, are characterized by upbeat tempos, major harmonies, lively rhythms, and communally oriented lyrics. In contrast, worship songs generally feature slower tempos, more poignant contrasts between major and minor harmonies, and intimate lyrics expressing devotion, love, and desire for God. (6)

Scholars and journalists writing about North American Christian popular and congregational musics sometimes use "praise and worship music" rather than "contemporary worship music" to refer to the musical repertory (see Price 2004a, 2004b, 2008; Woods and Walrath 2007; Busman 2015); however, a growing number are using "contemporary worship music" as their preferred umbrella term (Redman 2002; Ingalls 2008; Nekola 2009; Reagan 2015; Porter 2016; J. Dueck 2017; Lim and Ruth 2017).[10] In explaining their choice to use "contemporary worship," Lim and Ruth 2017 (124–131) notes that "praise and worship" often carries strong pentecostal-charismatic theological and liturgical connotations that might or might not carry over to North American evangelical or mainline Protestant settings where it is found. For these reasons, *Singing the Congregation* generally uses the designation contemporary worship rather than praise and worship while conceding that the latter term may be more useful in referencing the repertory outside the North American evangelical context.

Another popular name for the repertory within some circles is "modern worship music." Nashville-based Christian music industry executives originally devised this category in the late 1990s as a marketing term for a new style of contemporary worship music that musically paralleled the "modern" or "mainstream rock" radio format (Breimeier 2008; Ingalls 2016). The genre label modern worship separated this newer style from older contemporary worship songs that no longer sounded "contemporary" and eventually came into common usage, particularly among younger generations of evangelicals. Finally, for the increasing number of younger evangelical worshipers with either limited memory or no firsthand experience of the conflicts between "traditional" and "contemporary" styles, this body of songs is often simply designated "worship music." The "contemporary" prefix is unnecessary when this musical repertory is normative for congregational singing rather than a "new" repertory defined in opposition to an older one.

For many years, scholars largely ignored contemporary worship music; however, beginning in the mid-2000s, there has been an upsurge of academic interest in the music. Perspectives from across academic disciplines illumine various aspects of contemporary worship music's history and cultural influence, including its intertwining development alongside the Christian- and gospel music recording industries (Ward 2005; B. Johnson 2008; Nekola 2009; Mall 2012; Ingalls, Nekola, and Mall 2013; Busman 2015a; Thornton 2015); its influence within evangelical youth movements and events (Fromm 2006; Ingalls 2011; Eskridge 2013; Busman 2015a); its place within "worship wars" discourse and practice (Nekola 2009; Justice 2012; J. Dueck 2011, 2017); the influence of charismatic, Pentecostal, and "new paradigm" theologies and circulation networks throughout its history (Ward 2005; Ingalls and Yong 2015; Riches 2010; Reagan 2015; Webb 2015; Porter 2016; Lim and Ruth 2017); its reliance on electronic media and digital audiovisual technologies for its creation, transmission, and reception (Nekola 2013; Nekola and Wagner 2015; Evans and D. Thornton 2016); theological and ethical assessments of its message and social structure (Ward 2005; Woods and Walrath 2007; Evans 2006; Busman 2015b; Porter 2016; Lim and Ruth 2017); the ways in which singing it engages and disciplines the body, both individual and corporate (Althouse and Wilkinson 2015; Carl 2015; Myrick 2017; Moore 2018b); its transnational spread by means of mobile individuals and global media (T. Wagner 2014a, 2014b; Evans 2015; Ingalls 2016); and its localization into a variety of congregational settings (Johnson 2013; Smith Pollard 2013; Justice 2015; Webb 2015; Klaver 2015; Porter 2017).[11] While "worship wars" discourse often treated contemporary worship music as an undifferentiated repertory or conflated it with presentationally oriented Christian pop, scholarly work has emphasized the internal diversity of the contemporary worship repertory, as it is an amalgamation of several subgenres that reflect differing contexts, convictions, and concerns since its beginnings in the late 1960s. Many of these sources are concerned to note shifts in themes, lyrics, music, style, and relationship to the music industry, over contemporary worship music's history. In previous work (see especially Ingalls 2012a, 2017; Ingalls, Nekola, and Mall 2013), I have traced the broad shifts in the North American commercial worship music mainstream as the predominant styles moved from folk-influenced choruses of the 1970s, to "adult contemporary" style ballads of the 1980s–1990s, to the youth-oriented, radio-friendly pop-rock of the late 1990s and 2000s, to a more eclectic genre that is nonetheless still dominated by pop-rock in the 2010s. Examining these several important subgenres of contemporary worship music affords an understanding of the different historical contexts out of which each style developed, along with which genre characteristics were adopted from mainstream popular music and their associated meanings that had to be negotiated as a result.

If the contemporary worship music is an amalgamation of nearly fifty years of songs with differing lyrical, musical, and performance characteristics, what characteristics hold this broad repertory together and make it a recognizable phenomenon? Liturgical historians Swee Hong Lim and Lester Ruth (2017) propose several common features of contemporary worship in US context (with "contemporary worship" conceived broadly to include all practices within a church worship service, including preaching, prayers, and sacraments in addition to music). Lim and Ruth write that contemporary worship is a "multifaceted worship style . . . that within the last several decades has come to be an identifiable, widespread liturgical phenomenon" (1). Though contemporary worship lacks a single point of origin and takes on slightly different forms with different denominations and traditions, Lim and Ruth identify nine elements, parsed into the three categories—presumptions, musical characteristics, and behavioral and media characteristics—that are generally present within those practices designated as "contemporary worship" within the North American context. Lim and Ruth write that three fundamental presumptions undergird the practice of contemporary worship: "using contemporary, nonarchaic English, a dedication to relevance regarding contemporary concerns and issues in the lives of worshippers, and a commitment to adapt worship to match contemporary people, sometimes to the level of strategic targeting" (2). In characterizing the musical features of contemporary worship, they enumerate three general tendencies: "using musical styles from current types of popular music, extended times of uninterrupted congregational singing, and a centrality of the musicians in the liturgical space and in the leadership of the service" (3). Finally, Lim and Ruth discuss the behavioral and media components of contemporary worship, which include "greater levels of physical expressiveness, a predilection for informality, and a reliance upon electronic technology" (3).

In describing prevalent orientations and concrete practices, this list of characteristics provides a useful starting point for identifying contemporary worship within the North American context. It is important to note, however, that as a dynamic and far-reaching congregational practice, contemporary worship music's characteristics have shifted and are bound to shift again over time. Even within a given present-day context, performances of contemporary worship music may exhibit some but not all of the characteristics Lim and Ruth describe. The chapters of *Singing the Congregation* each approach contemporary worship music as a contingent social practice that both shapes and reflects the religious collectivities that create, circulate, perform, and critique it.

LOCATING NORTH AMERICAN EVANGELICAL
CHRISTIANITY THROUGH MUSICAL PERFORMANCE

Because contemporary worship music is such a widespread phenomenon, attempting to group together the religious communities where it is performed proves a formidable challenge. Nondenominational megachurches or Pentecostal church networks are often held up as representative of the religious communities in which contemporary worship music is created and circulated; however, this music has become an integral part of worship within many other types of Christian congregations, including progressive mainline Protestant congregations, rural self-described fundamentalist churches, and even Catholic parishes. Though there is no one designation capable of holding these disparate religious communities together, I put forward the term "evangelical Christianity" as the one best suited to this task, while acknowledging that it is a complex and contested designation. Evangelical Christianity refers to a transnational, interdenominational religious group: evangelicals number between 300 and 550 million Christians worldwide[12] and can be said to comprise anywhere between 60 to 100 million Christians in the United States alone, or between 22 percent and 35 percent of the US population (Eskridge 2012). In its various usages worldwide, the term "evangelical" carries many different connotations; in much of Latin America, for instance, an evangelical is a synonym for "Protestant Christian" of whatever variety, whereas in many countries in Europe, the term references "free church" Protestant congregations that are not state supported. Many Christian groups that scholars consider paradigmatic examples of evangelical Christianity do not use the designation "evangelical"; in South Korea, where nearly all forms of Protestant Christianity have been influenced by the practice and ethos of evangelical Christianity, adherents of these groups would generally label themselves Protestant.

In the US context, the designation "evangelical" has long carried complex and intertwined theological and political connotations, with the relative weight of each element varying along with shifts in national political discourse. The difficulty of defining evangelical Christianity in the contemporary United States is that the designation itself is understood differently, depending on who is using it. Christian writer and blogger Jonathan Merritt describes the problem succinctly: ". . . individual observers are left to decide how to define what makes someone or something evangelical. To the pollster, it is a sociological term. To the pastor, it is a denominational or doctrinal term. And to the politician, it is a synonym for a white Christian Republican" (2015). Scholars and some journalistic observers use evangelical as an ascription, grouping together religious individuals and congregations that share certain beliefs or practices whether or not they would self-identify as evangelical. In most political polls and the quantitative studies based on them, the category "evangelical" is more often purely a self-designation; thus, the definition of "evangelical" relies entirely on those characteristics of individual respondents who are willing to identify with the category. Danielle Kurtzleben, in an NPR broadcast conducted during the 2015 campaign season in advance of the national primary elections, remarks that the way the US media uses the term is "squishy" and "remarkably poorly defined" (2015). She points out that the differing ways that pollsters define evangelicals results in a widely varying estimate of their total numbers, ranging from 6 percent of the total US population (Barna Research, which uses a nine-question doctrinal litmus test to define its sample) to 35 percent (Pew Research, based solely on respondents' self-identification with the terms "evangelical" or "born again" Christian) (Kurtzleben 2015).

Trying to define what individuals or groups are currently considered (or consider themselves) "evangelical" in the United States can be like trying to hit a moving target. Demographic shifts as well as changes in how individuals choose to self-identify are continuing to influence how this group is represented and how it understands itself. The report "America's Changing Religious Identity," which summarizes results from the Public Religion Research Institute's a landmark 2016 research study based on telephone interviews with over 100,000 Americans, observes a marked demographic shift along ethnic and racial lines in who self-identifies as either an "evangelical" or "born again" Protestant:

> Like all Christians in the U.S., evangelical Protestants are experiencing a substantial racial and ethnic transformation. Young evangelical Protestants are far more racially and ethnically diverse than previous generations. Only half (50%) of evangelical Protestants under the age of 30 are white, compared to more than three-quarters (77%) of evangelical Protestant seniors (age 65 or older). Twenty-two percent of young evangelical Protestants are black, 18% are Hispanic, and nine percent identify as some other race or mixed race. (Cox and Jones 2017)[13]

The importance of positions on national political issues in defining what type of Christian self-identifies as evangelical has shifted over time in response to broader cultural trends and key social moments. In the process, how the broader public understands American evangelicalism and how the constituency understands itself are subject to change as well. There was a notable shift in the popular usage of the designation "evangelical" in the United States between the time period that ethnographic research for this book was conducted (2006–2013) and the time of its writing and publication.[14] At the time of this writing, evangelical has taken on a much stronger political resonance: many evangelical leaders are celebrating the Trump administration as a political victory for US evangelicalism, while others believe that the 2016 election precipitated a full-blown crisis of evangelical identity (see particularly Labberton 2018). The term "evangelical" was used throughout the 2016 presidential campaign and post-election to describe a key constituency responsible for the Trump administration's rise to power. Sometimes this group designation was qualified with the other terms "white" and "conservative," while at other times these two characteristics were simply assumed; either way, the statistic that 80 percent of (white, conservative) evangelicals voted for Trump continues to be widely cited.[15] Many have attributed the outcome of the election to a degree of unity in the conservative Protestant voting block not seen since the heyday of the Religious Right (Pew Research Center 2016; Zauzmer 2016; FitzGerald 2017), while other observers have declared that the term has lost its ability to refer to a coalition of Protestants united by shared beliefs and practices rather than a shared religio-political ideology (Carter 2016; Campolo and Claibourne 2016; Goodstein 2016). Further fueling the flames of the evangelical identity crisis was the Alabama state senate election in late 2017 that involved Republican candidate Roy Moore, who during the campaign was accused numerous times of sexually assaulting women and girls as young as fourteen. Though Moore, a staunch supporter of the Religious Right, was defeated by a narrow margin by Democratic rival Doug Jones, exit polls show an identical level of support for Moore among Alabama evangelicals as had supported Trump a year earlier (80 percent) (Bailey 2017). Media coverage of the overwhelming evangelical support for Moore led to a renewed outcry among many moderate and progressive (but also some conservative) evangelical leaders, many of whom advocated for complete dis-identification with the term (de la Torre 2017; Krattenmaker 2017; Wehner 2017; Zauzmer and Bailey 2017; Keller 2017).

It remains to be seen whether the designation "evangelical" in the United States will retain a religious meaning independent of a Christian nationalist political affiliation. However, I choose to use the term in this book because I believe there is no other more suitable term to delineate the large religious coalition whose musical practices I seek to interpret. Even before the definitional challenges caused by the current US political regime, scholars of evangelical Christianity frequently disagreed about where its boundaries were located. Scholars of evangelicalism often feel compelled to make explicit a position on a number of frequently asked definitional questions: does evangelical Christianity include Pentecostal and charismatic communities, or should these groups be separated in analysis? To what extent can a mainline Protestant, Catholic, or Orthodox church—or some subset of its members—be considered evangelical? Is "evangelical Christian" in the U.S. context synonymous with "conservative white Protestant," or can the designation include African American, Asian American, and Latinx Christians, or those from other racial or ethnic minorities? How much relative weight should demographic factors (such as race and ethnicity, institutional affiliation, or political persuasion), self-identification, and doctrinal adherence be given in defining this group?

Larry Eskridge, former director of the Institute for the Study of American Evangelicals, describes three of the most common ways evangelical Christianity in the United States has been defined (Eskridge 2014). The first approach is theological, seeking to identify a set of doctrines or theological emphases that all evangelicals hold in common. One widely adopted framework, taken from British historian David Bebbington's *Evangelicalism in Modern Britain* (1989; see also Balmer 2010), has been dubbed the "Bebbington quadrilateral." This framework has been adopted by the National Association of Evangelicals (NAE); on the organization's website, the NAE paraphrases Bebbington's four key theological emphases as follows: "1) Conversionism: the belief that lives need to be transformed through a 'born-again' experience and a life long process of following Jesus; 2) Activism: the expression and demonstration of the gospel in missionary and social reform efforts; 3) Biblicism: a high regard for and obedience to the Bible as the ultimate authority, 4) Crucicentrism: a stress on the sacrifice of Jesus Christ on the cross as making possible the redemption of humanity" (National Association of Evangelicals 2016). The NAE presents these characteristics as immutable, apolitical, and transcultural, stating that "these distinctives and theological convictions define us—not political, social or cultural trends" (2016). Secondly, evangelical Christianity is often treated as a constellation of shared orientations or attitudes embodied in modes of speech and devotional habits. A final approach focuses on institutions, including denominations and parachurch organizations such as the NAE, which define themselves as, or are commonly acknowledged to be, "evangelical."

These modes of definition are useful up to a point, but there are many situations in which each approach falls short. The doctrinal and attitudinal approaches do not allow for the possibility of significant shifts in evangelical belief and practice. By drawing hard boundaries around what constitutes religious orthodoxy, doctrinal approaches fail to capture many individuals' and institutions' dynamic—and often selective—engagement of normative evangelical practices and discourses. In addition defining evangelical Christianity by means of institutions runs the risk of ignoring less strictly organized yet highly influential networks and the influence these have on the collective imagining of evangelical community.

In order to describe in a more nuanced manner the way evangelical Christianity is constituted and experienced, I rely on a synthesis of two other approaches: religious historian Michael Bergunder's model of religious discursive networks and religion and media scholar Birgit Meyer's idea of aesthetic formations. Bergunder focuses on global Pentecostalism; however, his observations are readily applicable to academic explorations of evangelical Christianity. In exploring definitional challenges that global Pentecostalism poses for researchers, Bergunder advances the idea of Pentecostalism as "neither as a nominalistic nor as an idealistic category but as a contingent discursive network" whose boundaries are subject to constant negotiation (2010, 54). In seeking to understand the Pentecostal network's limits, Bergunder advocates moving away from the search for an inherent essence, considering any traits shared across the broad scope of Pentecostal history and culture as discursive articulations. Rather than seeing beliefs and practices that Pentecostals share in common (for instance, glossolalia, prophecy, or Spirit baptism) as essential traits, he advocates that they should be understood as contingent articulations that depend on mutual affirmation of people and institutions within the network (55). The contingency of the discursive network implies that the researcher must acknowledge conflicting claims of inclusion and exclusion (who is considered "in" and who is considered outside the community) and situate the network in relationship to other discursive formations. (In the case of Pentecostalism, these include evangelical Christianity, fundamentalism, Protestantism, Christianity, and religion more generally.)

Media and religion theorist Birgit Meyer (2009b) provides a compelling framework for explaining how religious discursive networks operate and are articulated through material practices. Meyer integrates the processes of collective imagining, mediation, and embodied experience as ingredients in the process of "making [religious] communities" (2). Drawing from and expanding upon Benedict Anderson's notion of "imagined communities" Meyer asserts that, in order to be experienced as real, religious imaginations "must become tangible outside the realm of the mind . . . [and] need to materialize in the concrete lived environment" through such mechanisms as the structuring of space, the performance of ritual, and the production of religious emotion (5). She proposes the notion of "aesthetic formations" in order to move beyond ideas of religious community that are fixed and bounded and to capture the performative roles "played by things, media, and the body in actual processes of community making" (6). She uses the term "formation" similarly to how I use "congregation": to describe both a social entity and the *process* by which that group is formed. This process relies on shared imaginations materializing through what Meyer calls "sensational forms" (7). Sensational forms are religious media and associated practices that are "attributed with a sense of immediacy through which the distance between believers and the transcendental is transcended" and thus are used to "invoke and organize . . . access to the transcendental" among religious practitioners (12). Miranda Klaver (2015) and Joshua Busman (2015b) each notes that contemporary worship music is a sensational form par excellence within contemporary evangelical and charismatic Christianity; here, music is "part of a larger domain of meaning, encompassing doctrines and ideas that not only are expressed in material forms but also generate new meanings by the constitutive power of social practices" (Klaver 2015, 101).

Singing the Congregation follows Bergunder and Meyer in describing evangelical Christianity as a discursive network that is articulated through concrete, embodied practices—in this case, the musical practices within the activity marked as "worship." Both of these approaches provide ways to approach a large religious community like evangelical Christianity as a social formation that is actively performed into being.[16] By foregrounding the performative nature of evangelical Christianity and not insisting that its adherents belong to a specific set of institutions or normative beliefs, this book is able to highlight shared practices that unite the North American evangelical Christian community as well as the conflicting tendencies that produce tension and sometimes threaten to divide it. For present-day North American evangelicals, contemporary worship music has become a primary conduit through which worshiping assemblies become nodes of discourse and aesthetic formations. It provides the Christians who engage it with a common language, a set of themes to engage, and a shared vocabulary of expressive practices; further, for those approaching the music in a posture of devotion, it often induces religious experiences that defy the power of words to categorize, rationalize, or control. The next section builds from the theoretical foundation these models of religious community provide to suggest a new way to understand the social formation of the congregation, and by extension, congregational music-making.

CONGREGATION AS SOCIO-MUSICAL PRACTICE: WORSHIP, MUSIC-MAKING, AND MODES OF CONGREGATING

Because participatory music-making powerfully imparts a sense of community and is a "strong force for social bonding" (Turino 2008, 29), congregational music-making is often one of the central participatory activities within Christian religious gatherings. Within North American evangelical Protestantism, the presence of participatory music-making has become, in some cases, the sole component that defines the activity as "worship." A Google image search for "worship" provides compelling evidence of how closely the term is linked in the popular imagination to the activity of singing contemporary worship music. In the screenshot shown in Figure I.1 depicting twenty-nine separate images of worship, one bodily stance predominates: individuals and communities are shown raising their hands, a common evangelical physical expression connoting ecstasy or surrender and used nearly exclusively in times of congregational singing. Most of the images depict assemblies that look much like concerts, with large crowds facing brilliant stage lights. In a few of these images, singers and instrumentalists are out of focus but visible on the stage. Though the cross appears in a few of the images, only one depicts a space with recognizable ecclesiastical architecture. The activity of worship, as

Figure I.1: Results of a Google image search for "worship" (2017).
Screenshot by the author.

seen through these commonly used images, does not carry within it a necessary association with local church congregations.

Evangelical commentators are often at pains to insist that congregational music-making and worship are not synonymous; the felt need of so many leaders to insist continually that "worship is more than singing" evidences how widespread the conflation is. This evangelical "mantra" (Hill 2016) has even been incorporated into worship song lyrics.[17] In describing what he refers to as the evangelical "sonicization of worship," Joshua Busman (2015a) writes that, beginning in the 1970s as an outgrowth of practices within evangelical youth movements, "worship became a category of experience that was increasingly indistinguishable from music. Even more specifically, worship became equivalent to singing along with pop-styled songs that featured acoustic guitar accompaniment" (46). As evangelicals accepted the practices and associated beliefs grounded in pentecostal-charismatic theologies of worship as divine encounter, their own understanding of worship shifted in the process. According to Busman, "the category of worship within evangelical Christianity was reconfigured to focus more explicitly on cultivating and sustaining an individual experience of the divine rather than the execution of identical, discrete, liturgical elements each week" (Busman 2015a), and, as a result, became a highly portable practice that could happen anywhere.[18]

The affective, collective practice of singing contemporary worship songs, then, has become for many contemporary evangelicals the sum total of worship. Musically centered worship is not limited to performance within local church congregations. The previous section demonstrated that, as a mass-mediated popular music, contemporary worship music engenders multiple modes of encounter. If worship equals assembling to sing contemporary worship songs, then this music can transform nearly any space or gathering in which it is performed into a place of worship. Individuals have numerous opportunities in a typical day to engage in the musical activity defined as worship: contemporary worship music has saturated many domains beyond church worship, including concert and conference circuits, radio airwaves, the commodity marketplace, and social media, as well as informal music-making. The evangelical concert and conference circuits run through metropolitan areas small and large; live-streamed events and prerecorded devotional worship videos are always on offer via social media; and smaller affinity groups—whether Bible studies affiliated with churches or with parachurch organizations—offer individuals a chance to engage in worship, as it is defined and mediated by contemporary worship music, on a frequent basis.

The rise of contemporary worship music, and with it the proliferation of opportunities to engage in participatory musical worship, has challenged the local congregation's authority within evangelical religious life (Nekola 2009, 2013). For an increasing number of evangelicals, other institutions or networks serve as the dominant modes of social connection and, in some cases, as the primary sites of religious formation. This situation has created disconnections between the way Christian leaders, scholars, and lay evangelicals understand and experience evangelical religious community. Some scholarship still privileges church congregations as the central loci of music and worship practice, parsing religious practices into those that take place within local church congregations and lumping everything outside of it into one broad "parachurch" category. Within this binary, the local church congregation is often privileged as the ritual space where everything significant for the spiritual life happens. In this way, the presumed relationship between congregational music-making and the local church context is similar to the relationship that popular music theorist Mark Butler describes between electronic dance music and the dance floor, a space often treated in fan and scholarly discourse alike as the "authentic locus of musical experience" (2006, 15). In seeking to extend an understanding of the electronic dance music genre beyond this context, Butler writes that, "although the significance of this site cannot be denied, it could also be argued that other important aspects of [this music] have been neglected because of the tendency to focus on this most immediate and obvious of social contexts" (16).

The local church congregation is undeniably a significant and formative institution within evangelical Protestant religious life. Nancy Ammerman (2011) provides a classic sociological definition of congregation as a social and religious institution shaped in great part by various aspects of the US cultural context:

> Congregations, in their prototypical American form, are locally situated, multi-generational, voluntary organizations of people who identify themselves as a distinct religious group and engage in a broad range of religious activities

together. They are usually, but not always, associated with some larger tradition and its affiliated regional and national bodies (i.e., a denomination). The space where they meet may or may not be an identifiably religious building, but congregations do typically have a regular meeting place and regular schedules of religious activities (usually, but not always, at least weekly) (Wuthnow 1994). With well over 300,000 such congregations, more than 80 percent of them Protestant, this American pattern has helped to shape how the term is defined. (2011, 562)

Ammerman is one of the architects of congregational studies, an interdisciplinary subfield that comprises sociology of religion as well as theological ecclesiology and takes the local congregation as just defined, rather than denominational structures or macro-level population surveys, as the structure to be analyzed (see Ammerman 1997, Ammerman 1998, Ammerman 2005). But congregations are not only a central unit for academic analysis; their centrality is also quite literally an article of faith for church networks and denominations with congregationalist polities, in other words, those who define the local congregation as either the ontological or phenomenological center of the Christian church.[19] The ecclesial ontology that regards local church congregations as normative examples of faith and practice prevails even in some denominational structures with more formal hierarchies. R. Stephen Warner has observed that even North American denominations with more hierarchical governmental structures, such as Episcopal, Presbyterian, or Roman Catholic churches, tend toward a "de facto" congregationalism in the US context (Warner 1994, 76). The congregation also occupies the central role in theological reflection, particularly within contemporary ecclesiological discussions in the field of practical theology. James Nieman and Roger Haight, writing from Lutheran and Catholic perspectives, respectively, advocate that the local church congregation should be the focus of theological reflection because "the primary unit of church that people experience is the congregation" (2012, 29). They propose, however, a significant shift in how scholars understand and represent this social formation, noting that "those who study congregations know how difficult it can be to specify where the boundaries of such groups are actually located. Religious behavior, identity formation, and so forth occur in diverse parts of the lives of congregants" (26). They propose the focus of congregational studies, then, be on shared practices that unite participants across the bounds of local congregations, advocating a shift in focus to from the structure to "the *activity* of those who gather through congregations" (26).

Rather than redefine or rehabilitate the term congregation, other ecclesiologists have sought to decenter it by advocating the importance of other social spaces for forming Christian community. In *Liquid Church* (2002), British practical theologian Pete Ward points out that there is a fundamental disconnection in how ecclesiologists understand traditional church institutions, on the one hand, and more loosely organized Christian gatherings and communication networks occurring largely outside this domain, on the other. Ward poses a question of significance that he believes scholars have not adequately addressed:

> What is the place of various productive and creative processes that characterize contemporary Christian culture? By this I mean festivals, worship music, evangelism courses, and other processes. At present the institution of the church, local or national, seems to be largely irrelevant to these creative and productive activities. . . . Liquid church would address this issue by saying that as these individuals, organizations, and groups carry out their activities, they are being or doing church. Moreover, as we participate in and use these groups' events and products, we are also being or making church. (2002, 3)

Ward proposes the concept of "liquid church" to describe the ecclesial result of the ongoing transformation of religious social forms by new media and communications technologies. Ward lays out three characteristics of liquid church. First, these Christian gatherings are frequently informal, taking place outside the purview of traditional religious authority. Second (and in parallel fashion to Nieman and Haight 2012), Ward argues that liquid church is constituted by practice rather than structure: the basis of the liquid church "lies in people's spiritual activity rather than in organizations patterns or buildings" (2). (Ward later gives an example of these spiritual activities by describing the participatory singing of a contemporary worship song at a popular British Christian music festival.) Third, Ward's liquid church "does not need or require a weekly congregational meeting" (2); rather, it often comprises a far-flung network of people who sometimes meet in person but more often experience connection through shared consumptive and media practices.

Extending aspects of Ward's model to music-making specifically, Dutch theologian Mirella Klomp observes that performances of Christian music outside church congregations pose significant challenges to the definition of "congregational music" and point to "the difficulties of distinguishing the 'ecclesial' from the 'extra-ecclesial' domain" (Klomp, forthcoming). She argues that theologians must develop notions of Christian community "that are commensurate with flexible, fluid gatherings around music" (Klomp, forthcoming).[20]

Ward's observations about the extra-ecclesial spaces that have come to define Christian community and Klomp's underscoring of the importance of extra-ecclesial music-making resonate strongly with my observations of how contemporary worship music forms evangelical collectivity. However significant the local church congregation may be for evangelicals' participation in contemporary worship music, privileging this social context above all others fails to take account of the lived experience of many Christians whose devotional activities are facilitated by common practices—particularly participatory music-making—across many different social spaces. Likewise, within North American evangelical Christianity, religious authority is diffuse and participation diverse; thus, gatherings that happen beyond local institutional settings are sometimes accorded greater authority to inculcate belief and determine practice, particularly concerning the meaning and activity of worship (see Ingalls 2011, 2012b; Mall 2012; Nekola 2013; Busman 2015a). Spaces that facilitate collective performance of contemporary worship music have introduced a particularly potent challenge to church authority. Over the course of my field research, my conversation partners often described their experience in worship spaces outside their local church, contrasting church worship unfavorably in relationship to "worship experiences" in which they had partaken elsewhere. Some participants found worship at mass concerts to be, in one participant's words, "more sacred than church." Other participants in national conferences described their collective singing as "what heaven is going to be like." A few individuals I met online admitted that they felt able to most "authentically" worship when viewing devotional song videos shared on social media. And many leaders at local evangelical churches confessed a strongly felt imperative to adapt, adopt, or reject the current musical and worship practices modeled by large parachurch conferences, powerful megachurches, and the transnational Christian commercial music industry.

In this book, I seek to retool the concept of what constitutes an evangelical congregation by bringing scholarly representations in line with these on-the-ground—and sometimes conflicting—understandings of what the religious community is and should be. As such, *Singing the Congregation* is a thick description of North American evangelicals' "lived ecclesiology."[21] In other words, rather than presuming or prescribing on the basis of a set of normative assumptions how evangelicals *should* congregate, it examines the various ways and reasons evangelicals *do* congregate for worship. I use the term "modes of congregating" to describe the active creation of various evangelical social formations that have gathered for the express purpose of worship. For evangelicals, the use of contemporary worship music immediately marks an activity as "worship"; thus, this song repertoire is an important lens through which to understand evangelical modes of congregating and how each of these different modes structures expectations and changes understandings of what constitutes worship. The modes of congregating examined in *Singing the Congregation* include but extend far beyond gatherings of local institutional churches. Contemporary worship music provides the conceptual glue between the activities of singing together with a few dozen friends at a local church Sunday service, joining one's voice with thousands at a concert or mass event, singing with hands raised while processing down the street in a public demonstration, or singing along with an online live-streamed musical event. Each of these experiences is marked as worship and involves participation in the same musical repertory; however, each is distinguished by its unique affordance—in other words, the socially defined associations and activities that it permits. An intimate local gathering, a public space, online performance, and a regional or national large-scale event each provides a different set of possibilities for worship, and as a result, each one has a bearing on participants' expectations and understanding of what worship and, by extension, the worshiping congregation, are.

In introducing this model of musical modes of congregating, my aim is to refine and reinvigorate the conceptual category of congregation, and along with it, congregational music. By expanding the notion of "congregation" beyond the local church setting to any gathering where participants understand the primary activity as being religious worship, *Singing the Congregation* offers scholars a way to connect different types of gatherings and performance spaces that participants experience as experientially linked and continuous. By doing so, this model is able to account for the continuity of religious experience between different performance spaces, the ways that religious sociality is influenced by media and mobility, and the lived experience of participants for whom the local church is just one of several modes of congregating that are meaningful to them.

EVANGELICAL CONGREGATIONS AS "HOME" AND "AWAY": NAVIGATING DISTANCE AND PROXIMITY IN THE FIELD

Growing up in a deeply religious family who attended an independent Baptist church in central Arkansas, I cannot remember a time I was not intrigued by the practice of evangelical congregational music-making. As a teenager, I watched my church go through "worship wars" conflicts in which organ, choir, and gospel hymn repertory were sidelined by contemporary worship songs led by bands and small ensembles of singers on microphones, resulting in more than a few people leaving the church. I saw how church leaders' and congregants' experiences at concerts, camps, and conferences influenced what songs were chosen for Sunday morning worship, what musical styles were permissible, and what movements and gestures (or lack thereof) were used to accompany them. And sometimes I was a conduit for these changes, arranging solo piano renditions of my favorite contemporary worship songs from youth camp or recordings, or singing the songs along with other teens in my youth group in the church's Sunday evening service. These firsthand observations of musical and cultural changes in the churches and gatherings in which I participated were what initially fueled my interest in the academic study of religious communities and their music. This section lays out the field-research activities that inform this book and explains how my shifting positions as observer, participant, interpreter, and sometimes critic have shaped the way I have researched evangelical music-making and culture.

The field research that informs *Singing the Congregation* spans seven years of multi-site ethnographic work between 2006 and 2013 within several strategically chosen locations in North America. I have chosen as my geographical focus the cultural region of "North America" rather than the United States alone because of the dense (if under-explored) interconnections between US and Canadian evangelical and charismatic musical networks (see J. Dueck 2011, 2017; Lim and Ruth 2017). Though the field research that this book draws from is largely limited to my work in the United States and Canada, preliminary research in the United Kingdom as well as conversations over phone and Skype with evangelical interlocutors in such places as Germany, Scandinavia, Australia, South Africa, Brazil, Mexico, and Malaysia have informed and enriched my perspective on evangelical Christianity in global perspective.

Because North American evangelicals are populous and widespread geographically, I based the bulk of my research around important nodes of evangelical cultural production networks. Nashville, Tennessee was the center of gravity for much of the field research that informs this book; I carried out the bulk of the field research for Chapters 1 and 3 of this book while I was residing in Nashville between 2006 and 2009, with a two-month follow-up stint in the summer of 2012 and several additional shorter visits. Nashville has been dubbed the "buckle of the Bible belt" not only for its large number of evangelical residents but also for its central role in US Christian cultural production. It houses denominational headquarters and/or national publishing houses for the Southern Baptist Convention, the largest Protestant denomination in the United States, as well as the National Association of Free Will Baptists, the United Methodist Church, and the National Baptist Convention USA. Since the late 1980s, it has been the center of the Christian music recording industry. As such, it is a central hub that draws individuals involved in creating and producing worship music from all over the world. Much of the research I conducted while I lived in Nashville focused on local church contexts (see Chapter 3) and conversations with those who worked in the worship music recording industry.

Nashville remains an important center for the production of evangelical worship music and the print and Internet discourse surrounding it. However, as changing media technologies spur the production of material cultural products and discourse to decentralize or relocate, other important network hubs have arisen. For this reason, my research involved frequent trips to conferences, concerts, and festivals located mainly in the southeastern and central United States. I made frequent trips to Atlanta, Georgia but also attended events located in St. Louis, Missouri; Kansas City, Kansas; Grand Rapids, Michigan; and Mount Union, Pennsylvania.[22] In each of these locations, worship events lasting from two days to one week afforded me the opportunity to meet evangelicals from across North America and often from around the world. I attended two widely known and influential conferences for college students, in St. Louis and Atlanta, respectively, during two-week periods in December/January 2006–2007 and December/January 2012–2013. The field research that informed Chapter 4, centered on individuals and evangelical church congregations that sponsored Toronto's annual Christian parade, was carried out in 2010–2011. And, though Internet research and social networking were used throughout the project period, I completed the bulk of the online ethnography that informs Chapter 5 in 2012–2013.

While physical locations that facilitate face-to-face encounters are important for promoting the powerful, embodied experiences that constitute congregations, online sites are increasingly significant. Following organization's online sites and social media has become increasingly necessary for keeping up with developments within evangelical Christianity and its worship music. Throughout this project I have closely monitored the circulating discourse about worship and music online, and have also observed evangelicals' interactions with online media as sites of the worship experience itself. Facebook groups, YouTube channels, organization websites, and the increasingly old-fashioned online platform of email have provided ways for me to locate and stay connected to conversation partners in the field, regardless of my current location.

The standard ethnographic field-research narrative often centers on the researcher's journey from distance to proximity, as he or she becomes more deeply integrated within the community and as knowledge about a group of people and their practices deepens. However, for ethnographers who are also what Mellonee Burnim has called "culture bearers" (1985, 433) conducting fieldwork "at home," the process is often inverted.[23] Ethnomusicologists Jonathan Stock and Chou Chiener describe John Blacking's perspective on ethnographers who conduct research in cultural context familiar to them: for them, musical ethnography is "a way to move back from focusing on musical specifics that were already deeply familiar, a means of envisioning broader concerns, musical and human alike" (Stock and Chou 2008, 109). This degree of proximity often entails entanglement within the social expectations and political dimensions of group life, and a space for critical distance must be formed. Renato Rosaldo (1993) has called this process "de-familiarization," whereby familiar and thus often overlooked cultural practices are rendered as a visible source of scrutiny (39). Stock and Chou observe that distance and proximity must be negotiated even more intensely by those whose research projects intersect closely with their everyday lives (111); however, just as the ethnographic field is actively constructed, so also what constitutes "home" may shift repeatedly during research. Theoretical work on intersectionality, in highlighting the multiple, mutually influencing aspects of identity that any individual must negotiate, has challenged any straightforward designation of cultural "insider" or "outsider"; in parallel fashion, Stock and Chou caution that this binary risks "reducing the often shifting and multiple identities a researcher carries during fieldwork to a single valency or position" (113).

My subject position as a straight, white, able-bodied woman with an American middle-class evangelical background meant that I was able to gain access to and establish trust relatively easily within North American evangelical networks and events. When I embarked on dissertation research in my mid-twenties, I wondered whether being a woman who was young in relationship to many of my key interlocutors would hinder me from gaining access or prevent my project from being taken seriously. Many North American evangelical groups and denominations promote traditional gender roles, and as a result women are frequently prohibited from occupying pastoral leadership roles in many evangelical churches and denominations. Though there are prominent exceptions, women are also vastly underrepresented within evangelical university and seminary faculties as well as in public intellectual leadership more generally. Early on in field research, I found my age and gender to be more of a help than a hindrance in gaining access during field research. As I continued my work, however, I realized that these markers influenced—sometimes significantly—what my interlocutors chose to share with me. Though I developed reciprocal and lasting friendships with some middle-aged and older male interlocutors, in conversations with others, I often had the sense I was perceived as a daughter figure—if somewhat of a curiosity—that they felt a paternal(istic?) inclination to help with her "school project." My age in particular helped me to build rapport among college-age and twenty-something evangelicals. Being only a few years out of my undergraduate work at the beginning of my field research meant that I shared many age-related church and broader cultural experiences with this demographic. Maintaining some of these relationships over social media has helped me to keep up with trends in youth-oriented evangelical worship music circles.

While it is expected that researchers will reflect on how their age, gender, sexuality, race, class, and ability influence their interactions in the field, the effect of their religious (or non-religious) subject positions remain comparatively under-theorized. Within the field of ethnomusicology, Melvin Butler (2002, 2005, 2008) and Jeffrey Summit (2000, 2016) have provided two helpful models of reflexive religious subjectivity that I have drawn on for theoretical insights and practical help as I navigated my complex and shifting relationship with evangelical Christianity. In his position as an African American Pentecostal Christian musician studying Pentecostal music-making in the Afro-Caribbean and its diaspora, Butler describes the "rhetorical acrobatics" involved in the dialogue of faith and scholarship as a researcher who occupies simultaneously the positions of ethnographic and religious "observer" (2005, 48). Butler writes that his experience of Haitian and Jamaican Pentecostal music is "not simply as one appreciating and studying musical sound, but also as a Pentecostal observant believing in the Holy Spirit and seeing in each musical encounter an opportunity to feel the power of God through song... [but] as I have discovered, connecting with God is not always easy to do in a musical style one experiences as foreign" (51–52). Butler notes that, while sharing aspects of religious faith and practice with his research consultants initially reduced the awkwardness and sense of intrusion that often accompanies field research, a series of tensions were brought to the fore and intensified as he developed deeper relationships within his communities of study. He experienced firsthand the contested nature of "blackness," tensions between religious and secular epistemologies presented as mutually exclusive, and sometimes fraught disagreements with his field-research consultants between what musical styles and practices were considered acceptable/sacred and objectionable/profane.

Jeffrey Summit (2000) describes his subject position as a rabbi studying Jewish congregational music-making by using the metaphor of a traveler who is already familiar with a location's terrain. Over the course of his fieldwork, Summit describes encounters with "people who were simultaneously 'me' and 'not me,'" adding that "as I studied others' identities, my identity was constantly in flux, a situation common to researchers engaged in fieldwork" (6). Summit also makes the crucial observation that the ethnographer is never the only one navigating a complex subject position in relationship to others. He reflects that "I do not think my experience 'tacking between the inside and outside of events' here was radically different from that of other informants I interviewed in these groups.... [Many] brought a well-honed reflexivity to their observations about Jewish worship and music as well as their participation in these worship communities" (2000, 9). This was a helpful reminder to me to afford my interlocutors in the field the possibility of experiencing similar degrees of tension, contradiction, and complexity in their relationships to evangelical worship as I was experiencing.

As a practicing Christian raised in southern US evangelical Christianity who has participated in and led contemporary worship music in several church settings, my research demonstrated both the assets and the liabilities of fieldwork as what Butler calls a [religiously] "observant participant" (2000, 48). Throughout my field research, I have constantly been forced to negotiate my relationship to North American evangelical Christianity and its music, considering often how my own religious affiliation positioned me relative to my interlocutors, and how this position intertwined with my and my interlocutors' racial, social class, and gendered subject positions. My relationship to those I encountered in the field varied widely on the basis of the particular event or network under examination. Evangelical Christianity itself is complex and conflicted, embodying many of the same paradoxical— and sometimes contradictory—impulses that characterize Christianity itself (see Cannell 2006); therefore, I found deeper resonance with some of the congregations described in this book than with others. In those places of resonance, I sometimes found myself caught up as a participant in the affective experiences of worship I had come to observe; in other situations in which I found aspects of musical worship ideologically or ethically problematic, I actively resisted becoming caught up in a "worship experience." And, in other situations, I came to regard my ethnographic observing and reflecting as activities that were worshipful in and of themselves, reflecting my Christian vocation as a researcher and providing an academic worship-practice perspective that I hoped some evangelical leaders and worshipers might find illuminating.

My background and lifelong experience within North American evangelical communities gave me thorough understanding of evangelical terms and categories for describing worship and religious experience, what some have parodied as "Christianese"[24] ; my ability to "speak the language" fluently was usually enough to establish instant rapport. While useful for eliciting participants' perspectives, this instant trust I was often accorded sometimes also posed an ethical dilemma. In certain situations, I feared that allowing my interlocutors to assume that I was "one of them" would be misrepresenting my own position or my intentions to subject the event to critical scrutiny. In the few worship events at which I found aspects of belief or practice deeply problematic, I felt the need to distance myself because I did not want my analytical interest or engagement interpreted as tacit approval. On these occasions, I chose not to sing or to participate bodily in worship, since these actions are generally interpreted by other worshipers as a sign of agreement with a gathering's beliefs or practices. When I engaged in conversation in events like this, one effective way of creating distance was to lead out with my denominational affiliation as an Episcopalian. For some conservative evangelicals, the mere mention of my affiliation with a progressive mainline denomination signalled strongly that I might not share certain of their theological beliefs or political persuasions. In a small number of instances, positioning myself in this way actually shut down conversation; more often, however, my conversation partners continued to engage in dialogue while subtly shifting their language away from an assumed "we."

My position relative to the community of study was also influenced by my own personal religious trajectory of increasing distance from evangelical beliefs and practices. Over the course of the seven years of research represented in this book and the four years of writing that followed it, my theological and political views became increasingly distinct from those of my evangelical upbringing and from what many evangelical institutions in the United States tended to espouse. During this time, I began also to step away from musical leadership in contemporary worship settings. While my own distance from the mainstream of evangelical belief and practice may have increased, I still remain in the general evangelical orbit. I currently teach at a Baptist-affiliated university, where the majority of my students are preparing for leadership positions in evangelical churches or seminaries. I have many friends and professional colleagues in evangelical church leadership, in Christian university of seminary faculty positions, and in Christian media and culture industries. Some of my more recent field-research opportunities have been coupled with offers of a public platform to present my research for lay audiences; I am approached on a regular basis to give practically oriented talks and to write popular press articles about contemporary church music. Though I am occasionally conflicted about the extent to which the field remains intertwined with both my personal and professional lives, I have come largely to accept my role as an ethnographer regarded (sometimes incorrectly) as an insider within North American evangelical worship music circles. I seek to use the influence this platform gives me in both strategic and ethical ways, whether in challenging elements of mainstream evangelical discourse (e.g., the pervasive denial of human agency that serves to mystify power relationships and often to uphold a white conservative status quo) or in showcasing the role of congregational music in efforts to promote justice and social inclusion. Contrary to media stereotype, I continue to find evangelicals like the Jewish practitioners Jeffrey Summit describes whose relationship to their own religious tradition is characterized by a "well-honed reflexivity" (Summit 2000, 9). These evangelicals find scholarly perspectives on worship informative and helpful for critically evaluating their practice, as they seek to make their worship conform more closely to their theological and ethical ideals. And, though my work has entailed its share of frustrations and challenges, I have found sharing an ethnomusicological perspective on evangelical worship a fulfilling way to give back to those evangelicals who find value in academic perspectives on their musical and worship practices.

BOOK STRUCTURE

Each chapter of *Singing the Congregation* examines a different mode of congregating in the performance spaces where evangelicals most frequently encounter and participate in contemporary worship music. These congregations comprise worship gatherings at concerts, conferences, local churches, public events, and online sites. Each chapter focuses primarily on one of these spaces but also describes what connects and differentiates these five types of congregations, highlighting the range of practices and modes of sociality that these performance spaces afford and the many ways that they intersect through the mobile individuals and music that traverse them. Through concert congregations, evangelicals actively negotiate the boundaries between participatory worship and popular music performance. In conference congregations, singing with others across regional and ethnic boundaries enables evangelicals to imagine and embody worshiping communities on earth and in heaven. In church congregations, worship music is as a strategic means whereby individual congregants and congregations as a whole position themselves relative to other area churches, Christian networks, and denominations. In public congregations like the praise march, evangelicals choose worship music to represent their community to the broader society as they define what it means to be part of that community through their collective performance. Finally, evangelical worshipers become part of diffuse networked congregations as they share, listen to, and engage in devotional practices centered around online live and recorded performances of worship songs.

Because contemporary worship music draws from current popular music styles, its performance is always in danger of running afoul of the boundaries between entertainment and worship. Chapter 1 uses the worship concert, a mass gathering marked by certain markers of participatory engagement intended to differentiate it from a "mere" concert, as a lens to investigate the interplay between pop-rock performance conventions and evangelical congregational singing. It examines the range of performative strategies whereby a contemporary worship music concert crowd becomes authenticated as a concert congregation united in worship. Through musical style, song lyrics, and discourse about music-making, many of the activities associated with arena rock concerts are reframed as public acts of worship. This reframing has musical and political consequences: understanding the concert gathering as worship shapes evangelical expectations of the "worship experience," influencing aesthetic ideals and expectations of local church music-making. The desire to realize these ideals, in turn, fuels the sale of a range of worship music commodities on which the Christian music recording industry has come to depend. In examining the transformation of fan to worshiper and the conflation of consumption and participation, this chapter shows the extent to which the Christian recording industry shapes and produces notions of congregation within contemporary evangelical Christianity.

The book's second chapter focuses on worship music at evangelical conferences, which are large, frequently interdenominational multi-day events sponsored by one or more nonprofit ministries that gather a specific demographic (e.g., high school or college students, men or women) for several days of intensive worship, prayer, and teaching. Chapter 2 examines the Urbana conferences in St. Louis and the Passion conference in Atlanta—both conferences for college students that have influential "brands" of worship music—as pilgrimage sites and eschatological communities. Conferences like these serve as focal points where devout believers come together across regional and increasingly national boundaries to partake in a powerful spiritual experience that promises to transform their lives. When they sing contemporary worship songs together, participants are encouraged to imagine the conference gathering as an embodiment of the heavenly community. This evangelical vision of heaven serves as a blueprint for social relationships on earth: as conference attendees collectively perform their devotion to God, they also imagine their relationships to others both within and outside the gathering. Comparing lyrics, musical performance, and social organization of congregational music-making at each conference reveals that the two events encourage participants to conceive the heavenly community very differently, resulting in diverging understandings of their relationship to Christians of other gendered, racial and ethnic, and national backgrounds.

The focus of Chapter 3 turns to worship in the local church congregation, often considered the paradigmatic mode of congregating. In a gathering that meets on a weekly basis, congregational worship music becomes an important—and often strategic—means of positioning through which the church signals its relationship with other area church congregations, denominational traditions, and church networks. An ethnographic portrait of St. Bartholomew's Church in Nashville, Tennessee reveals how the strategic choices of congregational music repertory, style, and performance practice enable the church to navigate relationships with charismatic and evangelical church networks while remaining part of the mainline Episcopal denomination. Highlighting what Jeffrey Summit has called musical "junctures of choice" (2000, 19) between a myriad of competing options for congregational worship, in this chapter I pay close attention to the way musical songs and styles are understood by local congregational leaders and congregants and how contemporary worship music, in particular, is used to stake out a church's respective places within the local religious setting. The choice of worship songs and styles on the local congregational level serves as a powerful signifier of what one church leader referred to as the church's unique "voice," in other words, its congregational identity and position relative to other congregations and within networks. Though the church's voice is constructed from broadly circulating discourses and practices within contemporary worship music, the case study of St. Bartholomew's shows that this song repertory is also subject to imaginative reinterpretation within the local church context.

The book's fourth and fifth chapters move progressively further outside the US frame to investigate how contemporary worship music informs the formation of congregation within public spaces. Chapter 4 examines what happens when congregational music "goes public," through the lens of the praise march, a public procession in which evangelical Christians sing contemporary worship songs in the streets of their cities. It examines two consecutive praise marches in Toronto—the UK-initiated March for Jesus (1992–1999) and the Jesus in the City Parade (1999– present)—which both use contemporary worship music for similar purposes: to display spiritual (and political) power, to negotiate the relationships among their religious and other identities, to rally the evangelical community while emphasizing its diversity, and to promote receptiveness to their message in the hopes of provoking bystanders' curiosity, with the hopes of their eventual conversion. Though both marches employ the same basic musical repertory and many of the same worship practices, two models of the public congregation emerge, each shaped by differing performance and ethical ideals. Exploring how contemporary worship music is used within public congregations like these is key to understanding not only how evangelicals shape their public image, but also how they define the boundaries of their community and manage diversity within those boundaries. Further, it shows the degree to which musical engagement with the broader society through public performance has influenced evangelical modes of congregating.

Chapter 5 builds from the foundation provided in Chapter 4, moving from physical to virtual space to examine the new worship gatherings that have emerged as evangelicals have taken contemporary worship music online. Digital audiovisual worship media—whether live-streamed worship services, user-generated YouTube worship videos, or prerecorded audiovisual materials for use in "live" worship—form the nodes of these diffuse congregational networks and serve both as extensions of congregations into the virtual realm and as sites for the creation of new networked congregations. These technologies have enabled networked congregations to expand globally, as far as digital technologies and the internet reach. Drawing from ethnographic field research in the United States and the United Kingdom and an online ethnography study centered on fifty online worship video "fieldsites" that include the perspectives of individuals from across the world, this chapter argues that the new avenues of online communication not only give participants new ways to transmit and share worship songs, but they also have enabled new ways of worshiping. Online musical media serve as both sites for worship and as expressions of individual devotional practice in which once-separate aural and visual strands of evangelical devotion are drawn together into a powerful experiential whole. From media resources for private devotion to live congregational music-making in churches, conferences, and concerts, the evangelical worship experience has become increasingly dependent on digital audiovisual technologies. The resulting networked mode of congregating challenges boundaries between public and private worship, between worship and other types of religious activities, and between aural and visual dimensions of the worship experience.

The conclusion of *Singing the Congregation* draws together the book's themes by returning to a performance of the contemporary worship song discussed in the introduction. It highlights a source of continued conflict within evangelical Christianity: the tension between the worship music "mainstream" and its alternatives. It shows the mainstream to be an influential matrix that combines a specific understanding of music, worship, and congregating and sets itself forward as a model for the way these three activities should relate across geographical and cultural space. Understanding how music makes evangelical congregations matters for understanding how other religious social formations throughout the world constitute and understand themselves. Thus, remodeling and reinvigorating the analytic categories of "congregation" and "congregational music" may enhance their usefulness for scholars working on religious musical practices among religious groups facing similar social changes and pressures.

NOTES

1. Following Ingalls, Landau, and Wagner 2013, I frequently use "congregational music-making/music" rather than "congregational singing/song" in this book so as not to privilege the voice a priori as the only or primary mode of expression in evangelical worship. In our introduction to *Christian Congregational Music: Performance, Identity, and Experience* (2013), we note that the activity of singing is often privileged within study and reflection on Christian musical performances "for a variety of practical and ideological reasons related to the association of 'presence' with the human voice. We chose 'music' in recognition that instrumental music, while often subservient to vocal song, is an evocative and necessary component of many Christian worship traditions, sometimes stepping out of its accompanying role and driving powerful spiritual experiences. Further, the broader term music also emphasizes the ephemerality of sonic performances in which there is not a clear script, creating space for the many Christian traditions around the world in which musical improvisation occurs within or among pre-composed pieces" (2). While singing may be the central means of communal participation within contemporary worship music, playing instruments in the worship band, certain bodily movements and gestures like swaying and raising hands, and contemplative or prayerful listening are other means of participating in the collective musical activity known as worship within evangelical Christianity.

2. I sometimes use "CWM" as a shorthand for contemporary worship music but acknowledge that this acronym never came into popular usage. It is used as shorthand almost exclusively by scholars and evangelical commentators. By contrast, "CCM" (Contemporary Christian Music) is a widely used acronym for Christian popular music among North American evangelicals.

3. My use of "global" here is intended to include both transnationally circulating musical repertories (mainly, but not exclusively, from Anglophone Christian media production centers) and those locally created by evangelical communities worldwide. Though worship music is often associated with North America, it emerged from cultural currents, institutions, and popular movements that are irreducibly transnational (youth movements, charismatic revivals, transnational media, etc.). In the early twenty-first century, the music is produced on local, regional, national, and international scales in evangelical communities worldwide. See Ward 2005; Ingalls 2014; Ingalls and Yong 2015; Evans 2015; and Ruth 2017a.

4. Though my focus in this book is on North American evangelicals, I seek to avoid attributing to this or any other religious group "ownership" of contemporary worship music. Though the dominant influences at the beginning of the music's history were mainly pentecostal-charismatic and evangelical coalitions,

it has since been incorporated into churches across denominational lines, including congregations affiliated with mainline denominations (e.g., Methodist, Reformed, Presbyterian, and Episcopal/Anglican). The emergence of contemporary worship music also dovetailed with the reforms of Vatican II, and there has been some overlap between North American evangelical and Catholic musical and liturgical trends. Parts of the CWM repertoire have been incorporated into Catholic worship, and Catholic contemporary-worship leaders such as Matt Maher and Audrey Assad have signed with evangelical record labels and have penned several worship songs widely sung in evangelical worship.

5. I follow Ingalls, Nekola, and Mall 2013, which suggests that, because of significant differences in their histories, audiences, discourses, and uses, CCM and worship music should remain distinct within academic analysis. For histories and cultural analyses of CCM in North America, see Howard and Streck 1999; Cusic 2002, 2012; Hendershot 2004; Stowe 2011; Mall 2012; and Young 2015.

6. The late 1990s and early 2000s saw a deluge of publications of church-focused resources for navigating the "worship wars." See, for instance, Peters 1994; Towns 1997; Byars 2002; York 2003; and Redman 2004, as well as other articles in a 2004 special issue (vol. 19, no. 4) of the Liturgical Conference's journal *Liturgy* entitled *Worship Wars*.

7. Some scholars and interpreters have proposed new categories in addition to the terms Christian communities use to refer to this music. For instance, see Tom Wagner's discussion of "popular worship music" (2017) and Daniel Thornton's appellation "contemporary congregational song" (2015). While both authors offer compelling reasons for their designations, the terms they devise have not yet been taken up by practitioners or other scholars.

8. The term "praise and worship" is preferable to "contemporary worship music" for referring to the genre as it has been localized in settings outside North America, particularly, but not exclusively, within pentecostal-charismatic communities. Many Christian communities worldwide use translations of "praise and worship" to designate this set of worship practices and their associated song repertory: e.g., alabanza y adoración (Spanish); хвала и поклонение (Russian); iyin ati adura (Yoruba); 경배와 찬양Kyŏngpaewa ch'anyang; Korean, lit. "worship and praise"); louvor e adoração (Portuguese); and 敬拜和赞美 (Jìng bài hé zànměi—Chinese, lit. "worship and praise").

9. For many African American Christian communities, much of what this book calls "contemporary worship music" is labeled as "CCM." The term CCM is often used by black Christians in the United States to describe Christian music in mainstream popular styles like rock that are racially marked as "white," while "praise and worship" denotes a participatory congregational musical practice that is often "gospelized" (see B. Johnson 2008, 2011).

10. There is considerable overlap between scholarship on contemporary worship music in contemporary global perspective and scholarship within the field of congregational music studies. For a history and characterization of this emerging area of study, see Porter 2014.

11. Many evangelical publishers and popular press publications provide valuable perspectives on the historical development of contemporary worship music as well. See in particular Frame 1997; Liesch 2001; Redman 2002; Beaujon 2006. And see particular the journalistic work of *Billboard*'s Deborah Evans Price (1999a, 1998b, 2003, 2004a, 2004b, 2008) and *Christianity Today*'s

Russ Breimeier (2007, 2008); see also http://www.christianitytoday.com for Breimeier's dozens of Christian pop and worship album reviews).

12. The large percentage differences in these figures illustrate well the differences how evangelicals are defined. Statistics for global evangelical Christianity are collected by two sources: the World Christian Database (WCD) at the Center for the Study of Global Christianity at Gordon-Conwell Theological Seminary and *Operation World* (OW), an evangelical missiological periodical. The WCD uses what the compilers call a "structural" approach to define evangelicals and evangelical Christianity. An evangelical is a member of a "church, congregation, or denomination" that is deemed part of evangelical Christianity by virtue of the institution's adherence to certain the beliefs and practices. The OW relies on a more inclusive, individually based parameters that defines evangelicals as those who subscribe to the four essential doctrines (Bebbington's quadrilateral discussed previously in the introduction), regardless of their church or denomination. For the OW, evangelicals are found not only in denominations with traditionally evangelical beliefs, but also in Anglican, Catholic, and Orthodox groups. For further discussion, see the report "Christianity in Its Global Context, 1970–2020: Society, Religion, and Mission" (Center for the Study of Global Christianity 2013). Another important factor is whether or not evangelical Christianity is seen to encompass or overlap with pentecostal-charismatic Christianity. For a discussion of overlaps and distinctions among these networks, see Coleman and Hackett 2015, 6–12.

13. Other smaller-scale studies have noted a wide discrepancy between the political affiliations of white and nonwhite Christians who claim beliefs considered hallmarks of evangelical Christianity. LifeWay Research, the research arm of the Southern Baptist Convention, conducted a poll one month before the 2016 presidential election and found that nonwhite evangelicals supported Hillary Clinton at nearly the same rate that white evangelicals supported Donald Trump (62 percent and 65 percent, respectively). The study also found party affiliation to be a stronger predictor than belief: while upward of 75 percent of Republicans who claimed evangelical beliefs planned to vote for Donald Trump, 75 percent of Democrats who claimed evangelicals beliefs planned to vote for Hillary Clinton (Smietana 2016).

14. During the "ethnographic present" of this book, a seven-year period that spans the final two years of the George W. Bush administration and the first six years of Barack Obama's presidency, there was a near-complete absence of national political discussion in the worship spaces in which I conducted my field research. From early on, I noticed a reticence and sometimes outright refusal among my interlocutors to mix talk of U.S. politics with the discourse or activity of worship, on both top-down and grassroots levels. Not once during any worship event I attended over eight years of field research—even at national conferences and public events in city streets and stadiums—did I ever hear a political candidate or party endorsed from the stage. And only rarely did a speaker at a worship event raise a contentious political issue (abortion came up on occasion, and I can recall two instances in which speakers expressed opposition to LGBTQ rights). This is not to say that contemporary worship music has never been used in conjunction with right-leaning political causes, as it is the music that is meaningful to a large number of US evangelicals, who as a group lean to the right. For instance, in the weeks and months leading up to the 2016 presidential election, at Dallas-area Gateway Church, a multi-site megachurch known for its worship music,

church leaders and congregants explicitly supported Donald Trump. This church was the subject of a March 2018 feature in the *New York Times* calling attention to the 2016 election as a breaking point causing an exodus of black Christians from predominantly white evangelical churches like Gateway (Campbell 2018). Contemporary worship songs were occasionally used on the 2016 campaign trail by candidates seeking to rally the Religious Right to their cause. National Public Radio reports that Chris Tomlin's song "Our God Is Greater" and other "gospel rock" songs were sung at a Ted Cruz rally at Liberty University, a far-right-leaning institution long affiliated with the Religious Right (accessed December 27, 2017, https://www.npr.org/2015/03/23/394906479/sen-ted-cruz-becomes-first-republican-to-announce-presidential-candidacy). In the rare instances that well-known worship leaders have ascended the stage at politically charged events (in over a decade of observation, I am aware of three such instances, including David Crowder's touring with Franklin Graham in 2017), their appearance has not been widely publicized. There appears to be a much closer connection between right-leaning politicians and Christian popular music that is not used in congregational worship. For instance, in 2016 Republican primary candidates Ben Carson and Ted Cruz both led prayers at the popular concert tour Winter Jam, considered a CCM performance rather than a worship music event (http://www.newreleasetoday.com/news_detail.php?newsid=1344).

I have not engaged in ethnographic research among evangelicals in the years immediately preceding or following the 2016 U.S. national elections and acknowledge that the relationship of evangelical worship and politics may change significantly as the result of this development and others on the national stage.

15. Mark Labberton and Richard Mouw, president and past president of a theologically moderate evangelical seminary in California, put out a statement immediately following the 2016 election on the effects of what they see as media misuse of the designation "evangelical." They write that "over the course of the campaign, the press increasingly referred to evangelicals as politically conservative, and predominantly white Christians." As a result of the strong political associations of the term "evangelical" pre- and post-election, Labberton and Mouw write that many who fall within this camp theologically or institutionally now feel compelled "to abandon the term, to adamantly reject further identification with evangelical and with groups associated with it" (Labberton and Mouw 2017).

16. For a parallel exploration that advocates for seeing evangelical Christianity as a community constituted through collective performance, see Stevenson 2013. Here, Stevenson focuses on five performance genres, including passion plays, museum displays, and megachurch worship services that each express a core set of orientations to popular performance media that she calls "evangelical dramaturgy" (24).

17. A cursory internet search reveals this equation as a source of considerable anxiety and criticism among evangelicals, bringing up scores of evangelical magazine articles and blog posts whose titles are variations on the theme of "worship is more than music" (Beach 2005; Hill 2016). See Chapter 1 for a discussion of the song "Heart of Worship," whose lyrics describe worship when music is "stripped away." Here, the worshiper declares to God in song, "I'll bring you more than a song."

18. See Lim and Ruth 2017 for a more in-depth explanation of the charismatic and Pentecostal practices and theologies that formed the backdrop for the equation of congregational music-making and worship.

19. According to Roger Haight (2004a), it is a common strand within historical Protestant ecclesiology to see the local congregation as both primary unit and complete encapsulation of the church. Churches and denominations considered to have congregational polities, where each church congregation is autonomous, often formalize an understanding of congregation along these lines in official church documents. See, for instance, Article 16. Church Order and Unity of "The Confession of Faith in a Mennonite Perspective" (available at http://mennoniteusa.org/confession-of-faith/church-order-and-unity/); Article 8. Congregational Ministries of the Disciples of Christ "Design of the Christian Church" (available at http://disciples.org/our-identity/the-design/), and the statement "Doing Church Baptist Style: CONGREGATIONALISM" from the Baptist History and Heritage Society (available at http://centerforbaptiststudies.org/pamphlets/style/congregationalism.htm).

20. Klomp and Barnard have proposed the theoretical concept "sacro-soundscape" to help academic interpreters "better understand gatherings around Christian music in and outside church in late-modern culture" (Klomp and Barnard 2017, 241); Klomp, forthcoming). My model of "musical modes of congregating" overlaps somewhat with Klomp and Barnard's notion of sacro-soundscapes, particularly in our commonly felt imperative to interpret the performance of Christian music outside church congregations. Where the model of musical modes of congregating parts ways with sacro-soundscapes is that the former describes gatherings within and outside churches for the *express purpose of Christian worship*, a participatory musical practice enabled by shared understandings among the gathered congregation. The sacro-soundscape concept, in contrast, describes the use of Christian congregational and presentational sacred music in secular spaces for nonreligious purposes. Here, individuals determine the degree to which the musical performance is experienced as "religious." In her interpretation of community singalongs of Bach's *St. Matthew Passion*, Klomp writes that it is one example among many in contemporary Dutch society in which "people freely shape rituals with Christian roots, and make sense of these rituals in their own manner, based on their own (personal) frameworks. Christian language and ritual practices thus moved from the 'ecclesial' domain to other domains: the private, public, and cultural domains . . ." (Klomp, forthcoming). She later observes that these communal gatherings around Christian music do not necessarily perform any religious functions: "many practices of Christian music are simply not informed by faith, or a desire for God, nor do they lead to such thing" (Klomp, forthcoming).

21. I am indebted to practical theologian Pete Ward for the term "lived ecclesiology" (2015), though my usage of the term here does not imply a theological project on my part. Rather, I seek to provide a detailed description and interpretation of evangelicals' theological, social, and ethical projects of community building through worship music.

22. Though contemporary worship music practices across North American share broad similarities, there are also important regional differences that shape how worship music is produced and performed. See Haynes (2017) for an account of Mars Hill, a now-defunct megachurch network that was a regional hub of contemporary worship music production in the Seattle area. The musical influence of many other such regional megachurch networks whose worship music has risen to national prominence within North American evangelicalism, including Bethel Church in Redding, California, and Gateway Church, in Southlake, Texas, remain unexamined within academic scholarship.

23. For anthropological and ethnomusicological perspectives on the challenges of fieldwork in one's home society, see Jackson 1987; Amit 2000; Stock and Chou 2008; and J. Jackson 2016.
24. For an explanation of over one hundred such words and phrases particular to evangelical Christianity, see Tim Stewart's online Dictionary of Christianese at http://www.dictionaryofchristianese.com.

CHAPTER 1

∽

Making Jesus Famous

The Quest for an Authentic Worship Experience in the Concert Congregation

CONCERT AS CONGREGATION

Since the early 2000s, North American evangelical worship music practices have grown increasingly intertwined with the spaces, practices, and discourses of the Christian recording industry. In the forty years since the production of the first "worship album" in the early 1970s for evangelicals on the countercultural margins, contemporary worship music has become a mainstream—and immensely profitable—commodity.[1] The definition of "modern worship music" as a radio format in the late 1990s and the subsequent reshaping of the Nashville-based US Christian music industry around the worship music subgenre have considerably broadened its reach (see Ingalls, Landau, and Wagner2013a; Ingalls, Nekola, and Mall. 2013). US Christians can now hear pop-rock style worship music not only in their churches and at Christian conferences, but also emanating from the stages of festivals and concerts and over the waves of FM stations, Internet radio, and music-streaming services. As a result, churches face an expanding marketplace for worship music, produced by both church-based and for-profit and record companies with expansive distribution networks and multi-pronged marketing strategies.

To investigate further the interplay between pop-rock performance and evangelical congregational singing and how their overlap informs evangelical understandings of worship, this chapter focuses on the performance spaces referred to as "worship concerts," "worship events," or sometimes "worship experiences," drawing from field research conducted between 2007 and 2011 at concerts in Atlanta, Nashville, and Toronto, as well as the United States' largest Christian music festival, the 70,000-participant Creation Festival Northeast in Mount Union, Pennsylvania. Recounting narratives and conversations from these events illustrates how performers and participants work together to mark off the activity in which all are engaged as worship and, in the process, perform a particular type of congregation into being.

To set the stage, I recount a worship concert I attended in Nashville, an event that illustrates well the multiple intersections between the spheres of arena rock[2] performance and congregational worship.

Fieldnotes, October 21, 2007

On a mild evening in mid-October, I arrive outside a sports arena, as excited, expectant concertgoers are descending on the venue in a steady stream of cars, buses, and vans with church names emblazoned along their sides. Celebrity worship leader and recording artist Chris Tomlin has extended his "How Great Is Our God" tour to include a stop at Lipscomb University's Allen Arena in Nashville, Tennessee. In the eight years since his debut album in 1999, Tomlin has become the best-known and bestselling worship artist and songwriter in North America, with a dozen or more of his pop-rock style worship songs becoming regular Sunday morning fare in US evangelical churches. I have seen Tomlin perform several times at annual conferences for college students but have never seen him on tour. As the snaking line moves through the lobby of the stadium, the first thing that greets the concertgoers is the prominent table that occupies a large part of the arena's foyer and is covered with a variety of colorful wares, from Tomlin's CDs and DVDs to branded apparel and other products. Many teenagers and young adults are browsing the product table, and a young woman is eagerly purchasing a ball cap emblazoned with the words "Made to Worship," the title of one of Chris Tomlin's popular songs.

By seven o'clock, three or four thousand people have filled the arena. All the overhead lights are turned off, and the music begins to play. The stage lights come on to reveal a five-piece pop-rock band with Chris Tomlin at center stage (Figure 1.1).

Nearly every seat in the square basketball arena looks down onto the stage, and two large screens have been placed on the sides of the stage so that every corner of the arena can read clearly the lyrics of the worship songs being performed. The energetic and heartfelt singing of the crowd to the projected lyrics marks the experience as "worship" for many evangelical participants; however, in many other ways the experience sounds, looks, and feels like a typical arena rock concert, complete with garish visual display. Bright lights of varying colors are flashing on the stage and onto the excited crowd. Following the song lyrics on the screen is at times dizzying—the words are placed overtop an ever-changing background, sometimes plain colored but other times featuring photographs or specially designed moving graphics. Looking out onto the sea of faces reveals an exuberant, predominantly

Figure 1.1: Chris Tomlin (far right) and his band play "Your Grace Is Enough" during the worship concert at Lipscomb University's Allen Arena. Nashville, Tennessee: October 2007. Photo by the author

youthful crowd. Nearly all participants are singing along enthusiastically with the worship songs as they sway or jump in time to the music.

Between upbeat songs, with one hand upraised, Tomlin animatedly exhorts the gathered audience to praise God by using words paraphrased from the biblical Psalms. On the slower-tempo rock ballads that follow, many participants, with their eyes closed and faces upturned, raise both hands above their heads as if in surrender. After one poignant slow ballad, Tomlin leads the gathering in prayer and then extemporizes for a few moments, concluding with an impassioned statement about the purpose of the evening. "I am not here to perform for you," Tomlin declares, but rather "to lead one massive concert to the living God." To loud applause and cheers from the crowd, Tomlin proclaims that "there is only one star of this show: the Lord Jesus!"

This vignette shows the strong resemblance between worship concerts and stadium rock concerts: both have extravagant multimedia and lighting displays, rock band instrumentation and amplification, and performer-audience interaction that characterizes musical entertainment events, such as cheering and applause. It also highlights the many elements of these events that resemble a church service. The large screens project song lyrics to encourage the audience to sing along. Leaders proclaim the words of biblical texts and lead public prayer, while modeling devotional gestures such as raising hands and faces as if toward heaven. These performative elements help to authenticate the gathering as more than a "mere concert" of Christian popular music, but as a congregation gathered for the express purpose of worshiping God.

Not just any concert of Christian music is considered "worship," and not all artists in the Christian popular music industry are considered "worship leaders." Fans of worship music constantly evaluate worship music artists and events not only for their artistic merit but also on grounds of theological accuracy and spiritual efficacy. Concert tours of celebrity worship leaders become proving grounds, where artists, brands, and products are authenticated if they inspire "real worship." While worship concerts draw from preexisting expectations of worship, they do not merely reinforce existing evangelical worship practices. Rather, they promote new songs and styles and, crucially, help to set aesthetic expectations and discipline the worshiping body in particular ways. In the context of a worship concert, participants learn to frame their affective experience as worship and thus experience the concert as congregation as well as an audience of fans. This chapter examines the range of performative strategies whereby concert crowds become worshiping congregations. It shows that a series of specific sonic moves and bodily gestures embedded in performance serve to authenticate the concert as worship, forming a "concert congregation." Through musical style, song lyrics, and extramusical discourse, many of the activities associated with stadium rock concerts are ritualized and reframed as acts of public worship. This reframing has musical and political consequences: understanding their worship concert activities as worship shapes what evangelicals expect of a "worship experience" in other settings in terms of aesthetic and ethical ideals. The desire to realize these ideals in communal and private devotional settings, in turn, has fueled the sale of commercial worship music on which the Christian recording industry has come to depend.

CONTEMPORARY WORSHIP MUSIC AND THE CHRISTIAN MUSIC INDUSTRY: MARKETING THE "WORSHIP EXPERIENCE"

A worship concert is a mass collective performance of contemporary worship music, generally led by a well-known celebrity performer and attended by a large audience. A worship concert is not simply a concert of Christian music; further, not just any Christian popular music performer or group can put on an event considered to be a "worship concert." Rather, there are additional genre rules, performance expectations, and experiential components involved. Before we delve more deeply into these aspects that define the worship concert, it is first necessary to understand the relationship of two interrelated forms of North American evangelical popular music: music for entertainment and devotional listening, often referred to as CCM (Contemporary Christian Music) and music for use in congregational singing ("praise and worship music," "contemporary worship music," or simply "worship music").

Beginning in the late 1960s, evangelicals started using pop-rock music both for concert performances and for collective singing in worship (Fromm 2006; Stowe 2011; Ingalls et al. 2013a, 2015b). A division of labor soon developed between performance-oriented music sung as a testimony by musical specialists (known as "message music") and participatory choruses oriented toward God and intended for an entire gathering to sing (known as "praise music"). It took less than a decade for the two genres to part ways and form recording industries that were to remain largely separate for another two decades. In 1980, Maranatha! Music, founded in 1972 as one of the first Christian pop-rock recording labels, chose not to renew the contracts of its "message music" artists, in order to focus exclusively on producing "praise music" (Redman 2002). "Message music"—in other words, performance-based Christian music produced by specialists for devotional listening rather than for corporate worship—was eventually renamed contemporary Christian music (CCM) and snapped up by Christian music labels seeking to capitalize on the success of Jesus Music artists with the evangelical youth demographic (Mall 2012).

Through there has always been some degree of overlap between worship music and CCM, the two related genres were produced by industries that remained largely separate from the late 1970s until the late 1990s (Redman 2002; Ingalls et al. 2013a, 2013b). As the audience for worship music expanded beyond charismatic churches into mainstream evangelicalism, and as CCM producers began looking at young worship leaders as new sources for inspiration, the musical division of labor began to unravel. *Campus Life*, a popular magazine for evangelical high school and college students, encapsulates in its January 2001 music column the sea change that was occurring:

> We're always getting new CDs here at *Campus Life*. We get all types—pop, rock, alternative, hip-hop, hardcore, gospel . . . you name it, we've probably got it. About the middle of last year [2000], we started noticing a trend. Seemed like every other CD that arrived here came with this label (or something like it): Praise & worship music. Sometimes it's called "modern worship." Sometimes simply "worship." But whatever they called it, we started getting tons of it. We started hearing it on Christian radio more and more. And we started singing the same songs in our churches and youth groups. And we still do. Of the more than 25 million Christian music albums sold in Y2K, about a quarter of them were praise & worship. The new year is starting out the same way. (Moring 2001, 20)

In order to capitalize on this new development, CCM recording labels and publishers scrambled en masse to break into the worship music business in the early 2000s. Some recording labels and publishers created new "worship music" arms. Many CCM labels began pushing the artists on their roster into writing songs for congregational worship or performing cover versions of worship songs already widespread. Many artists were also pressured by their labels to release one or more "worship albums" consisting entirely of songs for congregational worship (Ingalls 2008; Nekola 2009). And these efforts proved immensely profitable: by the mid-2000s, almost half of the top twenty albums on *Billboard*'s Christian music charts were classified as "worship albums." Over less than a decade, contemporary worship music, previously located outside the mainstream of the Nashville-based Christian recording industry, became Christian music's fastest growing subgenre (Ingalls et al. 2013a, 2013b).

In tandem with the growth of this new participatory Christian popular music subgenre, a new term for the divine encounter mediated in congregational singing insinuated its way into the evangelical vernacular: the "worship experience." This term is endemic within early twenty-first-century evangelical discourse about congregational singing; Anna Nekola notes that, beginning in the late 1990s and early 2000s, an increasing number of congregations have replaced "worship service" with "worship experience" (2013: 133, fn. 49). Since the early 2000s, the worship experience has become an important component of worship music marketing, commonly used in titles of conferences and concert tours and found in titles of several worship recordings. Figure 1.2 shows the album cover for *Casting Crowns: A Live Worship Experience*. This worship album from a popular CCM band was released in 2015 and made it to number 3 on the *Billboard* Christian music charts that year.

The album cover situates the worship experience geographically by designating the location "Atlanta, Georgia." Promotional material around the album reveals the degree to which the location is generalized: the album was recorded live in the band's church in McDonough, a city of 20,000 located thirty miles from the city center on the southeast edge of the Atlanta metro area. The album's title and cover image does not make immediately clear whether the recording was made in a church, concert, conference, or public event. It depicts a large group of people raising their hands—which evangelicals immediately recognize as symbolizing "worship," or congregational music-making—in a cavernous, darkened space illuminated by the multicolored lights of a front central stage. Visible in the midst of the glow at the front of the worship space is a stage with a guitarist on stage right and a vocalist on center stage who is singing into a microphone. Above it all hang three large screens on the left, right, and center of the stage.

This album cover captures well the intertwining of technological mediation, marketing, and participatory zeal within the activity known as the worship experience. In the following discussion, I trace the genealogy of the term "worship experience" through its three intertwined roots: evangelical piety, technological developments, and marketing trends within late

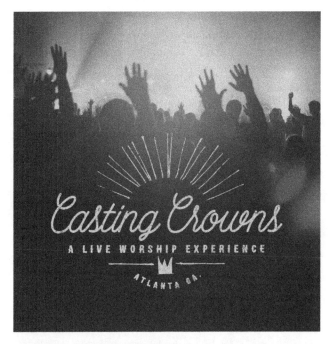

Figure 1.2: Album cover for *Casting Crowns: A Live Worship Experience* (2015).
©2015 Provident Music Group. Used by permission.

capitalism. Though these strands are often inseparable in practice, it is worth teasing them apart here in order to produce a more nuanced interpretation of this musically mediated experience that has become so formative within evangelical Christianity.

In the latter quarter of the twentieth century, companies and brands began marketing experiences, ushering in what business writers Joseph Pine and James Gilmore dub the "experience economy" (Pine and Gilmore 1999). They write that corporately produced, branded experiences draw techniques from the entertainment industry, "connecting with [consumers] in a personal, memorable way" (3). They do not seek to create passive spectators but rather actively engage customers who will act as willing promoters of their product through testimonies of life transformation. The Christian music industry was no exception to this marketing trend. Anna Nekola (2013) has described the ways that, beginning in the late 1990s, Christian music and media industries began to "echo worship leaders who urge their congregations to bring ecstatic, spirit-filled worship into everything they do," collapsing the boundaries between public and personal worship through the medium of contemporary worship music that ran as a common thread through both (134). She charts the course of the experience discourse in the marketing of contemporary worship music by examining the shifting textual and visual content of advertisements in *Worship Leader* magazine from the mid-1990s to the late 2000s. Worship music went from being marketed as a tool for congregational singing to a resource for personal worship whenever and wherever the devoted listener chooses to play it. Nekola writes that these ads "reinforce the discourse that worship is an 'experience' that should 'overwhelm' the listener with feeling" (131), and interprets this shift as contributing to a trend toward the privatization of the worship experience in which worshipers may turn "their ordinary, everyday life into an experience of divine immanence" (134). She notes that, by the late 2000s, the experience discourse had pervaded congregational worship as well, and she gives examples of churches that described their weekly worship services or special music-based events as worship experiences (133).

CONVERSATIONS ABOUT VALUE: AUTHENTICITY IN POPULAR MUSIC AND EVANGELICAL WORSHIP EXPERIENCES

That worship experiences can be produced, packaged, and sold is not lost on contemporary evangelicals. In the late 2000s and early 2010s, evangelical periodicals and blogs chronicled an eruption of anxiety—and sometimes cynicism—centered on the marketing of worship, and sometimes the language of the "worship experience" itself. In his 2009 book *The Divine Commodity*, pastor and evangelical magazine editor Skye Jethani includes an excerpt from a conversation between his co-editors and business writer James Gilmore, coauthor of *The Experience Economy* (Pine and Gilmore 1999). Here, Gilmore notes—and bemoans—the close parallel between the experience economy he describes in his book and the new economy of church worship. Gilmore observes that "increasingly you find people talking about the worship *experience* rather than the worship *service*" (72). One of the writers muses, "When people come to church, don't they expect an experience of some kind? Consumers approach the worship service with the same mindset as they do a purchase" (72). When asked if worshipers—and consumers more generally—will ever tire of seeking experiences, Gilmore predicts that the (over-)emphasis on experience will generate a desire for authenticity that will usher in a "transformation economy": "After a while, thoughtful people begin to ask 'What effect are all these experiences having on me? What am I becoming?'" (74).

And transformation is exactly the term Andrea Lucado uses in her 2015 article "Do You Worship Your Worship Experience?" in evangelical young-adult-oriented *RELEVANT* magazine. The article is headed by a photograph of a young white woman in a posture of personal worship: her hands raised, she stands alone in a bleak forest, her face turned upward toward the brilliant sunlight. Lucado voices her own worry that she has "allowed worship, to become . . . [simply] an experience that makes me feel good"; that in seeking churches with "amazing worship bands," entertaining services, and engaging pastors, she is merely consuming a product and not allowing God to transform her. In describing worship, she asks herself if she worships "the act of [worship] as it takes place in our church services? The music, the dark lighting, the instruments playing behind the prayer? Is this what I crave more than God?"[3] With her references to music, contemporary bands, lighting, and dark spaces, Lucado depicts a culturally specific backdrop that her evangelical readers can readily identify. And her article apparently struck a chord: garnering over 11,000 shares on social media, it became one of the most popular posts in the history of *RELEVANT*'s online archive.

These are but two of countless examples within print and online discourse of evangelicals' acute anxiety about the commodification of the worship experience, manifesting a pervasive worry that spiritual interests have taken a back seat to self-centered ones. In the early 2000s, coinciding with worship music's rapid commercialization, the category of authenticity became the standard for evaluating the overall performance of both worship and of worship music. Evangelical pastors, worship leaders, and worshipers filled books, magazines, and blogs with thoughts on what qualities or actions constituted worship— and worship music—that was "authentic," "genuine," or "real."[4] Evangelical conversations about authenticity in worship music parallel closely the authenticity discourses of other musical forms. Sarah Thornton describes the privileged place the discourse of authenticity holds within Anglophone popular music:

> Authenticity is arguably the most important value ascribed to popular music . . . Music is perceived as authentic when it *rings true* or *feels real*, when it has *credibility* and comes across as *genuine*. In an age of endless representations and global mediation, the experience of musical authenticity is perceived as a cure both for alienation (because it offers feelings of community) and dissimulation (because it extends a sense of the really "real"). As such it is valued as a balm for media fatigue and as an antidote to commercial hype. (1996, 26)

As a result, authenticity has become an important way to market commercial products, promising to contribute meaningful resources to the "identity projects" of those who purchase them.[5] Michael Coyle and Jon Dolan assert that "in the world of commerce, authenticity is simply a matter of trademark" (1999, 29). Within popular musical performance,

> the discourse of authenticity proposes to ground audiences and performers alike in a place outside discourse, a place somehow free of the star-making machinery, a place where audiences and artists yearning for what is genuine can commune with an ageless and priceless heritage. (29)

In evangelical discourse, authenticity performs many of the same functions as an evaluative category for worship music. It is used to distinguish between congregational worship in line with, in Coyle and Dolan's words, the "ageless and priceless heritage" of the Christian faith, on the one hand, and worldly "performance" that smacks of the recording industry's "star-making machinery" and "commercial hype." Like the popular music concerns for authenticity, ultimately, the evangelical authenticity discourse around worship and worship music centers on questions of trust: Are songwriters writing for the good of the church or to make a (considerable) profit? Are record labels promoting worship music that will promote spiritual growth, or are they simply churning out what will sell? Can celebrity "worship leaders" be trusted to write songs useful in church worship if they are constantly touring rather than serving in a local church? Ultimately, how does one decide whether a worship experience, artist, or setting is genuine?

Many commentators and Christian leaders have sought to work out evaluative principles that individuals could apply to worship in different settings. For an understanding of how the authenticity discourse is applied to evangelical worship, it is helpful to look carefully at a representative example. One such position piece, entitled "Real Worship," appeared as the cover article in the evangelical publication *Christian Leadership* magazine in 1999. The author, evangelical pastor and magazine editor Marshall Shelley, begins by articulating the widespread concerns about authenticity. He comments on the ubiquity of the term: "one word I hear a lot these days is 'authentic,' as in 'we seek authentic worship.'" Shelley gives his readers three diagnostic questions to ascertain whether or not a gathering is authentic:

1. Are we worshiping the real God? (Not ourselves or something we've created.)
2. Is the participation of the people real? (Not a charade or mere ritual.)
3. Is the response real? (After encountering God, do people serve him?). (3)

The three criteria that Shelley develops over the course of his article—that worship must be God centered, participatory, and personally transformative—provide a useful framework for considering if a concert can be authenticated as a "worship experience" and the gathered crowd widely understood to be a congregation united in worship. Widely circulating criteria like Shelley's allow individual worshipers to weigh for themselves the relative authenticity of worship gatherings on the basis of their own experience and interpretations of the events. Yet they also equip performers, artists, record labels, and the commercial sphere with rhetorical moves whereby they can legitimate themselves and insulate themselves from criticism. Indeed, as the following sections of this chapter demonstrate, successful authentication of worship concerts relies on boundary markers integral to mass-mediated discourses and embedded within the musical performance itself. These ritual elements include patterns of speech, song, and gesture that work together to deflect fame from the celebrity performers and redirect focus to God, to draw in attendees as participants, and to enable attendees to interpret their ongoing experience in worship music fan culture as personal transformation.

The worship concert has become the proving ground of evangelical worship music artists working in the industry. Whether or not an artist or band can provide participants with a "worship experience" deemed as genuine or successful ultimately determines their success in the genre. In other words, concertgoers have to feel part of a worshiping congregation, coming away with a sense that they "really worshiped" and utterly convinced that the artist on stage was an inspired "worship leader" rather than merely a skilled performer. Using Marshall Shelley's framework, the next sections of this chapter look at how authenticity is performed in the worship concert and take a close look at the performative moves used to bring the concert congregation into being.

"IT'S ALL ABOUT YOU, JESUS": SINCERITY AND FREEDOM IN GOD-CENTERED WORSHIP

Shelley's first criterion is that worship must be "God-centered"—an ascription that can be a challenge in a space that looks, sounds, and feels like an arena rock concert. Even though participants gather in a large space oriented toward a center stage with a celebrity band at the focal point of the lights, cameras, and gathered crowd, the focus of the gathering must be experienced as centered on God for authentic worship to occur. Throughout my fieldwork, I observed a common constellation of performative ways that evangelicals sought to establish a God-centered concert congregation. Each of these actions, including verbal avowals, song lyrics, and musical gestures, served to deflect focus from inappropriate human centers of attention onto a Divine center.

One principal way that worship concerts become God centered is through speech before, during, and in between worship songs. Many of my conversation partners at worship concerts told me that worship leaders' verbal remarks—what one participant called the "between-the-song-banter"—are helpful ways of encouraging a single-minded focus on God. Before a two-day event in Atlanta, Maria, a Latina college student from Miami, Florida recounted, "every worship leader will say something—they'll speak on a verse or on a song you're going to sing. What they say before the song . . . helps people understand [that] the focus is on God" (personal interview, 2008). At worship concerts, these all-pervasive framing remarks range from avowals of a singleness of purpose ("all we are here to do is to worship God") to reframing of the event ("you have come not to a concert, but to enter into a time of worship"), to exhortations to sing, clap, or engage in other actions associated with evangelical worship ("let's all sing to God, because he alone is worthy of our praise!").[6] Lionel Trilling has termed these verbal exhortations intended to communicate sincerity of purpose "rhetorics of avowal," or "the demonstration of single-minded innocence through attitude and posture" (1972, 70). These comments serve as ritual performative utterances (Austin 1962), helping to bring about the reality that they are intended to convey for participants.

These performative utterances extend beyond worship leader's reframing comments. In particular, musical sounds and gestures can help to affirm participants' sense of a God-centered focus by communicating sincere intentions. Worship leaders and participants alike avow, in the face of distractions or weakness, that their intentions are to focus on God alone. In the context of popular musical performance, Simon Frith writes that, for the performer to maintain a sense of "sincere utterance" in the face of the clear artifice of the pop song, musical gestures and textual markers that signify inarticulacy or uncertainty are employed:

> Sincerity may then be best indicated by an *inability* to speak (as in soul vocal convention) or through an aural *contradiction* between the glibness of the lyric and the uncertainty of the voice (as in much male country music). (1996, 168)

Frith's notion of an "inability to speak"—a performed inarticulacy—is useful when considering how worship song lyrics and performance are used to center participants' focus on God. An account from my field research at a Christian music festival highlights an example of the collective performance of one such song.

It is the evening of the second day of the 2007 Creation East Music Festival in rural Pennsylvania, then the largest Christian music festival in North America. The Creation East crowd, estimated to be around 70,000, has filled the outdoor amphitheater with a sea of camping chairs spread along on the grassy field. Up to this point, all of the performers during the festival's evening concerts have been CCM or Christian rock artists or bands; performers of worship music have generally been confined to the smaller mid-afternoon "worship tent" venue, which has drawn 200 to 300 attendees for the past two days. This evening's headliner, however, is Tim Hughes, a British worship leader whose songs are exclusively written for and performed as congregational worship. As Hughes takes the stage and begins to sing, song lyrics stream line by line below his image on the two Jumbotrons in the front of the amphitheatre (Figure 1.3). Participants near the front—whom I could make out with the aid of a friend's binoculars—are singing animatedly and raising their hands. From my seat in the middle of the vast festival audience, participation is more varied: some around me have their eyes focused on the screens as their lips

Figure 1.3: Tim Hughes leads worship on the main stage at the Creation Festival Northeast. Mount Union, Pennsylvania: June 2007.
Photo by the author

mouth the song lyrics, while others continue to chat loudly to their neighbors or to munch on popcorn and funnel cakes.

After several up-tempo, energetic worship songs, there is silence from the stage, and a relative calm descends upon the large gathering. Hughes begins to softly strum his acoustic guitar, evoking the intimacy of an "unplugged" moment. Seeming to recognize the familiar strains of the song's opening chord progression, many members of the gathered audience—even those at some distance from the stage—close their eyes and enter a posture of prayer while swaying gently to the music. From the image projected via the huge screens, I see Hughes close his eyes and, with an expression conveying a serious intensity of feeling, he sings the first verse in a hushed tone:

When the music fades
All is stripped away
And I simply come
Longing just to bring
Something that's of worth
That will bless Your heart

Hughes's voice grows louder and more confident and the instrumental texture builds as he sings the transitional material leading into the chorus:

I'll bring you more than a song
For a song in itself
Is not what You have required
You search much deeper within
Through the way things appear
You're looking into my heart

With rising volume and intensity of expression, Hughes and the worshiping crowd perform the chorus, whose lyrics express the worship leader's and audience's sincere intentions to return to a God-centered "heart of worship":

And I'm coming back to the heart of worship
And it's all about You, all about You, Jesus
I'm sorry, Lord, for the thing I've made it
When it's all about You, all about You, Jesus[7]

The song "Heart of Worship," a mainstay at worship concerts and festivals during my field research, begins with a striking combination of lyrics, music, and gesture that aims to re-center worship onto the divine object. In the song's opening lines, the worshiper's encounter with God moves (symbolically, if not literally) from an encounter mediated through music to an unmediated one: the mediation of music "fades," and all the trappings of performance are "stripped away." The song begins with solo vocals accompanied solely by acoustic guitar, suggesting a greater musical immediacy through a relative lack of technological mediation. In his performance, Hughes also makes use of vocal and bodily techniques that index effort, including straining to reach certain notes and contorting the face into a serious, impassioned expression. The song's use of filler words common within everyday speech evidence again an aesthetic of inarticulacy: the worshiper "simply" comes, longing "just" to bring God an acceptable offering. Within the very context of a song, the worshiper promises to bring God worship that is "more than a song," that God can see by looking into the heart. This is the worshiper's gift: the offering of his or her sincere intentions to make Jesus the center of worship. The perceived "artlessness" of this song's performance enables the shared expression of sincerity, and the collective performance of God-centered worship. This performance of the song "Heart of Worship" can be understood as a verbal, musical, and lyrical reframing of the concert space to focus on God, a collective performance comprising a reframing of a commercial concert event as sacred worship.

The performance of "Heart of Worship" shows the degree to which pop-rock performance conventions are used to construct authentic worship. In order to reframe their activity in worship concerts as "God-centered," worship leaders and participants collectively express sincerity—and to interpret their performances as sincere—through musical cues they instinctively draw from pop-rock music. Sincerity in worship becomes sonically attached to certain musical aspects such as "unplugged" acoustic guitar strumming and vocal straining, in addition to other performative expressions and gestures used by rock musicians to convey a sense of authenticity (Frith 1996, Moore 2002, M. L. Butler 2005). Because worship is a performative action undertaken by participants in the bleachers as well as the worship leader onstage, these God-centering moves adapted from the expressive language of rock become a part of the collective performance of worship to a divine rather than human audience.

For worship to be experienced as God centered, participants must feel the freedom to demonstrate the depth of their sincerity and their sense of love, awe, and devotion. While standing in line before a 2008 concert in Atlanta, I spoke with Rebecca and Emily, two young women growing up in Baptist churches in Ireland and Southwest Missouri, respectively, and attending the same college in Missouri. When asked what they thought drew people to concerts like these, Rebecca replied, "I think it's the freedom that events like this can bring. [Many] people aren't from church traditions where they can express themselves as freely." Emily chimed in later in the conversation, "We sing a lot of the same songs in my church [as in the concert]. But it's maybe not as free there as it would be here. Here it's very unique because people are free to worship in the way that they want. But in my church at home it wouldn't be as contemporary. So it's really good to come and share this." Both Rebecca and Emily invoked the traditional/contemporary binary to contrast the restraint they felt imposed by their home-church traditions with the freedom they anticipated finding during concert worship. For both, the worship concert was a space free of the perceived strictures of "traditional" worship where they could worship in a way that, as Emily put it, was "more real to expressing yourself."

Worship leaders actively help to construct the environment that participants like Emily and Rebecca interpret as "free." Over the course of the dozen-plus worship concerts I attended, worship leaders frequently exhorted participants from the stage, telling them "don't worry about what the people around you are doing" but to worship "in the way that the Spirit leads." Leaders often encouraged an exclusively God-centered focus that Martyn Percy has described as the "social abrogation" at the heart of many performances of contemporary worship. Percy writes that in charismatic worship settings, "God is experienced . . . in the deep interiority of experience that is socially abrogative and centered on the self. The body social is abandoned for the individualistic and supra-spiritual" (1996, 286).

Though freedom is understood to be highly individualized, its expression requires a range of bodily disciplines. For evangelicals, freedom in worship is expressed through personal choice of a finite range of worshipful gestures once considered to belong to pentecostal-charismatic worship. There are many expressive bodily gestures that have become standard in charismatic church worship and worship concerts but that may still raise eyebrows in conservative evangelical churches: hand raising, swaying or hopping in place, and sitting, standing, or bowing at will rather than in concert with others. For evangelicals from conservative churches in which there are still strong social inhibitions on expressive movements during worship, worship concerts provide a relatively anonymous space in which these practices associated with "freedom" are modeled and learned. Particularly for youth and young adult audiences, worship concerts provide a space for experimentation where they, along with self-selected members of their youth groups or college groups, can try out worshipful actions not encouraged or permitted in their local church congregations.

At several different moments during fieldwork, I observed the learning process first hand as evangelicals experimented with physical and vocal gestures associated with freedom in worship. Near the beginning of the Chris Tomlin worship concert described earlier in the chapter, Tomlin invited anyone who wanted to dance to God to flood the aisles and come up to the front. Shortly thereafter, as the holder of a seat on the side of the aisle, I became an unwilling member of a mosh pit comprising mainly middle-school girls. The girls screamed off and on during the song toward the stage as they jumped up and down in place to the beat with hands upraised. During the slower fourth song, "Made to Worship," I watched as some of the girls took cues from one another. A short middle-school girl looked up at the taller girl beside her who raised her hands during the chorus. At each iteration of the chorus thereafter, the smaller girl raised her hands, too. Another memorable instance took place at a 2007 Hillsong United Concert in Nashville's Ryman Auditorium. From my seat in the middle of the balcony, I had a profile view of several members of a large youth group to my right. My eyes were drawn to a group of four teenage boys in junior high or early high school. The shortest of the four, who also looked to be the youngest, was fairly undemonstrative in the beginning few songs of the concert, with arms folded across his chest. However, a change came about midway through the collective performance of the rock anthem "Fire Fall Down." As the band and most audience members were energetically singing the words of one of the song's middle choruses ("I know that You're alive / you came to fix my broken life"), the youngest teenager looked away from the stage and began watching older boys beside him. The teen to his left had his arms spread apart and lifted high in the air as he sang with an impassioned expression mirroring Hillsong's lead singer's, while the young man to his right was singing while jumping up and down in time with the music. I saw a huge grin spread across the youngest teen's face, illumined by the bright lights from the stage, as he began jumping in place during the chorus. With frequent glances to the boys on either side of him, he also experimented, somewhat self-consciously, with lifting his hands a few times over the next few songs.

For young evangelicals like these for whom the gestures that accompany contemporary worship music are novel, the worship concert provides a space free from the constraints of their home churches and the perceived strictures of their worship traditions. In a space together with a few close friends and away from others who may be uncomfortable with more demonstrative worship, they can experiment with different postures and levels of intensity as they sing. However "free" these may feel, however, expressions of sincerity and freedom require disciplining the body and voice with gestures modeled and learned in these spaces. In the process, "authentic" worship becomes intrinsically linked to these practices, which then become prerequisites for expressing sincerity.

"YOU ARE THE FAMOUS ONE": DEFINING PARTICIPATION, REFRAMING SOCIAL ROLES

Shelley's second criterion for authentic worship is that worship must be participatory. Words, music, and gesture are again marshaled in an attempt to construct boundaries between authentic "participation" and mere "performance." Evangelicals understand the term "performance" in the context of congregational worship as unequivocally negative, similarly to the African American Christians described by ethnographer Glenn Hinson:

> [They] use the word "perform" to suggest spiritual theatricality. Often cloaking the term in verbal italics, or prefacing it with a disparaging "just" (as in "they weren't real; they were just performing"), they speak of "performance" as the enactment of a put-on role for the purpose of "entertaining" an audience. (2000, 237)

Likewise, in contrast to an arena rock "performance," authentic worship must be, as worship leader Tim Hughes put it, "a participator sport in a spectator culture." (It is worth noting that Hughes uttered these words while performing as one of the headliners for the 70,000-participant Creation Festival East described earlier in this chapter.)

The contrasting categories of "performance" and "participation" within evangelical discourse correspond closely to two categories of live performance that Thomas Turino describes in *Music and Social Life: The Politics of Participation* (2008). Drawing from Bourdieu's practice theory, Turino conceives different types of music-making as distinct fields of practice characterized by differing goals, values, power relationships, and resources. These, in turn, "determine the role relationships, social positioning, and status of actors and activities within the field" (26). Turino describes live musical performances as belonging primarily to one or the other of two musical fields of practice: participatory performance or presentational performance. *Participatory performances* are those live performances in which there is no firm distinction between artists and audience members, though they may perform different music-making roles. The goal of participatory performance "is to involve the maximum number of people in some performance role" (26). As a result, these performances use several musical strategies to encourage participation, including repetition on several scalar levels within the musical performance; a deemphasis on virtuosity; and a consistently loud volume and dense texture that serves a "cloaking function" (46), encouraging novice musicians to join in without fear of embarrassment. In *presentational performance*, by contrast, there is a distinct separation between artists, who make the music, and audience members, who receive and appreciate it but are not actively involved in sound production. Presentational performances are well rehearsed, with musical works in more or less stable arrangements that feature frequent contrasts of many different sonic features. Variety, rather than repetition, is emphasized within the presentational-performance aesthetic. Presentational performances, further, are usually scripted into a prearranged order that provides variety in order to maintain the audience's attention. Though drawing a stark conceptual distinction, Turino acknowledges that, in practice, participatory and presentational performances frequently overlap. He gives an example of his own zydeco dance band as a "compromise" between the two types of musical activities (55).

The worship concert (and as later chapters show, the other modes of congregating that it influences) is another example of a performance space that comprises a hybrid of the differing values, goals, and social roles of participatory and presentational performances. Rather than understanding the worship concert as a space of compromise, however, worship leaders and worshipers often attempt to define the activity wholly as participatory performance. In order to be "authentic worship," the worship concert must be experienced as a participatory performance, in which the boundary between the worship leader at center stage and the audience in the stadium seats is collapsed because both are engaged in the act of worship. Attendees must understand both themselves and the worship leaders onstage as "worshipers"— equal participants in the activity of worship. They do so by emphasizing participatory qualities and values and distancing themselves from the social roles and the goals of presentational performance. Despite the rhetoric of disavowal, however, many of the aesthetic values and patterns of social organization that mark presentational performance profoundly shape the musical activities of the worship concert.

Concert attendees become a worshiping congregation through engaging in the same participatory actions that constitute congregational worship in evangelical churches. The most important of these is singing. Evangelical detractors of contemporary worship music sometimes uncritically assume that worship bands onstage performing at ear-splitting volumes discourage singing and lead the gathered crowd to espouse a passive "entertainment mentality." After attending over a dozen worship concerts, I did not find this assumption to be the case. Rather, the expectation that everyone in attendance participate in worship through singing is reiterated again and again in multiple ways. Celebrity leaders reinforce repeatedly throughout worship concerts the imperative that concertgoers sing. They exhort the worship concert crowd to sing more loudly or more fervently and give the crowd opportunities to sing verses or choruses unaccompanied by amplified voices or instruments ("just the voices"). As they sing, participants engage in other practices that often accompany worship in local churches, such as raising hands in praise and bowing heads in prayer. All of these performative actions serve to mark the activity as "worship" and reinforce the sense that concert audience members are full participants.

Electronic media technologies also play a crucial role in rendering performance participatory by enabling simultaneous presentation of all song lyrics. Projected onto large screens behind or adjacent to the stage and scattered around the arena or stadium, song lyrics are an important visual focal point of the worship concert. In arena rock concerts, audiovisual effects are generally centered fully on the "star," functioning to "preserve and create [rock stardom]" through using technology to "exaggerate and fortify audiovisual gestures" (Kärki 2005, 38). By contrast, in worship concerts, while elaborate stage lighting is used to highlight the band onstage, song lyrics are a necessary visual element on the screens. While a live video feed of the band onstage often provides a backdrop to the lyrics, at some worship concerts, the screens contain only the song lyrics atop colorful still backgrounds or moving images.

Though Christian symbols are often absent in the large multipurpose arenas and auditoriums in which worship concerts are held, participants' bodies become visual markers of participation in the act of worship. By raising their hands, closing their eyes, lifting their faces heavenward, or bowing their heads in a prayerful posture, audience members' bodily bearing inscribes the Godward focus of worship and evidences their participation as worshipers. During familiar worship songs in which participants know the words by heart, many attendees close their eyes or lift their eyes upward, denying their attention to the visual spectacle of the band onstage or to the screens. For many audience members in the bleachers, artists on center stage, and event organizers alike, these types of participatory behaviors serve as compelling evidence that worship concerts are indeed mass worship services.

At the same time as worship concerts emphasize aspects of participatory performance, they also embody many of the values and social roles of presentational performance. Obvious markers of presentational performance include the spatial centering of celebrity worship leaders and well-rehearsed, professional bands on a raised stage; demarcated social roles of performers and audiences, who pay rock concert ticket prices for the privilege of singing along with—and worshiping alongside—their favorite recording artists; and the amplified wall of sound that facilitates, even as it covers over, the gathered crowd's singing. One could argue that the wall of amplified sound is intended to facilitate maximum collective participation, to provide the "cloaking function" Turino references that encourages even the worshiper who believes she "can't sing" to join in. It does so, however, through the near-silencing of individual voices, subjugating them to a homogeneous crowd sound.

Worshipers know that they are expected to sing, and are often very invested in doing so. But to understand the dynamics of worship concert participation, it is important to ask what it is that concertgoers *hear* when they sing, and how they experience their own voices in relationship to the collective sound of the gathered concert congregation. The intense physical involvement and effort of concert congregations often belie their aural output. The following anecdote from my fieldwork at a worship concert at the opening of the 2007 Passion Conference describes my own experiences of singing and listening in one such worship concert.

After waiting over an hour in line to enter Atlanta's Phillips Arena, I finally make it through the doors fifteen minutes late and quickly try to find a seat in the nosebleed section of the arena. Guitarist and vocalist Charlie Hall and his band are at center stage as they lead worship in the massive space, illumined by colorful bright lights, and I can count at least ten screens arranged in varying heights and angles above the stage so that every corner of the square-shaped arena could see the words to the worship songs. I am used to overhead lights being dimmed during worship concerts, but it is so dark in this arena that I cannot see my field notebook. (And I am annoyed to find later that my attempts to jot down the names of songs and make other observations during the worship set are a garbled mess.) As I survey the crowd, the juxtaposition of the dazzling lights from the stage with the darkness of the arena creates a distinct visual dynamic. I begin to reflect on how the visual dynamic is shaping how I perceive other participants at the event. I cannot see clearly the people in my section of the arena—not even those sitting immediately next to me. Looking out across the arena from the view my nosebleed-section perch afforded, I find it easier to see concertgoers in the arena's middle section as lights from the stage swept over them. The crowd at a greater distance is punctuated by a few individual faces and gestures. To my eyes it is a billowing, boiling sea of moving, singing bodies.

Sound represents the other concertgoers to me in much the same way as the worship concert's visual elements do. The worship music being performed onstage and amplified by gigantic overhead speakers is so loud that, as hard as I strain to listen, I cannot hear anyone immediately around me sing. Indeed, when I sing along as loudly as possible, I can barely hear myself sing. I try yelling the words to make an audible sound, but it is still primarily worship leader Charlie Hall's voice, accompanied by guitars, keyboard, and drums, that I hear. Though I can't hear my own voice or those of the people sitting beside me, over the amplified wall of sound I can hear the aural sum of several thousand participants' voices, a youthful-sounding unison of men's and women's voices singing together the same tenor-to-alto range melody line. The crowd's volume ebbs and flows, often in response to exhortations from Hall to sing more loudly or to worship with abandon. Though the crowd's singing is an ever-present layer within the musical texture of the event, it is often subsumed by the amplified sound of the worship leader's voice and the worship band's instrumental offerings that together fill nearly all of the sonic space.*

In this worship concert as well as most others I attended, it was often difficult or impossible to hear individual voices of the people sitting nearby. (The exception that stands out is the outdoor music festival described earlier in this chapter where all-permeating amplification was not possible.) The crowd sound is a necessary authenticating layer within the sonic texture of a worship concert but one that often plays a relatively minor role in the overall sound experienced by worshipers in the space. Some worshipers in concert spaces describe their participation as "singing along." Joshua Busman argues that this description signals continuity of experience between worshipers' engagement with live concert performances and the commercial recordings of the celebrity artists and bands (2015a: 257). The aural experience of hearing one's own voice singing along with an artist onstage calls attention to the presentational-performance aspect of worship concerts. Turino notes that within participatory performances, "the etiquette and quality of *sociality* is granted priority over the quality of the sound per se" (2008, 35), often resulting in performances that miss widely the aesthetic mark and frustrate skilled musicians in the group. In this way, singing at a worship concert allows the experiential pleasure of participatory performance without compromising the aesthetic values of the presentational performance.

The sonic interplay of worship leader and crowd within creates a dynamic relationship between individual participants, the artist onstage, and the gathered concert congregation that participants can experience and interpret in different ways. A memorable email exchange after a worship event illustrates this complex and sometimes contradictory relationship. When

I asked Thomas, a nineteen-year-old college freshman from Ohio, if and how worship at the event had influenced him, he responded,

> I was most affected by the number of people with whom I was worshiping. It was just amazing to be a part of that loud voice praising God. From this experience I learned how to let go and give my all in worship. Before Passion, I had a hard time focusing only on God, and worried about how I looked with my hands raised in praise. Now, I have been reminded that we are in God's presence, and it doesn't matter what other people are doing. (email correspondence, 2007)

Thomas's response contains an intriguing contradiction: while he states that, ultimately, his experience helped him "let go" and not worry what others did or thought during worship, he begins by observing that it was the social, participatory element of the worship event—being "part of that loud voice"—that was most experientially powerful. What is an interpreter to make of Thomas's statement that, on the one hand, what others do should have no bearing on one's experience or expression of worship, and yet, on the other, that the actions of other worshipers matter profoundly?

 Here, it is helpful to group other worshipers into two distinct categories that I will designate "specific others" and "imagined others." Specific others are individuals who are known and knowable to concertgoers. The majority of participants come to worship concerts with members of their churches or other ministries and sit together as a group during the main conference sessions. The dazzling visual array often renders invisible the specific others in close proximity, at the same time as the wall of sound emanating from the stage drowns out their individual voices. In many concert spaces, even those well acquainted with the people sitting immediately next to them find it difficult to pick out their voices in the saturated soundscape, just as the visual spectacle of stage and screens divert their focus away from the movement of their bodies. In other words, the sonic and visual affordances of participation at worship concerts make it challenging to relate to specific others in worship. The worship concert's remove from the sphere of local church religious authority, as well as the specific others that inhabit it, is an important part of the dynamic that enables the experience of freedom Thomas and others from earlier in the chapter describe.

I use the term "imagined others," in contrast, to refer to other participants who are experienced as a temporary embodiment of the evangelical imagined community within the context of large events like worship concerts (see Chapter 2 for further discussion of the importance of the "imagined community" in worship). These are the other people whom an individual worshiper does not and will probably never know personally, though they are in close proximity to her in this particular space. In a conversation before a worship concert in 2008, Rachel, a twenty-something attendee from Missouri, articulated the power of the experience of worshiping with imagined others. For her, the most powerful part of the event was the experience of "the body of Christ, united together." She compared the event to a heavenly gathering of Christians:

> And it's almost like a small reflection of what it will be like in heaven, when you're there for one purpose: you're there to glorify God, and you're going to be amazed by his presence. And it's almost like a small, tiny part of what it will be like in heaven to [be with] people that you don't even know, but you're united in God and through Christ . . . it's such an amazing thing. (personal interview, 2008)

It is singing together with "people that you don't even know"—the voices of thousands of imagined others—who come together to form the one powerful voice of the crowd. The aural sum of participants' singing is heard as a single congregational voice (Thomas and many others used "voice" in the singular to describe their experience of singing) that conveys an aural experience of *communitas* in which individual voices are rendered indistinct. This single congregational voice is the one I heard when I experienced the sublimation of my own voice into that of the collective; further, this unified crowd voice can also be heard on most live worship recordings. Thomas's and Rachel's comments both demonstrate that participants relish knowing that they are worshiping together with others from all over the nation and the world; yet these are imagined others whose proximity is experienced under the cover of darkness and through a wall of amplified sound.

In worship concerts, it is primarily participation in singing that reframes the social roles of worship concert attendees from "spectator" to "worshiper," though it is the incorporation of certain values and social roles of presentational performance that lends the activity of singing much of its experiential power. Given that these social roles must be effaced in order for attendees to experience the event as "authentic worship," it can be an even more formidable challenge to reframe the social role of the celebrity performer to "worship leader" when hundreds or even thousands of fans have paid an admission fee to see them in concert. In worship concerts, the social role of the popular music celebrity is often consciously and repeatedly denied in an attempt to frame the worship leader and band as fellow worshipers. Before a concert in Atlanta, Will, an attendee in his late twenties, commented on how pervasive rhetorical disavowals from the stage were:

> I think there's *such* a focus on it not being about [the worship leaders]. If you had a negative spirit, [it's] almost to the point of redundancy that they keep pointing it back to God [with] *every* song, *every* lyric, *every* between-song banter. . . . When you come to one of these things they don't want you looking at the stage: they want you either closing your eyes, or looking up, not just outwardly, but they

want your attention and affection to be on God . . . They don't want you saying, "that was a really sweet guitar riff," or "it sounds so great," or "oh, good, they're going to play my favorite song next . . ." [They reiterate] "It's all about God, It's *all about God*, guys, and it's not about us." That's a really admirable thing that as big and popular as they are, they don't want any of it on themselves. (personal interview, 2008).

Here Will aptly describes how, in worship concerts, well-known figures take great care to represent themselves as <u>worshipers, rather than performers,</u> stars, or celebrities. They reframe the problematic social roles of arena rock stars by disavowing or denying their celebrity status, as in the vignette from the worship concert at the beginning of this chapter in which worship leader Chris Tomlin's insisted to the crowd that he had not come to "perform," but to lead a "massive," collective worship service for a Divine audience.

Celebrity worship leaders also seek to redefine their social role by deflecting fame away from themselves to God, through verbal and musical rhetorical actions. The Passion Conference, which has propelled several of its worship leaders to evangelical stardom,[8] has as its stated purpose "to make Jesus famous." In between yearly and regional conferences, concert tours of Passion's immensely popular worship leaders further spread the self-proclaimed worship "movement." <u>Disavowals of the culture of celebrity</u> and fame have made it into several worship song lyrics of artists associated with Passion. One such lyric is Chris Tomlin's 2002 worship song "Famous One." The chorus lyrics of "Famous One" paraphrase and expand on the first half of Psalm 19:1 ("the heavens declare the glory of God"):

> You are the Lord
> The famous One, famous One
> Great is Your Name in all the earth
> The heavens declare You're glorious, glorious
> Great is Your fame beyond the earth[9]

Tomlin discusses this song at some length in his book on worship *The Way I Was Made*, sold at the resource table at the 2007 concert I attended. Here Tomlin states that he wrote the song "Famous One" to cultivate the virtue of <u>humility in worshipers.</u> Tomlin interprets the virtue of humility in an intriguingly <u>self-referential</u> manner: for Tomlin, the opposite of humility is not pride, but *fame*. Tomlin defines humility as deflecting fame away from the self and "influenc[ing] the world without ever seeming to be in the spotlight," instead ensuring the spotlight is placed on God (Tomlin 2005, 73–74). In the song "Famous One," Tomlin interprets biblical ascriptions of God's glory through the lenses of superstardom, pointing to Jesus as "the supreme celebrity" (69). The second verse begins with the lyrics, "The Morning Star is shining through / And every eye is watching You." In Tomlin's reading through the lenses of fame, the "Morning Star," a reference to Jesus in the biblical book of Revelation, becomes a rock star on center stage—"the Famous One" who has the rapt attention of the entire cosmos, whom "every eye is watching."

Understanding the song lyrics of "Famous One" through Tomlin's interpretation shows that some worship songs can be read as attempts to break down the social roles of fan and celebrity that inhere to the arena rock concert. Because they are performed by the entire concert congregation, these lyrics become the disavowals of fame for both the worship leaders and audience members, as stadium crowds deny their roles as celebrity and audience, and through this denial perform their roles as "worshiper." Even as worship leaders and audiences seek to redefine their social roles, they imagine worship using the categories of the very popular music culture from which they are attempting to distance themselves. God becomes the celebrity, the Divine Performer, whose power is felt in the powerful emotional experiences during worship. God is also (and sometimes simultaneously) conceived of as the Divine Audience, who sits back in his heavenly throne and listens. Indeed, the descriptor of "audience of One" in reference to God recurred again and again during worship concerts throughout my fieldwork. And it has found its way into sung affirmations as well; according to the Christian Copyright Licensing International's SongSelect database, the phrase "audience of One" has been used in over twenty-five worship songs, some of which have been popularized by well-known worship leaders and bands (http://www.ccli.org.) As God becomes a celebrity on center stage, the fame metaphor that is used to de-center the performer gives audiences a new way to understand God. Further, it uses the stardom of popular music performance as a lens through which to understand the Christian virtue of humility. Evangelical worshipers who sing this song at worship concerts are invited to imagine God as a celebrity and themselves as God's fan community, committed to spreading his "fame" in their daily lives and throughout the world.

"MADE TO WORSHIP": CONSUMPTION, FANDOM, AND THE WORSHIP LIFESTYLE

Speech, song, musical style, and gesture are each performative means of establishing authenticity within worship concerts. They redirect focus to God and redefine the social roles that inhere to the space of the arena rock concert. However, to be considered "real" or "authentic," worship must be transformative; in other words, a worship concert must be perceived to have a lasting effect outside the event itself. Worship is transformative when it effects personal change and elicits practical response. This sense of transformation is imparted to participants by providing resources for living a "worship lifestyle" long after the concert is over.

The idea of worship as transformative encounter that interprets the mundane through the lenses of the sacred is intimately related to a second discourse that is pervasive within worship concerts: the idea of worship as a lifestyle. Anna Nekola has situated this discourse as being "part of a larger popular movement within American evangelical Christianity in the twenty-first century that sought to identify one's personal life choices—including one's musical choices—as 'worship,' enabling worship to be framed as a lifestyle, or 'the outward and inward expression of evangelical identity'" (2011, 131). Despite the fact that their claims to authority rest on musical performance, celebrity worship leaders are often the first to acknowledge and emphasize that worship is *more* than music and should extend to all activities in life.

Worship concerts are well equipped to offer lifestyle products that promise to help continue the life transformation inaugurated by affective worship long after the event is over. The enduring transformation on offer is membership in a fan culture centered on a trusted figure or organization and enabled by a range of lifestyle products. Similarly to any popular music fan culture, living a "lifestyle of worship," as it is enabled through the worship concert experience, relies upon what Matt Hills has called "performative consumption" (2002, 159). Building from Hills's theory, sociologist Garry Crawford argues that such "consumption does not end with the purchase of an object, but rather that consumer goods can (and frequently are) lived with, experienced, and utilized by their owners," who actively use these products as resources for constructing and negotiating identity (2004, 122).

At worship concerts, music-related commodities act as signs of transformation. Evangelicals are invited to enter into a "worship lifestyle" through purchasing one or more of an array of worship-related commodities available at worship concerts. These goods usually encompass all the typical trappings of a popular musical fan culture, including musical recordings and DVDs, apparel, and books, most of which are also available through Christian music magazines, retail stores, and internet sites.

I recount a particular moment in field research to highlight the close connection between musical performance and worship lifestyle products.

Before the beginning of Chris Tomlin's worship concert in Nashville, an enthusiastic man in his early thirties walks onstage with his arms full of merchandise. After welcoming the crowd, he demonstrates several examples of apparel from the tables in the foyer of the arena, including a ball cap embroidered with the words "Made to Worship" (Figure 1.4) and a hooded sweatshirt whose scripty text proclaimed "How Great Is Our God," the name of both the tour and of Tomlin's hit worship song,

Figure 1.4: A "Made to Worship" hat for sale at the foyer resource table at Chris Tomlin's concert at Lipscomb University's Allen Arena. Nashville, Tennessee: October 2007. Photo by the author.

which, according to church copyright licensing statistics, was currently the most frequently sung worship song in North America. After describing the CDs and DVDs, the man admonishes the crowd in parting to "make sure to check out the resource table!"

A few moments later, the concert begins. After three upbeat songs, the opening strains of the fourth song take on a more serious tone and are played in a slow, deliberate tempo. As Tomlin begins to sing the first verse, the large screens display song lyrics describing God's originary act of creation. As the song's dynamics gradually build in intensity, participants around me raise their hands toward the sky and together proclaim the climactic chorus line that describe humanity's purpose; "You and I were made to worship." The chorus lyrics consist of a parallel series of "you and I" statements proclaiming both the identity of the worshiper and elaborating what he or she is called to do. The ending line of the chorus promises that, in living this lifestyle of worship, the worshiper's core identity will be discovered and realized:

> You and I are made to worship
> You and I are called to love
> You and I are forgiven and free
> When you and I embrace surrender

When you and I choose to believe
Then you and I will see
Who we were meant to be[10]

*Though I do not know the song well at the time, I experience a sensation of déjà
vu as I look up at the lyrics on the screen; the text that is presented in stark white
letters on a black background seems so familiar. My eyes are then drawn to a teenage
girl with hands upraised who is standing a few feet in front of me. The song's chorus
lyrics are emblazoned on the back of her T-shirt in white text on a dark background,
under larger, flowery letters proclaiming "I Was Made to Worship."*

At this worship concert, "Made to Worship" is a multivalent signifier of identity, operating on multiple levels as song hook, theological statement, musical performance, and brand slogan. The T-shirt's message "I Was Made to
Worship" is at first textually ambivalent: it could be interpreted to mean "I
was made *to be* worshiped," placing it in the category of "diva" T-shirts popular among teenage girls in the mid- to late 2000s. However, the "Made to
Worship" products advertised at the beginning of the show and embodied by
members of the gathered audience are tied to the specific narrative provided
by the song. In this narrative, God is the author of the individual's story as it
is lived out on a daily basis. Singing provides an embodied way of performing
this identity, identifying with the divinely purposed roles and actions in the
song lyrics of worship, love, surrender, and belief. Through musical performance and performative consumption, the worshiper aligns herself with this
particular identity, embodying through song and dress her sincere intentions
to be transformed into who she was "meant to be." By wearing the "Made to
Worship" T-shirt and singing expressively, she is proclaiming her commitment
to a lifestyle of worship by identifying with a particular set of songs or
experiences that faithfully reflects these ideals. As Tom Wagner has similarly
argued in his work on the Hillsong megachurch and its worship music brand,
these experiential encounters help to "simultaneously distinguish [Hillsong]
from and connect it to other churches, adding value to worship by uniting the
brand, its music, and the God encounter in a single experience" (2014, 71).

Studies of early twenty-first century consumer culture have described how
advertisers and producers have sought to imbue certain commercial products
with "authenticity" by means of certain media and marketing practices. In *The
Soul of the New Consumer*, authors David Lewis and Darren Bridger assert that
authenticity is the key to selling products to the "new" consumer, expounding
upon many ways in which the ideal of authenticity informs the purchasing
decisions of consumers during the contemporary moment (Lewis and Bridger
2001). The resulting "authentic" brands can be used as resources for a particular lifestyle chosen by individuals, "cultural resources" that serve, according

to media studies and branding scholar Douglas Holt, as "useful ingredients to produce the self one chooses" (D. Holt 2002, 83). Holt also observes that perception of a product's authenticity is necessary for the product to be understood as a resource for shaping identity, and "to be authentic, brands must be disinterested; they must be perceived as invented and disseminated by parties without an instrumental economic agenda, by people who are intrinsically motivated by their inherent value" (83). The association of worship-related commodities with the sites and experiences of worship experienced as "authentic" invests them with spiritual significance, transforming them from mere "products" to "resources" for living the Christian life. Worship leaders emphasize the importance of a lifestyle of worship from the stage through speech and song, and frame their products as resources for living this life.

The branded products popularized by worship concerts serve to reference a powerful musical experience and to signal membership in a particular popular musical fan culture defined by a style, an organization, or a particular celebrity worship leader. Personal transformation is, in part, an entry into this fan culture, with a new identity formed through performative consumption of "lifestyle products" authenticated through their association with trusted bands and figures. One twenty-year-old participant explained his reason for attending a day-long worship concert this way: "I went because of the big-name speakers and bands. I knew I would be poured into and grow a lot as an individual" (personal email, 2007). For this concertgoer, the well-known celebrity names are integrally connected to the potential for personal transformation. Personal experience authenticates and effects the transformation of the musical performer on center stage to a trusted role model who can provide resources for living the Christian life, just as these "resources" popularize his music to an ever-widening audience of evangelical worshipers. The concert space is thus sacralized by the promise of transformation. The "resources" for living a worship lifestyle serve as both enablers and evidence of a transformation into a true worshiper.

CONCLUDING THOUGHTS: CONGREGATIONAL MUSIC AS POPULAR MUSIC

This chapter has shown how evangelicals use elements of musical performance—including speech, song, and discourse about music—to erect boundaries around "authentic" worship in worship concert settings. By performing a God-ward orientation, redefining social roles, and resourcing a "lifestyle of worship," stadium rock performances are transformed into participatory worship at the throne of God. In the process, congregational singing is redefined in light of popular musical performance, as performers deflect their fame to God, as God is represented as a Divine celebrity with a worldwide fan culture, and as the "worship lifestyle" is made available for purchase. The worship concert, then, can be conceived as a space that mediates between popular music performance and worship in evangelical churches: where practices that can't be defined as exclusively "sacred" or "secular" interpenetrate and influence one another. Phil Bohlman's observation of these dynamics within sacred popular music in the Mediterranean can be applied to worship concerts as well:

> The sacred enlivens the popular, and the popular intensifies the experience of the sacred. The sacred and the popular interact in particularly powerful forms of mutual dependence . . . Indeed, in an era of global connections, religious practice has benefited in countless ways from mass mediation and the growing presence of religion in the public sphere. (2003, 290)

Through musical performance at worship concerts, evangelicals produce the boundaries between their culture and mainstream society, rejecting elements that do not fit their vision or sound concept of what worship *should* be. Yet, as they experiment with new possibilities for songs, sounds, gestures, and practices as part of a concert congregation, their concept of worship is transformed in the process. The worship concert is a place where elements of pop-rock performance—including stadium rock's high production values and elaborate visual spectacle, performer-audience interactions, and pressures of the Christian commodity marketplace—influence congregational worship practices in an experimental space outside the church, governed by the logic of the commercial music industry.

In my conversations with concertgoers, many of the people I chatted with expressed eager anticipation for the next concert they would attend. Not infrequently, describing their experiences participating in concert congregations elicited unfavorable comparisons to worship in their local church congregations. At the Chris Tomlin concert in Nashville, I sat by Jim, a middle-aged man from a small Tennessee town a few hours' drive away. Jim attended what he called a "traditional" church and had been introduced to Tomlin's music on Christian radio. He told me wistfully that his church did not sing Chris Tomlin's songs in worship, and that he had become familiar with most of Tomlin's songs from listening to his recordings. He was hopeful that with "changing times" his church would eventually sing Tomlin's songs and introduce more contemporary musical styles into worship. For Sara, a college-aged woman I encountered at a concert in Atlanta, the concert worship experience was "more sacred than church," both because of the enveloping multi-sensory experience and because it allowed her to gather with other believers who were more "like-minded." Sara considered the other worshipers like minded in part because they were part of the same generation she was;

more importantly to her, they shared an understanding of what constituted "real" worship.

These conversations and others like them reveal that, even as evangelicals use musical performance to reframe and reinterpret elements of popular musical performance, their incorporation of elements from pop-rock performance actively shapes their understandings of worship. Worship concerts are crucial agents in the production of desire in that they generate in attendees a sense of lack where previously none may have been felt. Not only can the signature "worship experience" on offer at a worship concert mold large, self-selecting crowds into a worshiping congregation, but it can also conform to a high degree to the aesthetic standards of pop-rock concerts. Most small to mid-sized North American evangelical churches are characterized by more diverse membership—not all of whom will be fans of worship music—and struggle over whether or not to attempt to attain worship concerts' high production standards. Participants' experience at worship concerts powerfully forms attendees' ideas and expectations of what congregational worship can and should be. The desire that evangelical church services conform to the worship practices of the concert congregation has had numerous effects on local church musical practices, aesthetic principles, and material culture. In his research into the Passion network of conferences and concerts, Joshua Busman writes that several of his interlocutors in the field had left small churches incapable of living up to (or unwilling to accommodate) the expectations formed by these events "to find larger, more media-savvy churches that could more accurately reproduce the specific and high-production standard for worship that they had experienced" (2015a, 183). To respond to the danger of congregational members leaving, many evangelical churches feel the pressure to purchase higher- and higher-tech sound systems and sophisticated multimedia packages and screens for projecting lyrics. And committed evangelical musicians, whatever their stylistic inclinations, feel compelled to develop musical and other performance competencies in particular pop-rock styles in order to reproduce concert stadium-like worship experiences.

In the case of the evangelical worship concert, then, the performative boundaries put in place in order to differentiate the worship concert from the pop-rock concert serve to mask the way the two spaces are integrally linked. A product of the Christian media industry, the worship concert serves as a powerful and formative intermediate space between the modes of congregating found in rock concerts and churches and, as such, is important for understanding the dynamics of contemporary evangelical worship. Further, it shows the fluid boundaries between evangelical worship and other kinds of experiential "secular" ritual performances. The worship concert is an important mode of congregating in which evangelicals negotiate the extent to which contemporary popular musical culture can be incorporated into the heart of worship while attempting to remain "in but not of the world."[11]

NOTES

1. For more detailed accounts of the Contemporary Christian Music (CCM) recording industry and contemporary worship music's relationship to it, see Redman 2002; Fromm 2006; Ingalls 2008; Nekola 2009; Mall 2012; Ingalls, Nekola, and Mall 2013; and Busman 2015a.

2. I use "arena rock" in this chapter to reference both setting and musical style. Also called stadium rock or corporate rock, arena rock is a rock subgenre developing in the 1970s that derives its name from the large-scale gatherings, often held in large sports arenas and stadiums, that both accompanied and drove the popularization of rock music. For further exploration of rock subgenres and commercial discourse, see Shuker 2005 and Skanse 2006.

3. The article was posted to *RELEVANT* magazine online on April 3, 2015, accessed June 28, 2016, http://www.relevantmagazine.com/god/church/do-you-worship-your-worship-experience#yA1C8RYjAkvdTtl6.99.

4. See, for instance, the following representative accounts of the evangelical concern to define "real" or "authentic" worship: Morgenthaler 1998; Shelley 1999; Webber 2000; Wiersbe 2000; Ryan 2010, and Eldridge 2011.

5. For ways in which the authenticity discourse is used in early twenty-first-century marketing and advertising, see Lewis and Bridger 2001; D. Holt 2002; and Botteril 2007.

6. Each of these statements is a comment from worship leaders I heard while attending worship concerts and conferences, including Passion 2007 (January 1–4, 2007, Atlanta, Georgia), Chris Tomlin's *How Great Is Our God* concert tour (October 6, 2007, Nashville, Tennessee), Passion Regionals 2008 (April 16–17, 2008, Duluth, Georgia), Hillsong United's Gospel Music Association Week concert (April 22, 2007, Nashville), and worship concerts given by worship leaders including Tim Hughes, Casting Crowns, and Matt Maher at The Creation East Festival (June 29, 2007, Mount Union, Pennsylvania).

7. THE HEART OF WORSHIP (WHEN THE MUSIC FADES). Beth Redman and Matt Redman. ©1999 Thankyou Music (PRS) (adm. worldwide at CapitolCMGPublishing.com excluding Europe which is adm. by Integrity Music, part of the David C Cook family. Songs@integritymusic.com). All rights reserved. Used by permission.

8. Louie Giglio, founder of the Passion Conference, started the record label sixstepsrecords in 2000 to market the music of worship leaders affiliated with Passion. Sixsteps has had a distribution agreement with EMI's Christian Music Group and has included artist/worship leaders David Crowder (and the former David Crowder*Band, Chris Tomlin, Charlie Hall, Matt Redman, Kristian Stanfill, and Christy Nockels. As of the August 2014 US Christian Copyright Licensing International report, Tomlin wrote or cowrote five out of the twenty-five most frequently worship songs in US churches, while Redman wrote or cowrote three, and Stanfill and Nockels cowrote one. Tomlin's 2013 album, *Burning Lights,* debuted at number 1 on the *Billboard* US Top 200 chart for the week of January 16, beating out albums from some mainstream pop acts as Taylor Swift and Bruno Mars (Caulfield 2013). See Chapter 2 for a more detailed exploration of worship at the Passion Conference itself.

9. FAMOUS ONE (YOU ARE THE LORD). Chris Tomlin, Jesse Reeves. ©2002 worshiptogether.com Songs (ASCAP) sixsteps Music (ASCAP) Vamos Publishing (ASCAP) (adm. at CapitolCMGPublishing.com). All rights reserved. Used by permission.

10. MADE TO WORSHIP. Chris Tomlin, Ed Cash, Stephan Sharp. ©2006 worshiptogether.com Songs (ASCAP) sixsteps Music (ASCAP) Vamos Publishing (ASCAP) New Spring Publishing Inc. (ASCAP) Stenpan Music (ASCAP) (adm. at CapitolCMGPublishing.com) / FORMERLY ALLETROP (BMI). All rights reserved. Used by permission.
11. This popular evangelical catchphrase is taken from John 17:14–15 (New International Version).

CHAPTER 2

❧

Singing Heaven Down to Earth

The Conference Congregation as Pilgrim Gathering and Eschatological Community

The worship [at Urbana] draws you in so much. It goes past the superficial, the regular. And it intensifies and you get closer to God. Being in that realm is amazing.
                    —Danae, twenty-year-old participant in the
                    Urbana 2012 Conference, St. Louis, Missouri

It's the coming together of other believers that makes [Passion] almost more . . . more sacred than church. Coming together here and uniting is like a little piece of heaven.
                    —Sarah, nineteen-year-old participant in the
                    Passion 2008 Conference, Atlanta, Georgia

Look around and try to imagine heaven.
                    —White letters projected on a large black central screen
                    during the final night of the Passion 2007 Conference, Atlanta, Georgia

These three statements were each made in reference to worship at large evangelical conferences. Like the worship concert examined in Chapter 1, conferences gather evangelicals across denominations, regions, and sometimes nations to a central location where a powerful, memorable mass "worship experience" with thousands of other believers is one of the main draws. Over the course of attending several regional and national conferences, I talked to numerous participants, who spoke in rapturous terms about their experiences during musical worship. The two college-aged women quoted previously describe conference worship as powerful because it is "intense," "amazing," out of the ordinary, and unifying, qualities that make the gathering seem even "more sacred than church." And the words on the screen at the Passion Conference sought to encourage participants to interpret their experience in a particular way: as transcending earthly divisions and prefiguring the heavenly gathering of Christians from across space and time.

This chapter examines the discourse and practice of music and worship at the triennial Urbana Conference and the annual Passion Conference, two well-known multi-day events for evangelical college students that are similar in scope, length, and age demographics. Every three years, Urbana and Passion are held back to back over college students' winter break, straddling the New Year's Day holiday. I attended each national conference twice, in December 2006 and January 2007, then again in December 2012 and January 2013. The Urbana conference, held in St. Louis's Edward Jones Dome and Convention Center, gathered 21,000 predominantly college-aged participants in 2006 and 17,000 participants in 2012, while the annual Passion Conference's attendance grew markedly from 22,000 college students in January 2007 to over 60,000 in January 2013.

I investigate the dynamics of and discourse about worship at these two events in order to theorize music's role in forming the unique social constellation of the conference congregation. Conference congregations share two primary characteristics: they are pilgrim gatherings and they are eschatological communities. As centers of sacred travel, conferences serve as focal points where evangelicals travel—sometimes thousands of miles—to partake in a powerful spiritual experience that promises life transformation. Taking participants out of their familiar religious and social contexts allows them to experience a vision—and, as I will argue, a sonic representation—of heaven; in other words, a glimpse of an ideal moral order built around the tenets of their faith. Extraordinary experiences facilitated by lack of sleep, hours upon hours of seminars, singing, and intense times of spiritually centered social interaction—create a sense of liminality. Evangelical participants step outside the purview of regular religious authority and are invited to try out new kinds of religious identities forged in the crucible of intense spiritual experiences. The collective identity and values associated with it do not simply dissolve, however, when the conference is over. Students carry with them the ethos, beliefs, and practices of these conferences with the help of pilgrimage "souvenirs" such as worship albums recorded live at the conference and can remain in the conference orbit throughout the year by purchasing additional resources and remaining connected on social media.

Describing the conference gathering as heaven is not a designation that arises spontaneously from conference-goers' transcendent experiences; it also happens because conference organizers and leaders intentionally frame the conference gathering as a means of participating in the heavenly community. At both conferences, leaders frequently invoke language about and descriptions of heaven—what I refer to as the eschatological discourse[1]—when framing musical worship. In doing so, they encourage conference participants to understand their singing as participation with the heavenly community, as an aural contribution to the "sound of heaven." This eschatological discourse is pervasive, embedded not only in song lyrics and verbal framing of music-making, but also in elements of musical style and social organization of music-making. The eschatological discourse also serves as a powerful moral argument: if the conference's worship is modeled on what it will be like in heaven, it follows that the conference's musical worship should serve as a model for local church and other gatherings. How heaven is represented sonically in times of worship—the unique ways that conference congregations sing heaven down to earth—thus comes to influence participants' desires and expectations of musical worship when they return to their local churches. As this chapter demonstrates, choices of musical performance, style, and social organization are laden with ethical significance. Through collective music-making, conference attendees perform not only their devotion to God, but also their relationships to others both within and outside the gathering. Like other utopian narratives, the evangelical vision of heaven serves as a blueprint for social relationships on earth.

Worship music, as both commodified product and embodied experience, is a souvenir of the conference pilgrimage, one that is both highly transportable and easy to integrate into local contexts. Both conferences examined in this chapter are instrumental in propelling worship music's meteoric rise in popularity and have strongly influenced music's adoption at the local church level. Studying music of the conference congregation, then, is necessary for understanding current evangelical worship music more generally because of its pronounced influence on worship in other kinds of evangelical congregations. And as the sights and sounds of conference worship encapsulate evangelical visions of heaven, they acquire the moral authority to influence evangelicals' relationship to other groups within North America as well as globally.

GATHERING AT THE (POST)MODERN TENT OF MEETING: EVANGELICAL CONFERENCES AS PILGRIM CONGREGATIONS

You have come on a pilgrimage to experience an event in which God will speak . . .The point of being here is to meet God and to let him shape the direction of your life.
—Urbana Conference director Jim Tebbe, Urbana '06 opening address

We have come, not for the music or the speakers . . . we have come here to meet God.
—Passion Conference founder and director Louie Giglio,
Passion '07 main session address

Opening remarks from the Urbana and Passion conference directors explicitly frame these conferences as pilgrim journeys whose goal is a personal experience of God. To experience this transformative encounter, evangelicals do not need to travel to sacred Christian sites in Israel or the Mediterranean, or to important places in US Christian history; rather, they more frequently converge upon sports arenas and stadiums for multi-day conferences generally geared to a specific demographic.[2] As they travel to these conferences on planes, buses, trains, and subways, evangelical pilgrims frequently strike up conversations with strangers who often turn out to be fellow travelers. Downtown hotels in major US cities sell out of rooms as large groups of conference-goers fill their lobbies. In anticipation of the conference's opening session, snaking lines spill out of the doors of the sports stadium in which it will be held. While standing in line, veterans of previous conferences share memories of their past experiences while new attendees describe animatedly the parts of the conference they are looking forward to the most. The atmosphere is both festive and expectant. Although spending time with friends and exploring a new city are certainly draws, most attendees say they have come for a more serious purpose: to "meet God" and to allow God to change their lives through the multifaceted, multi-day conference experience.

Conferences like Passion and Urbana have antecedents within North American evangelical Christianity that include tent revival meetings and multi-city evangelistic crusades. These multi-day regional and national events have long been sites of evangelical spiritual formation and transformation (McLoughlin 1980; Hatch 1989; York 2003; Stowe 2002). Since the mid-twentieth century, interdenominational rallies and conferences more specifically focused on high school and college-aged students have become an evangelical mainstay (Eskridge 1998; Wuthnow 1988; York 2003). Events for college students are often sponsored or promoted by evangelical college campus organizations such as Campus Crusade for Christ, InterVarsity Christian Fellowship, the Navigators, or the Fellowship of Christian Athletes. In 2001, the combined membership of evangelical campus organizations in the United States totaled an estimated 210,000 students (Schmalzbauer 2007, 2).[3]

The Urbana and Passion conferences are both national events, drawing evangelical college students from every region of the United States and from many other nations, though Passion far surpasses Urbana in its influence on evangelical worship music. Since its first conference in 1946, the triennial Urbana Conference has been organized and sponsored by InterVarsity Christian Fellowship, a Christian campus organization active on over 600 US campuses with approximately 40,000 participating students.[4] The Urbana Conference was named for its original location at the University of Illinois at Urbana-Champaign but has retained its name with its recent move to the Edward Jones Dome and St. Louis Convention Center. Though Urbana traditionally focused on encouraging students to pursue full-time cross-cultural mission work, since the 1990s it has highlighted many professions, including law, medicine, social work, and education, as Christian vocations that help to fulfill "the global mission of the church" (InterVaristy Christian Fellowship 2015).

In his PhD dissertation on the Passion Conference and media network, Joshua Busman (2015a) describes Passion as "one of the most influential Christian media networks on the planet" (8). The Passion Conference grew out of a college campus ministry originally called Choice Ministries, founded in 1985 by Louie Giglio at Baylor University in Waco, Texas. The first Passion conference was held in Austin, Texas, in 1997, and subsequent regional and national conferences have been held in Memphis, Tennessee; Nashville; and Atlanta. From 2007 through 2015, Passion "has staged fifty-two large-scale events in thirty different cities in twenty-two countries" (Busman 2015a, 9). Passion has been popularized by denominational and interdenominational college ministries including CRU (formerly Campus Crusade for Christ)—the largest Christian campus ministry, which as of this writing claims over 100,000 participating students and faculty in 2,300 chapters in the United States alone—and by its popular live worship recordings and the solo albums of celebrity worship leaders, including Chris Tomlin, David Crowder, Matt Redman, Christy Nockels, and Kristian Stanfill.

Martyn Percy has argued that journeys to charismatic Christian revivals such as the "Toronto Blessing," which drew tens of thousands of travelers to a suburban Toronto church and later to satellite churches across the United Kingdom and Europe, can be considered forms of "postmodern pilgrimage." These pilgrimages are centered not on physical objects or sites, but on a particular kind of experience: they are "journey[s] to a place that is beyond 'ordinary' religious control, in order to gain an extraordinary religious experience" (1998, 282). Like charismatic revivals, evangelical conferences do not depend on attributes of a specific geographical place for their spiritual authority; conference leaders point to nothing inherently sacred about sports stadiums or convention centers, or intrinsic to downtown Atlanta or St. Louis. And, like these revivals, a major draw to evangelical conferences is an "extraordinary religious experience," at a different register of intensity and "seriousness" than weekly church or small group worship.

Indeed, when I spoke with students before and during these conferences about what drew them to the conference, the most frequent response I received—even above hearing from well-known speakers or engaging in Bible study—was worship. Participants described their experience during times of corporate worship as "amazing," "awesome," "life-changing," or "like being in heaven." Worship, which in the context of each conference is used to refer to a fifteen-to forty-minute period of congregational singing, is central to the evangelical-conference experience. Framing the times of preaching and teaching, worship facilitates a divine encounter that often acts as a catalyst for personal and communal transformation. The daily schedules for Passion 2012 and Urbana 2013 (Table 2.1) illustrate the ways in which musical activities are woven into nearly every one of the day's events. Conference attendees begin the morning by singing a few songs before the smaller group Bible studies. Morning and evening main sessions are structured like a charismatic or evangelical church service, with speakers bookended by worship sets, during which a designated vocalist or team leads the gathered throng in congregational singing. Congregational singing usually comprised anywhere from one quarter to one half of these two-hour general sessions. Afternoon main sessions at Passion included congregational singing, while at Urbana, worship music was among the variety of topics addressed in elective afternoon seminars. Worship opportunities extended even into the late evening at both conferences, integrated formally within special late-night events and informally into small group prayer time.

The role of congregational singing is integral to the conference experience because it is one of the primary practices that create sacred space, marking the conference meeting as a sacred event through sound and embodied participation. Simon Coleman and Martyn Percy have argued that the "sacred center" of Protestant pilgrimage comprises not specific places or physical objects, but rather portable practices and discourses intended to be "transferable back into more localized ecclesial contexts" (Percy 1998, 284), which charismatic personalities at center stage help to interpret for participants (Coleman 2004). The sacred center of the evangelical conference pilgrimage can be conceived as a space of ritual enactment created in large part by the activity of singing worship music together.

Table 2.1. DAILY SCHEDULES FOR THE URBANA 2012 AND PASSION 2013 CONFERENCES

Urbana 2012		Passion 2013	
8:45 a.m.–10:15 a.m.	Morning Bible Study (2–3 songs)	9:00 a.m.–9:20 a.m.	Community Groups (2–3 songs)
11:00 a.m.–12:30 p.m.	Morning Session (6–8 songs)	10:45 a.m.–12:45 a.m.	Morning Main Session (6–10 songs)
2:00 p.m.–5:00 p.m.	Afternoon Seminars	1:30 p.m.–3:30 p.m.	Afternoon Main Session (1–5 songs)
7:30 p.m.–9:30 p.m.	Evening Session (5–8 songs)	7:30 p.m.–9:30 p.m.	Evening Main Session (11–17 songs)
10:15 p.m.–11:00 p.m.	Small Group Prayer with Roommates	10:30 p.m.–11:40 p.m.	Community Groups (2–3 songs)

In addition to creating the sense of sacred space, worship music also imparts a sense that the mass gathering is not simply an amalgamation of individuals and smaller groups, but also a congregation united in worship. Worship is a mass spectacle that helps to form the congregation and mediate a sense of community. Sonic and visual elements of this spectacle are equally important: large screens set up around the arenas depict leaders and musicians on stage and also frequently pan the gathered crowd, showing hands raised in the air and rapturous faces turned heavenward. In her study of Pentecostal television viewing in Ghana, Marleen de Witte has argued that, through on-screen visual representation, worshiping bodies become "'living icons," serving as models of an appropriate receptive posture and evoking "an experience of spirit presence" (2011, 193). Conference gatherings come to experience themselves as congregations visually, through the aid of roving cameras and screen media, and aurally, through the mass collective sound they generate. Through engaging these sights and lifting their voices together, participants at conferences like Passion and Urbana bring into being a conference congregation comprising three distinct communities: the conference gathering itself, the heavenly community, and the imagined community of Christians worldwide.

COMMUNITIES IMAGINED AND IMAGINARY: CONFERENCE CONGREGATIONS AS ESCHATOLOGICAL GATHERINGS

In conversing with participants before and after Urbana and Passion, I found that one particular interpretation of the event emerged from their accounts: the idea that the conference gathering was an experience of the heavenly community on earth. One nineteen-year-old Filipino student who attended Passion '07 commented that the worship times were "a taste of heaven" that made him "really look forward to that time when I will be part of worshipping the Lord with countless more than 24,000" (email correspondence, January 12, 2007). When I asked nearly two dozen participants what one word summed up Urbana for them, more chose "heaven" than any other. A twenty-year-old Urbana participant from Detroit explained to me, "It's because [worship] is a picture of what heaven will look like in terms of what it says in Revelation. Every tongue, tribe, and nation coming together to worship our Lord. This is my third Urbana, and [worship] is my favorite part" (personal interview, December 31, 2012). A young woman from Lesotho told me that her most memorable experience at the Urbana conference was "to sing with people, with this many people from different countries from different cultures, coming together for God. It was something great and that changed my life: that even though we are different, even though I feel like . . . we are the same. I [have] heard about heaven, but oh my goodness, here I experience it!" (personal interview, December 31, 2012).

These conversations highlight a prevalent discourse surrounding worship at both conferences: a conversation about heaven or the end of time that I call the "eschatological discourse." This discourse—particularly in reference to musical worship—formed the set of interpretive lenses through which participants were invited to interpret their musical actions, to understand the purpose of the gathered community, and to explain the meaning of the conference as a whole. One of the most powerful and pervasive forms of eschatological discourse could be heard resonating within and around the conferences' congregational singing. At the 2012–2013 conferences, one song that featured prominently at both conferences was "Revelation Song," a musical setting based on the fourth chapter of the biblical book of Revelation that describes worship around God's throne in heaven. The first part of the chorus is a near-direct setting of the angelic song in Revelation 4:8: "Holy, holy, holy, is the Lord God Almighty, who was and is and is to come." The following field accounts show how prominently heaven features as a theme in each conference's worship. Through the performance of these worship songs, conference congregations' singing becomes the "sound of heaven," linking the gathered crowd with the heavenly community.

On the opening night of the triennial Urbana conference on December 27, 2006, I sit in the midst of an excited crowd of an estimated 23,000 college students gathered in St. Louis's Edward Jones Dome. Attendees stream into the stadium, filling the sloping bleachers on three sides of the dome, which face a wide front stage (Figure 2.1). The gathered participants cheer loudly when the twelve members of the Urbana worship team ascend the left side of the stage. Worship leader Daryl Black, an African American man who looks to be in his late twenties, takes his seat at the keyboard and welcomes the crowd. After leading the gathered congregation in two upbeat gospel-inflected and rock-style songs, the team begins to play an energetic, jazz-inflected instrumental introduction, with two trumpets playing close harmonies over a chord riff established by the band's guitarists. The excited crowd begins clapping on the offbeats as the worship band vocalists sing in unison a prayer for the strength "to exalt and to extend Jesus' name globally." The vocalists break into three-part, gospel-inflected harmonies to express the chorus's petition: "Cover the earth with Your glory / Cover the earth with the sound of heaven."[5] The second verse of the song continues the theme of the first: a prayer that the "sound of heaven" be used to extend God's kingdom on earth. After repeating the chorus at a louder dynamic level, the crowd joins the worship team in the prayer that forms the song's bridge: "Open up the heavenlies / Let a new sound be released." As the worship team and crowd repeat the bridge several times, the crowd raises a loud shout in the sonic spaces between the song's lyrics.

Figure 2.1: The Urbana '06 worship band leads worship from the main stage. St. Louis, Missouri: December 2006.
Photo by the author.

One week later, on January 3, 2007, I find a seat in Atlanta's Phillips Arena a few minutes before the beginning of the evening session on the third day of the Passion Conference. Cheers erupt as the band led by well-known worship leader David Crowder, a lanky white man in his late twenties who sports a hipster look with large glasses and bushy hair, ascends the central stage along with his band of five other young white male musicians. Bright lights of all colors flash from the stage, and a series of screens arranged in varying heights and angles show elaborate camera shots of the band and alternate with abstract imagery underneath the song lyrics (Figure 2.2). Across the expanse of the arena, the excited conference crowd forms a billowing sea of moving, singing bodies.

Crowder leads the conference participants in singing several rousing rock anthems; then, in the middle of his set, comes a moment of silence. A hush falls over the crowd. As the screens reveal the next song's title to be "O Praise Him," Crowder begins strumming softly an eighth-note rhythm over a four-chord vamp, subdued but with latent energy.[6] With minimal instrumentation, Crowder sings the opening strains of the song softly, as if in a posture of listening: "Turn your ear / to heaven and hear / the noise inside. . . . " A transitional section between verse and chorus exhorts the gathered crowd to join in so that the strains of their song can be added to the sound of heaven.

At the chorus, the rest of the band joins Crowder, and the gathered crowd sings loudly, "O praise Him / He is Holy, yeah!" The song's second verse exhorts participants to "turn your gaze / to heaven and raise / a joyous noise." After singing the words "a joyous noise" comes an extended pause between the lyrical phrases, and participants let out a collective roar, filling the arena with yells, screams, and whistles. After repeating the song's chorus twice, Crowder leads the crowd in a long

Figure 2.2: David Crowder and his band lead worship at the Passion Conference. Atlanta, Georgia: January 2007.
Photo by the author.

bridge section comprising the repeated vocables: "Oh, la la la la la . . . ." After another three iterations of the chorus, the song ends on an unresolved chord and the crowd breaks into loud cheers and applause.

Both songs described in the previous accounts afford the gathered conference participants a way to perform the eschaton, inviting them to extend the song of heaven to earth and, in the process, to imagine their gathered conference community in relationship to the ideal heavenly community. In the Urbana participants' singing of "Cover the Earth," a song that juxtaposes eschatological imagery from various biblical sources, the dominion of God's kingdom covering the earth is represented by sound. The chorus's repeated prayer ("Cover the earth with your glory!") asks for God to bring God's kingdom to earth, represented sonically by a "new sound" being released from heaven—a sound that is then extended to earth through the agency of singers serving as God's "instruments." Speech, song, and shouting—the joyful sounds of the faithful—are all sonic agents in preparing the way for God's kingdom to come to earth.

Likewise, the performance of "O Praise Him" at the Passion Conference provided a telling illustration of how the worship space is imagined and performed as a sonic interchange between heaven and earth. In the first verse, the lyrics depict the singers as listeners eavesdropping on the sound of heaven, who are then invited to join the unceasing song. In the second verse, the gathered crowd is exhorted to raise a "joyous noise," which is then taken up in heaven. Up until the bridge, the song's lyrics largely comprise singing about singing: the verses describe sacred sound (heaven's "noise," "the sound of salvation," "the sound of rescued ones") and the content of the heavenly song. The chorus exhorts the gathered crowd to sing ("O praise Him!"), and grounds the singing in the transcendence of God ("He is Holy!"). The bridge section is where this musical action is finally accomplished: the sung vocables can be understood as the "joyous noise," as earthly and heavenly songs become one.

The eschatological discourse that is a recurrent trope in these conference songs also informed the interpretation of the event that prominent speakers and worship leaders advanced from the stage. As conference attendees sang songs that explicitly linked their corporate sound with the loud voice of the heavenly community, worship leaders urged participants to worship together around the throne with the hosts of heaven, and speakers compared the large gatherings to eschatological worship around the heavenly throne. On the last night of the Passion '07 Conference, as participants gathered outside for a candlelight rally, the words on a large central screen instructed participants to "[l]ook around and try to imagine heaven."

Through the pervasive link made between actual conference worship and ideal heavenly worship, attendees' musical performances became a space in which social ideals and religious beliefs became conjoined and mutually reinforcing. In her account of Brazilian popular Catholic pilgrimages, Suzel Reily describes this "musical mode of ritual orchestration" as "enchantment," and explains music's mediating role as follows:

> Through musical performance, religious discourse and aesthetic experience become inextricably intertwined, inclining participants to experience the ritual space as an encounter with the moral order of the sacred. In such an enchanted world, participants construct and simultaneously experience the harmonious order that could reign in their society. (Reily 2002, 17)

As in this Brazilian pilgrimage, the centrality of communal singing at Passion and Urbana foregrounds the overriding importance of sound—especially musical sound—in an encounter with the heavenly social order on earth. Music enables evangelical conference attendees to experience their beliefs about the afterlife by enfolding them in the "sound of heaven." The experience of being part of a vast gathering of Christians singing together, so indelibly imprinted within participants' memories, is used to interpret biblical accounts of the ideal community at the end of time. One such commonly invoked passage from the book of Revelation describes a large multitude comprising "people from every tongue, tribe, and nation" gathered in worship around the throne of God (Revelation 7:9–10). In performing these songs corporately, the gathered conference assemblies are in effect enacting the beliefs, ethics, and aesthetics of the Christian eschaton.

Through collective music-making at conferences, evangelicals create and conflate earthly and heavenly communities. The community that results can be interpreted to embody an "evangelical imaginary" in two distinct ways. First, the gathered throng becomes a conference congregation through the collective activity of imagining. Here I draw from Byron Dueck's understanding: "'imagining' is . . . an orientation to a public of strangers. It is a relationship, facilitated by mass mediation, between people who, though unknown to one another, understand themselves to have something in common" (2013, 5). Through the collective act of musical performance, common belief is performed and an evangelical social imaginary becomes temporarily emplaced. As Dueck explains, "[imaginaries] come into existence as people perform and publish for unknown audiences, and especially as they acknowledge the previously circulating performances and publications of others—for instance, by training their minds and bodies to make music in ways that respond to those previous performances. Imaginaries emerge as performances, broadcasts, publications, and acts of bodily discipline respond to previous ones, and anticipate others to come" (6). Conferences, as pilgrimage sites enabled by a shared cultural amalgam of print, video, internet, and musical media, can be understood as spaces in which the evangelical imagined community becomes temporarily emplaced, embodied by the actions and expressions of conference participants and leaders alike. Conference worship is characterized, as one earlier conversation partner put it, by worshiping alongside "other people you're not ordinarily with," and among a gathered throng so large as to be nearly as anonymous as the evangelical community itself. Fellow conference attendees from across region and nation represent to one another the translocal evangelical community.

Not only does conference worship serve as a space in which the evangelical imagined community is (re)presented to itself; participants are also encouraged to interpret their corporate worship experiences as a foretaste of worship with the heavenly community. For an explanation of this added dynamic, the category of social imaginary can be put into fruitful dialogue with literary critic Phillip Wegner's notion of the imaginary community. For Wegner, imaginary communities are formed by a common vision provided by a "narrative utopia" in utopian literature, in which "description itself serves as what in other contexts we think of as action or plot, so that social and cultural space and communal identity slowly emerge before our eyes" (2002, xviii). Wegner argues that people use narrative utopias not for mere escapism but to imagine and create new constellations of social relations; in other words, narrative utopias enable the formation of imaginary communities that "have material, pedagogical, and ultimately political effects, shaping the ways people understand and, as a consequence, act in their worlds" (2002, xvi).

In the context of corporate worship at evangelical conferences like Passion and Urbana, commonly held beliefs about heaven function similarly to

Wegner's narrative utopia, with the important caveat that participants ardently believe in the physical existence of the idyllic place described in biblical accounts. For participants, biblical narrative and personal experience become conjoined: the experience of conference worship is used to interpret evangelical narratives and beliefs about the eschaton, even as these beliefs inform participants' worship experience. The collective performance during conference worship serves to fuse powerfully the evangelical social imaginary (i.e., the translocal evangelical Christian public) with an eschatological imaginary community (the throng worshiping around the throne of God in heaven). In other words, as the conference gathering represents the evangelical social imaginary across space, it also comes to represent the imaginary community beyond the limitations of earthly time.

THE SOUND OF HEAVEN: MUSICAL STYLE AND SOCIAL ORGANIZATION AS ESCHATOLOGICAL DISCOURSE

The Passion and Urbana Conferences, as transformative sites of sacred experience, rely heavily upon the eschatological discourse as both a rationale and an interpretive frame for their worship. Sung and spoken discourse, including song lyrics and words of exhortation and encouragement from the stage during the worship songs, helps participants interpret their experiences in a way that conflates the imagined community on earth and the imaginary community in heaven.

Verbal discourse about the eschaton, however, forms only a small part of the blueprint for heavenly community; indeed, musical style and social organization play an even more crucial role as meaningful elements of these conferences' eschatological discourse. While many aspects of verbal discourse about the eschaton may be shared at both Urbana and Passion, crucial differences between the conferences' choices of musical style and socio musical organization reveal a wide divergence in how their conference participants are invited to understand social relationships between members of their heavenly— and, by extension, their earthly—communities. While ostensibly the same evangelical beliefs form the blueprint of the imaginary community in each conference, distinctions that arise within each conferences' collective musical performance suggest very different ways evangelical college students are taught to understand difference and relate to members' global Christian community.

Evangelical Protestantism is one of many religious communities that use musical style as a form of ideological or ethical discourse. Timothy Rommen suggests that for Trinidadian Christians, musical style is employed and interpreted discursively, "put to use in order to achieve certain goals . . . [which] are informed by overarching ethical concerns" (2007,

35–36). In his exploration of the meaning of musical style within Estonian Orthodox congregational singing, Jeffers Engelhardt discusses ways in which the "rightness" of congregational singing "registers an emergent moral order and reveals how religious ideology and musical ontology conflate in notions of musico-religious orthodoxy" (2009, 33).

The Urbana and Passion conferences held in common certain aspects of an "evangelical musico-religious orthodoxy," including musical practices, basic beliefs about worship, and musical ontology. During both conferences, professional or semiprofessional musicians on a front stage led the gathered crowd in singing worship songs in current popular music styles. Worship song lyrics were projected onto large screens throughout the arenas underneath images of the worship leaders onstage. During musical worship, participants employed a common language of evangelical expressive practice. While singing, worshipers raised their hands, closed their eyes, and alternately raised their faces to heaven or bowed their heads in deferent prayer. Leaders and participants at the two conferences also shared many beliefs about the role of music in worship and spiritual life, including participants' expectation of a personal encounter with God during congregational singing. During these times, worshipers described what God was doing in their lives in terms of "speaking into," "ministering," or "being real to me."

Yet, it is in examining the differences between the range of musical styles and social organization of music-making at these conferences that key differences most clearly emerge in how conference organizers seek to position their conference congregations in relationship to broader North American society and the global Christian social imaginary. The following sections recount key moments from both the 2006–2007 and 2012–2013 conferences to show how the two conferences present a markedly different vision of the constitution and social ideals of the Christian eschatological community.

Heaven as "God's After-Party" at the Passion Conference

At both the Passion '07 and '13 conferences, nearly all of the worship songs were performed in a guitar-driven pop-rock style, a genre sometimes referred to as "modern worship music" (see Ingalls 2012a, 2017) Passion's celebrity worship leaders have been instrumental in defining the genre of modern worship music, characterized by rock band instrumentation, standard pop-rock song forms, harmonies built upon cyclic chord riffs, and rhythmically complex tunes often based on short melodic motives. With two notable exceptions (David Crowder's bluegrass-inflected worship sets and the full evening concert given by gospel hip-hop artist Lecrae in 2013), the congregational songs performed at both Passion conferences conformed to these genre characteristics of modern worship.

The modern worship music at Passion drew not only from the sounds of rock, but also from its normative social organization, which scholars in popular music studies have noted is often centered on white male subjectivity (Frith and McRobbie 1990; Walser 1993; Cohen 1997). The Passion '07 program given to each attendee at the beginning of the conference advertised six worship leaders for the main sessions, each of whom was a white male at the helm of a small band of five to eight other predominantly white and male instrumentalists and vocalists. Out of dozens of congregational songs sung during main sessions at 2007's four-day conference, there were only two exceptions to this pattern. In one evening session, Israel Houghton, a prominent African American celebrity worship leader guest-led one song (still in the predominant modern worship style). Singer Christy Nockels led one song during two different Passion '07 main sessions and served as a backup singer during the rest of the conference. Further reinforcing the individualistic dynamic of rock performance, during each Passion main session only one worship leader led the congregational singing at a time. In fact, during Passion '07, there was not one moment during the entire conference in which two or more Passion worship leaders ascended the stage to lead worship together as a team.

Further, there was only one instance during the 2007 conference in which a musical style outside the standard pop-rock modern worship was heard from the stage, and revealingly, this moment was used as part of the speaker's message related to heaven. At the Passion '07 Conference, two successive evening sessions were spent on the topic of heaven and the afterlife. Conference founder Louie Giglio's talk on the last evening of the Passion Conference used musical anecdotes that connected a specific vision of worship in the eschaton to understandings of Christian community on earth. In that talk, he ascended the square stage at the center of the large arena. The stage was unadorned except for a lone prop placed in the center: a large sheet-glass window. After reading a few verses from the book of Acts, Giglio launched his lesson for the evening on the topic of heaven, "God's after-party." He then walked across the stage to the window prop and told the crowd, "We're going to peek into heaven for a little bit because I want you to know what's going on up there. Something like this is going on in heaven." As he slowly slid open the window, sound began to fill the stadium: a West African call-and-response song accompanied by clapping and hand drums.

Giglio declared, "That's the party!" The crowd seemed confused; there was widespread murmuring punctuated by a few awkward claps. Giglio took the opportunity to give an impromptu lesson in world Christianity, exhorting participants to get excited about the sounds of heaven. Giglio said a second time, "[S]o the party sounds a little bit like this up in heaven." He again raised the window, this time to what sounded like mariachi music. This time the audience, on cue, cheered loudly. After closing the window a second time, Giglio told the crowd, "[T]ere'll be something for you up in heaven, too. Maybe when you get there, it will be something more like this." Giglio lifted the window a third time, and the strains of Passion worship leader Chris Tomlin's well-known rock-influenced worship song "Holy Is the Lord" filled the stadium. Loud cheers, whistles, and applause erupted from the crowd. Giglio spent the rest of his presentation in expounding the importance of spreading the Christian faith and ended with a challenge: "So let's get this party started by telling everybody on the planet that they have an invitation, and the party will start and the music of heaven will fill our lives."

This moment is instructive because it shows how musical style and social organization are connected within the Passion Conference's eschatological discourse and reveals the way Passion locates itself and its participants in re-lationship to both the heavenly community and the earthly global Christian community. Giglio admitted freely during his talk that he did not know what heaven's music actually sounded like; however, the musical illustrations he gave in this lesson carry strong implications for how participants are encouraged to imagine their earthly and heavenly evangelical communities. Giglio used a metaphor from the popular music industry as his governing met-aphor for the afterlife: heaven is presented as the ultimate after-party at the end of time. The Christian's responsibility to others is framed as extending to "the nations" a backstage pass to heaven.

In Giglio's anecdote, musical style serves as an icon of "nations" or "people groups," essentialized groups according to which Giglio's after-party of heaven seems to be segregated. In Giglio's segregated eschaton, there is recognition of the presence of (Christian) Others in heaven but there is little interaction be-tween the predominantly white, Southern US "self" and the global (Christian) Other beyond being in generally the same place (heaven) and worshiping the same God, albeit with mutually unintelligible forms of expression. In this model of the afterlife, relationships with o/Others, with the exception of foreign missionary endeavors, are not presented as part of the Christian so-cial ideal—indeed, they are not even imagined to be present in heaven itself. Instead, groups of people separated by race, nation, language, and culture are presented as discrete, independent, reified entities, worshiping in their own way in a musically bounded Paradise.

Giglio gave his "Heaven's After-Party" message as a preface to the following day's announcement of Passion's upcoming 2007–2008 conference tour to sev-eral major world cities on six continents. I learned from personal conversations that representatives from several of these cities in South America, Europe, and Asia had been flown in to experience the Passion conference in Atlanta and take word back to their respective countries. In the six years in be-tween the national conferences I attended, the Passion conference went on at least two multi-city "world tours," and its worship leaders rose to interna-tional prominence on their own solo tours as well. When attending the 2013 conference, I was curious to see how or if the Passion worship leaders' and speakers' experience on the world tour had influenced their representations of the earthly or heavenly communities and whether their experiences would be characterized by an increased cultural diversity or the continuation of white Christian hegemony.

At the 2013 conference, the Passion Conference had expanded its roster of worship leaders, and worship leaders nearly always appeared visually together on the central stage, even if there was generally only a single audible leader for each set. Guest artists beyond those affiliated with Passion's sixstepsrecords were brought in to lead single songs, in some cases, entire worship sets, and there was more frequent trading off of song leadership during each individual worship set. Stylistic diversity was enhanced by David Crowder's morning worship set offering of gospel classics set to an indie-bluegrass style, and by an evening concert by gospel hip-hop sensation Lecrae. Well-known women worship leaders Kim Walker-Smith from Redding, California–based charismatic megachurch Bethel and Kari Jobe from the Dallas-area multi-site megachurch network Gateway Church were brought in as guest leaders. Two black backup singers (both London-based artists who toured with British worship leader Matt Redman) added to the visual diversity onstage. While women and racial minorities may have been more visible at Passion 2013, a tally of total song performances shows that worship leadership was still dominated by conference's eight white male leaders. These men led the gathered throng in fifty-five out of a total of seventy songs performed over the four-day conference.

Some speakers and worship leaders at Passion explicitly voiced the need for Christian unity across national, ethnic, and racial lines. However, examining musical style as discourse and paying close attention to the subject positions of those chosen to lead the gathering suggest a conflicting interpretation. Despite an expanded international reach and professed desire to partner with Christians across the world, Passion 2013 still encouraged conference attendees to imagine the "sound of heaven" as being their signature modern-worship style, promoting the idea that Christian unity is achieved through assimilation to the cultural—in particular, the musical—norms of white North American evangelical Christianity.

Earthly Rehearsals for the Heavenly Choir at the Urbana Conference

At Urbana, as at Passion, frequent reference was made to the eschatological gathering, as participants voiced through song the biblical narrative of the end-of-time gathering, and as worship leaders and speakers drew comparisons between the present gathered community and the future heavenly one.

The Urbana worship leaders' intentional choices of a wide range of musical styles and diverse teams of musicians who shared musical leadership provided participants with social ideals and ways of envisioning their earthly and heavenly communities that departed in several important ways from that at the Passion Conference. The "sound of heaven" as it was modeled at Urbana signaled a very different eschatological vision.

Urbana's congregational singing intentionally emphasized the gendered, ethnic, and racial diversity of the Christian community in the United States and abroad. The 2006 Urbana Conference Handbook given to each registered participant framed the gathering and the worship leadership with the following statement:

> We who have gathered at Urbana 06 reflect the fullness of the body of Christ as described in Scripture—a unified group of people with different gifts, traditions, backgrounds, and cultures, praising God together. We will experience God and the splendor and complexity of his creativity through the style of worship from different nations and cultures. (InterVarsity Christian Fellowship 2006, 85)

The following account illustrates how Urbana used musical style and social organization to attempt to accomplish these ends.

On the third day of the 2006 Urbana conference, I find a seat in the sea of chairs on the floor of the Edward Jones Dome shortly before the evening session is to begin. The worship band is leading several upbeat urban gospel- and rock-inflected worship songs as participants gather for the evening session. The band is composed of twelve members who are always on stage at the same time. Each band member shares in the responsibilities of serving as principal vocalist, leading the conference gathering in prayer, and exhorting participants to sing. While all of the band members look to be in their mid-twenties to early thirties, the band is markedly diverse in terms of race, ethnicity, and gender, including Latinx, Asian, black, and white instrumentalists and vocalists under the leadership of an African American worship leader.

I have noticed an interesting progression in the worship band's choice of songs since Urbana began. During the opening session three days prior, the worship sets included mainly well-known contemporary worship songs set to either rock, folk, or contemporary gospel styles. In each session since, the Urbana worship team has introduced one or two new worship songs in other styles, frequently in languages other than English, often—though not always—led by the cultural "representative" on the worship team. The music chosen during this particular evening's session serves to reinforce the trend. Achlaï Ernest, a Caribbean-born Canadian pianist and vocalist, leads the gathering in singing "Il Ma Sauvé" (He's My Savior), a calypso-inflected chorus in French, and teaches them a simple two-step dance pattern. Worship team director Daryl Black then leads the congregation in a contemporary

African American gospel song and then a slower worship ballad he composed, with verses that alternate between English and Spanish. Musical leadership is then passed to Asian American vocalist and guitarist Joshua Koh, who leads the assembly in the well-known worship song "We Fall Down" with alternating verses in Mandarin and English. With their eyes on the giant screens onto which the lyrics are projected, a group of white students behind me sing loudly the transliterated Mandarin words "wo hu han sheng jie, sheng jie, sheng jie," which correspond musically to the well-known English chorus lyrics "we cry holy, holy, holy." To my right stands a group of four Chinese and Chinese American college students from Arizona. The young man beside me sings softly the Mandarin words and he closes his eyes and extends his palms upward.

The range of musical expressions used at this session was by and large representative of worship sets at both Urbana conferences I attended. In both conferences, the main worship leader was a person of color: a black singer-songwriter and worship leader in 2006, and a Latina worship leader and pastor in 2012. Both worship leaders chose songs and musical styles that drew from contemporary popular musical traditions associated with the ethnic, national, or regional backgrounds of the other musicians in the worship band. Often, but not always, the "cultural representative" in the band was tasked with leading the song whose language and style represented his or her culture. Termed "multi-ethnic worship" by Urbana leaders and musicians, this intentional cultivation of diversity is an organizational value of the conference's sponsoring organization Intervarsity. Multiethnic or multicultural worship is also part of a larger trend within some evangelical circles to promote ethical and racial reconciliation among North American Christians.[7]

This emphasis on unity through diverse expressions of worship was often explained in terms of the eschatological narrative, relating the earthly community to the heavenly one. In one teaching moment in between songs, Urbana '06 worship director Daryl Black connected Urbana's musical worship to the ultimate eschatological gathering, telling the crowd, "We've been singing these songs to show the diversity of the Kingdom of God. We sing songs in different languages to help prepare you for what God has planned." He then connected God's ultimate plan for the community at the end of time with the relationships with others formed in daily life on earth, telling the assembly: "Your mission begins where you are . . . We need to know how to engage with other people."

In a group discussion with members of the Urbana worship team before the 2012 conference, I asked how the team approached Christians who aren't convinced that diversity should be a value in worship. Anthony, a white male member of the team, reinforced the moral importance of the eschatological discourse:

In terms of helping people who don't see the value of diversity see the value, I think Scripture is the easiest answer for that because there's examples, teaching all across Scripture of diversity. And talking about heaven, that's one of the reasons we always point towards heaven. You want your worship gathering to be like heaven and there's going to be people of every tongue, tribe and nation and all different languages and cultures clearly represented . . . and not in one melting pot mush. . . . If you're purely mono-cultural, you're not reflecting the kingdom of God. (personal interview, 2012)

Urbana's worship did sometimes reinforce the idea of discrete cultural groups, sometimes playing to stereotyped or essentialized portrayals. At the 2012 conference, a series of short videos on the theme of "Come to the Table" were played before the main session each morning. Each of these videos highlighted the distinctive culinary, cultural, and musical offerings of four major North American racial/ethnic groups: African Americans, Asian Americans, Latinx Americans, and white Americans. One of the implicit goals shared by both Urbana '06 and '12 teams was to unmask how the worship of predominantly white churches, groups, and music industries had become normalized as the dominant evangelical mode (see Van Opstal 2016). The "Come to the Table" video at Urbana '12 did this unmasking by categorizing Euro-American hymns and pop-rock-based modern worship songs as "white" contributions to Christian worship. The social structure of music-making, styles of music, and variety of languages used in the worship songs at Urbana was intended both to highlight unique contributions of cultural groups represented, and to encourage participants to appreciate the practices of o/Other worshipers and incorporate them into their own expressions.

And, in contrast to the view promoted at the Passion Conference of heaven as the ultimate goal—an eternal after-party at which Christian responsibility to other partygoers ends when the invitations are passed out—at Urbana, musical worship on earth was represented as a rehearsal for the worship in heaven. On the last evening of Urbana 2006, participants were given an opportunity to join in a musical representation of the ideal earthly and heavenly communities by participating in the Unity Choir. The choir of 200 participants, rehearsed by Urbana's worship team throughout the week, led the conference gathering in three songs sung in three-part gospel inflected harmonies. Gerardo Marti (2012) has noted that among North American Protestants who seek to cultivate ethnic diversity within their congregations, gospel choirs are seen as a necessity. They serve as both a symbol of a commitment to diversity and as a "radically specific, yet radically inclusive" means for including people across lines of ethnicity (168).

The Urbana Unity Choir's final song was "Hallelujah, Salvation and Glory," a song written by Flint, Michigan–based gospel songwriter and arranger A. Jeffrey LaValley and known in many African American congregations as

"Revelations 19:1" after the biblical passage it sets. In framing the final song, Daryl Black read to the conference choir a passage from the fourth chapter of Revelation that describes a vision of the great eschatological gathering around the throne in heaven, explaining to the students that this heavenly gathering should serve as the model for Christian worship on earth.

During the choir's performance, the video cameras that throughout the conference had focused almost exclusively on the members of the worship team onstage scanned the uplifted and often rapturous faces of the choir. As choir members of varied racial and ethnic backgrounds stood beside one another with faces uplifted and hands raised high, the colorful faces and hands that stood out against the choir members' uniform white tops became at once a representation of the Urbana conference to itself, an icon of unity across ethnic and racial barriers, and a foretaste of the eschatological gathering at the end of time. As the Unity Choir's final song, the performance of "Hallelujah, Salvation and Glory" served for participants as both a culmination and a foreshadowing, musically representing the eschatological image in which representatives from every tongue, tribe, and nation together sing the multipart, multivoiced song in overlapping but harmonizing parts in one heavenly choir. Choir members spoke of singing with the Unity Choir as one of their most powerful experiences at the Urbana conference.

The Unity Choir provided a unique opportunity for conference attendees to participate in leading worship and, in the process, to represent the conference community—and an idealized image of the global Christian community—to itself. For many conference attendees, the Unity Choir visibly and audibly evoked the great multitude at the eschatological gathering in Revelation where representatives from "every tongue, tribe, and nation" worship around God's throne, using the very words of "Hallelujah, Salvation and Glory" ("Revelations 19:1"). Interpreted as a form of eschatological discourse, Urbana's "multi-ethnic" worship became a powerful musical symbol of the earthly relationships that are viewed as essential features of the life to come. In this model, signified by the diverse Urbana worship team's modeling of musical reciprocity in both musical style and song leadership, participants were taught that relationships with o/Others are an important part of their worship.

The differences between Passion's and Urbana's eschatological imagination as expressed through musical style portray two very different ways of imagining both earthly and heavenly community, which are suggested by the two distinct governing metaphors they used to describe the social ideals established during conference worship. Passion participants were invited to understand their purpose on earth as extending invitations to heaven's grand after-party, while Urbana participants were invited to identify with other conference-goers across racial and ethnic barriers as a way to rehearse for the eschaton. As conference congregations imagine their place as members of the global evangelical Christian social imaginary, the next section illustrates how these differences extend to representing and identifying with the marginalized.

VOICING THE GLOBAL OTHER: DIALOGICAL PERFORMANCES OF MARGINALITY

In attending both conferences a second time over the winter break of 2012–2013, six years after my initial experiences in 2006–2007, I noticed one major development at both Urbana and Passion: both conferences placed a much stronger emphasis on social justice causes on a global scale, building in opportunities for student participants to identify with poor, oppressed, or marginalized groups, sometimes within North America but more frequently in other parts of the world. At both conferences, leaders of various justice-related nonprofit organizations' causes were given a platform to inform participants about their causes, and monetary donations were solicited for selected organizations. At Urbana '12, a number of causes were presented throughout the week, though the week's major emphasis was on helping sub-Saharan African communities affected by HIV/AIDS. Passion '13 placed its central focus on human trafficking around the world. At the conference, Passion also launched its own "End It Now" campaign, a social-media-based fundraising endeavor designed to raise awareness of the plight of human-trafficking victims and to raise money for various anti-trafficking organizations. In addition to panels and information sessions, both conferences also incorporated their respective causes in memorable moments of musical worship. Analyzing the dynamics of these two particular musical performances is key to understanding how the Passion and Urbana conference congregations marshaled the eschatological discourse to locate themselves in relationship to marginalized global Others.

Both of these musical performances can be interpreted as attempts at what I call "dialogic performances of marginality." Here I draw from the work of E. Patrick Johnson on what he calls the "dialogic performance of blackness" (2005, 72) extending his observations about blackness to marginality more generally. In theorizing a white, nonreligious Australian choir's affinity for African American gospel music, Johnson argues that there is more to the choir's performance of the music of a far-removed racial Other than simply another instance of white appropriation of black culture. Drawing from the work of Dwight Conquergood (1986) and his notion of dialogic performance in which "the performer comes to know himself or herself by performing the Other" (quoted in Johnson, 72), Johnson writes that dialogic performances "foreground the tensions between self and Other such that, despite evidence to the contrary, self and Other temporally and spatially come together and converse . . . Thus dialogic performance makes possible the sharing of ideas, beliefs, and values across barriers of difference" (72). Johnson argues for the transgressive, transformative effect of the white choir's gospel performances on its members, demonstrating that their performance of gospel music has encouraged choir members to become more self-reflexive as they identify with marginalized groups, a trend that has spurred activism on economic, social, and political fronts. After giving an extended description of the performances at Passion and Urbana, I use Johnson's model to theorize and examine the differing implications of each.

Passion 2013 Conference, Atlanta, Georgia, January 4, 2013

It is nearing lunchtime during the final session of the Passion '13 conference. Following an opening song set, talk, and second song set, conference founder Louie Giglio, comes out to announce the kickoff for End It Now, a social media campaign to raise funds for nineteen different organizations devoted to preventing human trafficking and rehabilitating its victims. Toward the end of his explanation, Giglio announces, "And we're going to stand up for freedom right now." Ushers have filled the aisles of the stadium and are passing materials down the aisles. I can't yet see what is being passed out, so I assume it must be an informational pamphlet about the campaign. Giglio explains that the ushers are handing out "the story of a real person." He gives an example of one such story, recounting a Filipina victim of sex trafficking named Maleah. Maleah was rescued by one of the organizations supported by End It Now and went on to testify in court against her molesters.

An usher has finally reached my aisle, and he passes a stack of materials down the row. When the stack gets to me, I take the one on top. It appears at first to be a strange fan: a flat stick attached to a round piece of cardboard. On one side of the card is the story of Busho, described as a seven-year-old "modern-day slave," who was rescued from forced labor in the mines of the Congo. I turn the cardboard over and there is a nearly life-sized face staring back at me: it the face of a young black boy with serious brown eyes and a crusty nose. I pass the stack of cards, faces up, to the white college-aged woman standing beside me. She foregoes the face on top of the stack—what looks to be a South Asian teenage girl, smiling—and sorts through the faces, choosing instead a young black child with a more somber expression.

A keyboard synth pad softly underscores with a sustained chord as Giglio continues. "When I hold Maleah's face today . . . I'm standing for Maleah today and her freedom and the other girls in Cebu who are yet to be free. I'm standing for freedom right now." As Giglio speaks, dozens of conference participants silently process onto the large circular stage. They hold the human-trafficking-victim face cards in front of their own faces as Giglio tells the crowd how the face cards are about to be used. "And that face is becoming your face today so that you can say 'it's not really all about me. It's all about those who have no voice.' So . . . together we're going to lift up our praise. The ones who are free seeking to bring freedom to those who still need it."

The background keyboard synth intensifies as Giglio loudly exhorts the crowd: "Hold that face up in a way that it obscures yours . . . Let's let the camera, as it pans this song, let's let it pan these faces and not our faces. And let's let the world see these men, these women, these children, and not us. And let's believe that Jesus is coming—freedom is coming—for the 27 million [victims of human trafficking], some 60,000 of them represented by you and me today. And let's believe God for what only God can do in Jesus' name."

At "Jesus' name," the background chord vamp resolves from a suspension to an open chord sonority. As the synth pad sustains the chord, a four-note electric guitar riff and powerful drum beat erupt from the band. Song lyrics appear on the large screens, and I recognize the first verse of "God of Angel Armies," a new worship song that was introduced in the conference's first main session. In a subdued tone and with minimal instrumentation, Chris Tomlin leads the crowd in singing the first verse, which uses martial rhetoric excerpted from biblical Psalms to declare the certainty of God's victory over the forces of darkness. Each four-line stanza of the verse ends with the rhetorical question "whom shall I fear?"

As they sing along, conference participants dutifully hold the face cards over their own. As the cameras pan the audience in different parts of the stadium (Figure 2.3), I see the same face cards repeated over and over again. The faces on the cards blanketing the faces of predominantly white, middle-class American college students overwhelmingly belong to people of color, some smiling, others serious, as the camera pans the crowd.

Figure 2.3: Screens show singers on stage at the 2013 Passion Conference as they sing "God of Angel Armies" with "modern-day slave" masks in front of their faces. Atlanta, Georgia: January 2013.
Photo by the author.

The volume increases and instrumental texture thickens as the melody jumps up in register, signaling the entry of the chorus. As participants hold the cards in front of their own faces, many worshipers raise their free hand toward the sky as they sing, as the chorus melody slowly but confidently ascends in pitch and volume:

> I know who goes before me
> I know who stands behind
> The God of angel armies is always by my side[8]

After two additional energetic songs, Chris Tomlin utters the final words of the conference, quoting the song "God's Great Dance Floor": "All the earth shouts, let the future begin!" Passion '13 officially ends. Exhausted and preoccupied thinking through the troubling implications of the surreal mask performance I have just witnessed, I follow the crowd slowly streaming out the doors of the Georgia Dome. When I stop to toss my empty plastic water bottle in the nearest trash can outside the stadium, I see a stack of face placards that have been discarded haphazardly on top of the overflowing bins.

The climatic masked performance at Passion '13 was presented explicitly as an attempt to identify with and speak/sing on behalf of victims of human trafficking, represented as predominantly nonwhite people from places far from Atlanta and the North American suburbs. Giglio's framing of the performance assumes that those who are in slavery cannot help themselves and cannot speak (or sing) until they are set free—a rescue mission that ultimately "only God can do." The mask performance at Passion construes the Other entirely in terms of victimhood as the traditional object of charity in need of a (white) Savior.[9] Paying attention to the sung performance, however, reveals a mode of partial identification that uses the marginalized Other as a way to reinforce a particular theological perspective. The juxtaposition of the mask performance with the worship song "God of Angel Armies" carries significant political and theological implications that are linked in the course of performance.

Singing as/for the Other can be conceived as a reversal of postcolonial theorist Homi Bhabha's colonial subject, an ambivalent subject position created through partial, but never complete, identification with the colonizer. Bhabha writes that "colonial mimicry is the desire for a reformed, recognizable Other, as a subject of a difference that is almost the same, but not quite" (1984, 126). In Passion's masked performance, participants use an act of musical ventriloquism to attempt to identify with and speak for the marginalized subject. Like Bhabha's colonial subject, Passion's "modern-day slave" is inherently ambivalent, an object to be identified against (the voiceless, powerless "they" defined vis-à-vis the "we" who have both metaphorical voices of representation and literal voices for singing) even as the individual stories ostensibly encourage identification.

Another aspect of the performance that encourages identification happens through the re-contextualization of the song "God of Angel Armies." The lyrics of this song both grow out of and reinforce tenets of the neo-Calvinist theology that subtly (and sometimes not so subtly) suffuses the conference. Neo-Calvinist theological anthropology is centered on the idea that human beings are ultimately depraved and therefore powerless to do good on their own, and that God is absolutely sovereign and thus the only true agent (see Busman 2015a, 2015b). The lyrics of "God of Angel Armies" narrate an unwavering confidence in an omnipotent Divine protector who is "always on my side": "you will deliver me / yours is the victory," the verse lyrics proclaim. Nowhere in the sung lyrics is the singer or community portrayed as a collaborator with God; God is the only active agent, and the singer-believer's sole action is having faith in God's sovereign control of all things. Performing this song as voiceless, powerless Others adds additional resonance to the song's message, giving student participants a powerful spiritual picture of who they are in relationship to God according to the theological perspective on divine-human agency that the conference advocates. Like the voiceless Others they sing for, worshipers are framed as undeserving, passive, grateful recipients of God's salvation. In this sense, they achieve at least partial identification with the victims whose stories they are attempting to embody.

Passion's masque offers partial identification with marginalized Others on a neo-Calvinist theological basis, but it cannot be considered a dialogical performance in Johnson's and Conquergood's sense. The trafficking victims in Passion's performance are (literally) disembodied, two-dimensional caricatures, powerless Others portrayed as voiceless and thus unable to contribute meaningfully the dialogue. Here, there are not two parties in dialogue with each other; rather, the Self temporarily shrouds and obscures itself with a caricature of the marginalized Other. These trafficking victims, in Giglio's framing of the performance, are victims in shackles in need of resources that only those who are "free" are able give them. Ending human trafficking—setting the "modern-day slaves" free—was presented throughout the conference as being fairly straightforward: it involves prayer for Divine intervention, raising awareness to those unaware of the plight of human-trafficking victims, and raising money to supply aid organizations with more resources. Indeed, as the name of the End It Now campaign suggests, human trafficking was presented as an evil that can be ended "now" by "this generation."

The victim mask is incorporated into a performance that makes marginalized people the objects of charitable consumption. My sobering find of the stacks of masks on top of arena trash cans suggests that, like the symbols used to represent them, these people are ultimately dispensable, used up after inspiring a ten-minute bout of emotional fervor. In spiritualizing the battle against human trafficking by insisting that only God can provide victory, and in lumping together the complex economic and social conditions that spur human trafficking into a generalized sentimental narrative of "setting slaves free," Passion marries an ostensibly progressive social-justice cause with an essentially conservative, neocolonialist politics. Similar to Bhabha's account of colonial mimicry, Passion's performance seems designed to mask structures of earthly power rather than to make participants aware of their own complicity with them, perpetuating what Teju Cole has called the "white savior industrial complex," in which marginalized places and peoples serve as "a backdrop for white fantasies of conquest and heroism" (Cole 2012). Many of the individual organizations within the End It Now coalition may have more nuanced approaches to human trafficking; however, this performance—along with many of the other panels and discussions from the stage—at Passion '12 presented the "wicked" problem of human trafficking as ultimately solvable by individuals "here" helping individuals "there," rather than through transforming or toppling unjust social structures. Passion's tens of thousands of college student participants were never encouraged to question their own countries' political structures or policies; likewise, no connection was made between the suburban North American lifestyle and the global economic and political structures that drive trafficking. As a result, no sense of responsibility was conveyed; rather, human trafficking was framed largely as voluntary charitable giving by the "haves" to the "have nots."

The third night of the Urbana '12 conference featured a musical performance analogous in some ways to Passion '13's masque. In this session, conference participants were similarly encouraged to come to the aid of HIV/AIDS victims across the world and, though their musical worship, to give voice a marginalized Other.

Third Evening Session, Urbana Conference: St. Louis, Missouri, December 29, 2012

Since the beginning of the 2012 Urbana conference, the organizers had hinted that something memorable would happen during the evening session on the third night of Urbana. At the session's beginning, Greg Jao, the event's MC, announced that the evening would feature a hands-on project: joining a large assembly line on the stadium floor to put together medical kits for volunteer community caregivers in Swaziland, the country that currently had the highest HIV/AIDS infection rate in the world. Jao framed the activity "not as an act of charity, but as an act of identification." Rather than singing along with a worship song set—how every other main session had begun—the crowd instead watched several short videos about the HIV/AIDS crisis in Swaziland; the documentaries showcased the importance of community caregivers' work providing in-home care. One of the videos was a short documentary about the day-to-day work of Shortie Khumalo, a Swazi nurse and caregiver. *After the video, Khumalo herself came onstage and extended to the conference an invitation on behalf of her team of Swazi caregivers to partner in being "the hands and feet of Jesus to our community." Her invitation was followed by a short report from a middle-aged white American medical-supply-company representative who had brokered a deal with his company to provide low-cost medical supplies to the Swazi caregivers. As he announced that conference-goers would be assembling 32,000 medical kits that evening, he told participants tearfully, "You're going to change the world."*

As the first wave of conference participants were ushered to the arena floor to assemble medical kits, the Urbana worship team entered the stage. Rather than the casual urban wear that they had worn in previous sessions, the worship-team women wore wraparound skirts in colorful patterns with black tops, while the men wore khakis and collared shirts (Figure 2.4). The team's Latina worship director began by teaching the crowd a set of traditional greetings used in southern Africa. Urbana worship director Sandra Van Opstal prefaced the first song by recounting aspects of her trip to Swaziland, where she learned the song from a group of young girls, some of whom were orphaned by HIV/AIDS. She extended an invitation to the gathered crowd: "Will you join us in coming to the table this evening with the workers and the children and the families in Swaziland?"

Swazi lyrics were projected on the large screens as the song "Siyabonga Jesu" began. The seven worship band vocalists sang in close three-part harmony, with Van Opstal interjecting an improvised line and leading the team and crowd in a call and response, as four worship band instrumentalists played interlocked hand percussion parts over a slow groove. The song's few words—translated as "thank

Figure 2.4: The Urbana Worship Team leads "Malibongwe." Urbana '12, InterVarsity's 23rd Student Missions Conference.

you, Jesus, you walk with us"—made it relatively easy for the crowd to learn. As conference participants streamed down from their seats to join the medical kit assembly line, the team started the next song, "Malibongwe." To the three vocal parts and hand percussion were added piano and bass guitar. As in the first song, the words were primarily in a southern African language—I assumed it was Swazi, or maybe Zulu—with an English translation given underneath the lyrics on the screen. As the song progressed, Ryan Cook, an African-American male vocalist in the worship band, and Van Opstal alternated leading the call and response parts.

At the end of the song set, Van Opstal led the gathered assembly in a prayer that framed their participation as an expression of solidarity: "God, we want tonight to be in solidarity with the heroes in Swaziland who are caring for their neighbors, who are extending their hands, who are lifting you up not only with their words but lifting you up with their actions. We ask, God, that you would give us a heart like they have, to reach out to our neighbors, to extend ourselves. To give energy, God, when we don't have it. To walk forty-five minutes in one direction just to be with someone and tell them that Jesus loves them. To bring them a tangible gift, God, so that they can feel love and actually experience health. Would you help us to lift you up that way?"

Over the course of this evening session, Urbana '12 modeled for its participant a very different understanding of and relationship to o/Others than Passion did. Economic and political aspects of the HIV/AIDS crisis were addressed in brief, and organizers chose a specific context—the small country of Swaziland—rather than a more generalized region or problem (e.g., "AIDS in Africa" or "the global AIDS epidemic"). A local aid worker extended an in-person invitation to the conference crowd to join her in her work. The local workers and the members of their communities were portrayed as social agents rather than victims, though one could argue that the portrayal was still somewhat two-dimensional. (Though not presented as helpless victims, Swazi caregivers were presented as "heroes" and larger-than-life role models.) The songs presented in the worship set were framed as meaningful to Christians in Swaziland and grounded in narratives of personal connection with them. The worship team attempted to incorporate musical elements of a generalized Southern African popular styles, and conference-goers were expected to sing the songs in their original languages.

Though Urbana's musical representation relied on some essentializing practices, it came markedly closer to a dialogic performance in "foreground[ing] the tensions between self and Other" (E. P. Johnson 2005, 72), encouraging greater self-reflexivity, and offering an opportunity for action. The performance at Urbana presented marginalized Others from elsewhere in the world as resourceful and competent. In reflecting on the evening service after the event, Van Opstal reflected on the goals that informed her musical choices:

the last thing we wanted was for people to walk away thinking, *How sad for these poor Africans. Let's pray for them and help them because they need us.* Instead we hoped the experience would be one of mutual exchange. We were being invited by the caregivers to be partners, yet we had something to receive from them as well. Through their strength, hope and joy we were to learn what it means to follow God and to live mission in the midst of struggle. (2015, 12)

By showcasing aid work organized and carried out by local caregivers, and by portraying these individuals as resourceful agents capable of assessing their own needs and initiating partnerships, student participants were invited to experience their participation as more than a one-sided act of charity, subverting some key elements of the white-savior complex.

The performance at Urbana comes closer to Conquergood's definition of dialogic performance but differs in one important respect. According to Conquergood, dialogic performance "resists closure and totalizing domination of a single viewpoint, a unitary system of thought. The dialogical performance counters the normative with the performative, the canonical with the carnivalesque, Apollonian rationality with Dionysian disorder . . . striv[ing] to bring as many different voices as possible into the conversation . . ." (1986, 47–48). Urbana's performance is presented as a more specific type of dialogue, an internal conversation between members of the same faith community. Students are encouraged to identify with others across national, cultural, and ethnic difference by understanding shared religious faith as the primary basis for identification.

From conversations with conference-goers, it seemed the third evening's activities and worship songs resonated with many participants. During the final afternoon of the Urbana '12 conference, I roamed the conference center's main concourse for several hours during the lunch break and early afternoon sessions, initiating conversations with participants who were usually clustered in small friend groups. I often started the conversation with an open-ended question about particular moments or experiences that stood out to them. Conference-goers in several of the groups immediately called to mind the evening when they had built the medical kits, and many mentioned their participation in singing the Swazi songs as particularly powerful, impactful, or revelatory. For Marissa, a twenty-year-old white student from Wisconsin, singing these songs before making the medical kits was one of the powerful moments of the conference. She explained,

When we were making the care packages, and then they introduced the song in the language of Swaziland. [*She then tries to sing part of the song's melody*]. I can't remember the words! [*laughs*] But it touched me how much pain and suffering they go through. Even in their suffering, you can just feel all that emotion and deep trust and faith—through the repetition of the words, and singing in that language, too. I really like the repetition, dwelling the words . . . it's like the words are marinating in our souls. (personal conversation, December 31, 2012)

Marissa's friend Rachel chimed in: "The moments when they bring in the international songs are really, really powerful because it helps you unite in solidarity with [other] Christians . . . To unite in solidarity and to *sing for* those people and to God, and to unite in [singing] that language, is just absolutely beautiful" (personal conversation, December 31, 2012).

Here, Rachel frames the singing at Urbana as an instance of "singing for" absent o/Others. Unlike Passion, at which a song written in North America was put in the mouths of absent Others, the words and music sung at Urbana was understood to come out of the lived experience of Christians elsewhere in the world. Though the tendency to essentialize and oversimplify remains, Urbana's leaders sought to build a shared understanding through singing songs that reflect a common faith and inspire common cause. Here, they use shared songs in an attempt to build a bridge between the conference congregation and that of the (absent, Christian) Other. Through musical performance, a conference congregation that seeks to include fellow members of their religious community from across the world was performed into being.

CONCLUDING THOUGHTS: CONFERENCE PILGRIMS RETURNING HOME

How evangelicals imagine the sound of heaven during conference worship matters profoundly for how they envision the shape of their community on earth. By providing a space for affective and meaningful worship experiences, conferences enable their participants to form a new sort of congregation, at once a pilgrim gathering and an eschatological assembly. Conference gatherings, often experienced as "more sacred than church," are outside the realm of ordinary religious control and embody for many of their participants a higher moral authority than their local congregations. Evangelical students go to conferences like Urbana and Passion to participate in powerful, memorable worship experiences. Through physical resources like worship recordings and through embodied practices, they often take home the beliefs, practices, and models that they encounter and to enact locally in their home churches and campus fellowships. The discourses and practices modeled at conferences and embodied in their collective musical performances, then, have far-reaching influence on evangelical belief and practice more broadly.

The eschatological discourse endemic within the congregational worship of the Urbana and Passion conferences demonstrate how evangelicals are encouraged to conflate the conference gathering with both the "imagined" heavenly community and the global evangelical imagined community. By audibly and visually representing a sacred gathering at the end of time to the conference assembly, conference worship embodies the images and sounds of worship around God's throne, shaping the sacred imagination of a large group of young evangelicals. And because these conferences draw individuals and groups from across regions and increasingly from around the world, they play an important role in mediating ideas and practices to local evangelical religious communities. Interdenominational conferences are excellent examples of what Timothy Rommen (2007) calls "alternative sacred spaces" (105), performance spaces outside the control of dominant religious authorities where a common set of convictions enable participants to encounter ideas and experiment with practices unfamiliar to them. While a pilgrimage is a journey out of the participants' ordinary time and place into a realm of spiritual experience, there is often a strong connection between these extraordinary rituals and the practices of daily life (Bohlman 1996; Greene 2003; Coleman et al. 2004). Philip Bohlman writes that the music of pilgrimage not only embodies the ideals of the religious community gathered in set-apart ritual space, but also provides a "means for mapping out the domains" of religious practice and daily life (1996, 407). Conference worship, as a portable practice carried by evangelical pilgrims back to their home churches and college groups, becomes a means for the local enactment of the eschatological community. Conference models of worship enacted on the local level carry with them the blueprint for eschatological communities and social imaginaries.

While the rhetoric of heavenly community used in both the Urbana and Passion conferences was drawn from the same biblical sources, how the conferences modeled the heavenly gathering's appearance and sound was markedly different. Over the course of the two conferences, musical style and social organization signified distinct orientations toward o/Others within and outside the community. The Urbana Conference was concerned with representing the sound of heaven as necessarily relational, presenting in its musical leadership a wide variety of evangelical subject positions that questioned—sometimes subtly, sometimes explicitly—the white North American norm. By contrast, the Passion Conference reinforced white male leadership and the dominance of North American evangelicalism as saviors of the disempowered victims on the global margins.

While local adaptation of conference practice rarely results in wholesale emulation, the effects of these differences in the two conferences' eschatological imagination and social relations nonetheless do become embodied in local worship practices. During field research in 2006–2007 and in subsequent informal visits to college student organizations, I had several opportunities to observe at first hand college campus ministry meetings and spoke with university student groups who sent large contingents to one or the other of these conferences.[10] Through these encounters, I saw and heard how music and worship practices from Passion or Urbana were translated to local spaces, as college-aged participants drew from their experiences and variously adopted and adapted the conference's songs, styles, and performance techniques. Among several college campus groups at both secular and Christian universities, Urbana's influence resulted in the inclusion of more musical styles and languages into worship. Individuals involved in these campus ministries who attended an Urbana conference spoke about their Urbana experience transforming the way they believed congregational worship should be practiced. In Urbana-influenced groups, I observed white students incorporating African and African American gospel songs they had learned at the conference; predominantly Asian student groups incorporating Latin-flavored songs in Spanish; and women students taking prominent roles in leading worship. Conversations with group members highlighted how influential Urbana had been not only on the group's musical choices, but also on expanding their notions of how the global Christian community is constituted and of their location within it.

Passion's influence on campus groups and college fellowships, on the other hand, was more generally characterized by a recommitment to personal piety rather than a shift in understanding. When asked specifically about the influence of Passion on their church and campus college fellowships, attendees pointed not to structural or ideological changes but rather to a change in the level of their own individual spiritual commitment. The Passion Conference produced recommitments to engage more frequently and seriously in such devotional practices as praying, Bible reading, proselytization, and musical worship. Tim, a college freshman attendee, summed up the influence of the Passion Conference on his college campus group: "Everyone in my college group has started worshiping from their hearts. All the songs are the same, but I think everyone is trying to concentrate on what they are singing to God. We are all taking our worship time much more seriously."

These differences between how community is imagined and constituted— for Passion, as a largely monocultural gathering with predominantly male leadership; for Urbana, an intercultural gathering at which leadership roles are taken up by those in marginalized subject positions—may be both a reflection and instigating factor for increasingly complex social and political affiliations among young evangelical Christians. It seems that, within congregations where contemporary worship music is performed in a relatively homogenous pop-rock style, the eschatological imagination is often limited to the dominant group and its concerns. However, where musical choices are consciously eclectic, worshipers are often more aware of systemic issues, whether or not they then work actively for justice and reconciliation.

And, as a growing number of sociological and journalistic studies are showing, evangelical religious identity is increasingly fractured across political lines, with younger evangelicals and nonwhite evangelicals moving left of the evangelical mainstream on social issues including immigration reform, economic policies, and climate change.[11] This chapter's comparison of worship at Passion and Urbana, where differing eschatological visions go hand in hand with diverging social ideals, is a performative entry point into understanding the political tensions that at the time of this writing are threatening to rend contemporary evangelicalism.[12] Contemporary worship music at student conferences like Passion and Urbana, then, is a window into understanding diverging ideological and cultural currents within the broad North American evangelical Christian social imaginary. More broadly, it serves to show how conference congregations—formed in a common pilgrimage and held together by a collective imagination—enable evangelical Christians to build community, negotiate difference, and construct a religious imagination.

NOTES

1. I use the term "eschatological discourse" to reference evangelical notions of both the (present) heavenly community and the community at the end of time, particularly as depicted in the book of Revelation. While formal theological discourse generally separates these ideas, I use the terms "eschaton" and "heaven" interchangeably throughout this section because (1) they both refer broadly to humanity's ultimate end, whether conceived as the afterlife (heaven) or the end of time (the eschaton), and because (2) these notions are frequently conflated within both the conferences and evangelical discourse more generally.

2. Conferences for the college-student demographic are currently the most visible and well-publicized type of interdenominational evangelical conference. However, several organizations organized highly successful series of regional and national conferences for adult men and women. The Promise Keepers conference drew over 6 million evangelical men to its regional and national rallies between 1990 and 2009, including an estimated 1.4 million participants to its 1997 rally at the National Mall in Washington, DC (http://promisekeepers.org/pk-history). The Women of Faith conference, the most well-known evangelical women's conference, has drawn over 4 million participants to its traveling weekend conferences since its founding in 1996 (http://www.womenoffaith.com/about/).

3. Evangelical campus ministries have thrived as religious observance has undergone a resurgence among American college students. In 2007, the Social Science Research Council commissioned a series of essays on collegiate religious practice as part of their work on Religion and the Public Sphere. The resulting essay collection from leading researchers entitled "The Religious Engagements of American Undergraduates" gives a detailed portrayal of US college students' religious practice, including a statistical overview of evangelical campus life, several essays on evangelical student groups, and a comprehensive bibliography. It is available at http://religion.ssrc.org/reforum.

4. Statistics are taken from InterVarsity Christian Fellowship (2015), "Vital Statistics," accessed 16 May 2015, http://www.intervarsity.org/about/our/vital-statistics.

5. COVER THE EARTH WITH YOUR GLORY. Cindy Cruse-Ratcliff, Israel Houghton, and Meleasa Houghton. ©2003 Integrity's Praise! Music, Lakewood

Ministries Music, and My Other Publishing Company (admin. by Integrity). Used by permission.

6. O PRAISE HIM (ALL THIS FOR A KING). David Crowder. ©2003 worshiptogether.com Songs (ASCAP) sixsteps Music (ASCAP) (adm. At CapitolCMGPublishing.com). All rights reserved. Used by permission.

7. For perspectives on the rise in concern for racial integration in US evangelical churches, see Marti (2012, 3, fn. 2). See also York 2014. A strong concern for racial inclusion and social justice in predominantly white US mainline Protestant churches has produced a standardized non-Western song repertoire known as "global song" (see Moore 2018a and 2018b). While many of the concerns impelling Urbana's use of songs outside the white mainstream overlap with the Protestant mainline use of global song, they represent two entirely different ecclesial, parachurch, and musical networks. A comparison of the songs outside the contemporary worship mainstream used at Urbana to the "canonical" global song repertoire as described by Moore 2018a reveals that the two are completely distinct.

8. WHOM SHALL I FEAR (GOD OF ANGEL ARMIES). Chris Tomlin, Ed Cash, Scott Cash. ©2013 Worship Together Music (BMI) sixsteps Songs (BMI) S.D.G. Publishing (BMI) (adm. at CapitolCMGPublishing.com) / Alletrop (BMI) / C/O MUSIC SERVICES (BMI). All rights reserved. Used by permission.

9. Here I reference Teju Cole's description of "The White-Savior Industrial Complex," accessed 12 June 2015, http://www.theatlantic.com/international/archive/2012/03/the-white-savior-industrial-complex/254843/?single_page=true.

10. Universities included during this period of field research included Wheaton College, Calvin College, Vanderbilt University, and Belmont University.

11. Scholarly observers have called attention to the growing rifts within US evangelical Christianity since the early 2000s, though the full-blown recognition of their seriousness did not come to the fore until after the 2016 US elections. Shortly before the 2008 US elections, ethicist David Gushee called cultural observers to "acknowledge that the evangelical political landscape is fragmented along right/center/left lines" (Gushee 2008b, 1). He goes on to comment that the "evangelical center" may be moving left, led predominantly by nonwhite evangelicals and young evangelicals between the ages of eighteen and twenty-nine. Other sociological and political studies and journalistic sources have emphasized the growing diversity of the evangelical political commitments. For further scholarly and journalistic perspectives on shifting evangelical political orientations, see Banerjee 2008; Freedman 2009; Goodstein 2008; Gushee 2008a; and C. Smith 2002.

12. For perspectives from within US evangelicalism on the severity of the crisis of religious and political identities instigated by the 2016 election, see Labberton 2018.

CHAPTER 3

⌒⌒

Finding the Church's Voice

Contemporary Worship as Musical Positioning in a Nashville Church Congregation

The preceding chapters have looked at performance spaces where contemporary worship music engenders two distinct modes of congregating. Exploring contemporary worship music within concert congregations highlighted the many intersections between ministry and entertainment, between worship and fandom, and, for evangelicals, between being in the world but not of it, and the fine line they must walk. Within conference congregations, contemporary worship music helped to unite the gathering into an eschatological assembly. Through the way they perform and frame times of musical worship that are experientially powerful, conference organizers shape their attendees' understandings of heaven and, in the process, shape how they imagine the evangelical religious community in their nation and world. In each performance space, contemporary worship music is a tie that binds and unites these disparate publics into a religious "community of feeling" that is as much a community of affinity as a community of descent (Shelemay 2011). Evangelical worshipers choose to congregate in these spaces on the basis of their common beliefs about worship and their expectations of what makes for a spiritually efficacious worship experience.

Congregational singing is one of the central participatory and experiential practices in the worship of local church congregations, which have long been considered the paradigmatic mode of congregating. However, the dynamics that govern musical choice and selection are different in a gathering that meets week in and week out and that must navigate its relationship with other area congregations, denominational traditions, and church networks. To understand how contemporary worship music forms and informs the dynamics of congregating unique to churches, this chapter will address two related questions. First, what cultural work does contemporary worship music accomplish within local worshiping communities that meet on a regular basis? And, second, how do congregations whose established worship traditions include other musical styles and repertories of congregational song understand and incorporate contemporary worship music? I address these questions through painting an "ethnographic portrait"[1] of an "evangelical Episcopal" church in Nashville, Tennessee in order to show how this congregation uses worship music as a means of positioning. Drawing from interviews with church leadership, congregants, and my perspective as an "observant participant" (Butler 2005, 48) within this congregation, the discussion highlights two related processes of musical positioning: first, how and where this church deploys the repertory of contemporary worship music itself within the service relative to other congregational song repertories, and second, how this church uses a particular blend of musical elements—what one leader called its "musical stew"—to locate itself relative to other individual congregations as well as denominational and interdenominational networks. Through detailed examination of the songs, styles, repertories, and discourses about music and worship within the life of a single congregation, interpreted through theoretical frameworks provided by perspectives from the ethnomusicology of Christianity and sociological congregational studies work, this chapter demonstrates how contemporary worship music shapes church congregations, even as its meaning and affective power is conditioned in turn by the local church congregations that use it in worship.

EXPLORING MUSICAL JUNCTURES OF CHOICE WITHIN CONTEMPORARY CHURCH CONGREGATIONS: A CASE STUDY

March 12, 2006—10:30 a.m. service at St. Bartholomew's Church in Nashville, Tennessee

A few months before relocating to Nashville, my husband and I visited an Episcopal church in the Green Hills neighborhood in the southwest part of the city. We arrived on an unseasonably warm Sunday morning in late winter during the penitential season of Lent. As we entered the main worship space, we were handed a thick bulletin containing the day's Scripture readings, spoken responses, and congregational song lyrics. As I leafed through the bulletin, I was surprised to find lyrics of many recent contemporary worship songs in addition to several hymns. Seeing no worship band on the central platform, I wondered how the contemporary songs would be performed. After an organ prelude and processional hymn, a middle-aged male minister welcomed the gathered assembly of 300 to the second of two Sunday morning worship services. He framed the congregation as an "evangelical Episcopal" church, which I found striking. Many US Christians I knew would consider these two descriptions a contradiction in terms. After reciting the Decalogue and chanting a contemporary setting of the Kyrie accompanied by piano, the congregation stood to the amplified sounds of an unseen band comprising acoustic guitar, piano, bass guitar, drum kit, and hand drums. Craning my neck backward, I saw the band members nestled behind the organ console in the back balcony. After a short instrumental introduction, a female vocalist in the balcony standing in front of a microphone led the congregation in "Your Love, O Lord," a popular worship song I recognized instantly from singing it at other gatherings, and from its frequent airplay on Christian radio. After repeating the first verse and chorus, the large pipe organ joined the band in what I thought would be the song's final chorus, as the congregation sang again:

> And I will lift my voice
> To worship You, my King
> And I will find my strength
> In the shadow of Your wings[2]

Despite the length of the service to come, the band led the congregation in four more repetitions of the chorus. During the chorus reiterations, congregation members in the pews and clergy standing near the front altar closed their eyes and raised their hands toward heaven.

St. Bartholomew's Church, known regionally as "St. B's"—is a suburban congregation of approximately 1,200 members located in the Green Hills area of south Nashville (Figures 3.1 and 3.2). At the time of my study, it averaged 450 attendees in its two Sunday morning worship services and hosted a separate Dinka-speaking Sudanese Anglican congregation that met concurrently in its educational wing. St. B's is one of twenty-eight churches in the greater Nashville metropolitan area affiliated with the Episcopal Church, USA (ECUSA), a mainline Protestant denomination that tends to position itself to the left of the evangelical mainstream both theologically and politically. These positions set apart Episcopal churches within the greater Nashville area. Nashville, sometimes called "the buckle of the Bible belt," has a religious landscape that is dominated by churches affiliated with evangelical Protestant denominations or networks. The Southern Baptist Convention, Churches of Christ, and nondenominational evangelical churches make up nearly one third of total religious adherents in the greater Nashville area, while Episcopalians represent less than one percent.[3] While it remains part of a denominational minority,

Figure 3.1: St. Bartholomew's Church, Nashville, Tennessee. Exterior.
©2016 St. Bartholomew's Church. Used by permission.

Figure 3.2: St. Bartholomew's Church, Nashville, Tennessee. Interior.
©2016 St. Bartholomew's Church. Used by permission.

however, St. Bartholomew's distinguishes itself from others in its denomination by gesturing toward the evangelical religious mainstream, as the minister framed it in my previously recounted first visit to the church. The congregation's self-designation "evangelical Episcopal" was unique within Nashville's religious landscape at the time of my study. Music serves as a powerful mode of differentiation and affiliation; St. Bartholomew's was one of the few Episcopal churches in the area with a worship band, and the only Episcopal church in the area in which contemporary worship music made up a significant part of its congregational song repertory. St. B's distinct social location as a denominational minority in the greater Nashville area and a liturgical anomaly within its own denomination makes it an excellent arena to examine processes of musical positioning.

While including an outline of the congregation's history, this chapter focuses primarily on the three-year research period between 2006 and 2009, with supplementary perspectives via follow-up interviews and observations gleaned in 2012 and 2016. During this three-year period, I was both a participant observer and what Melvin Butler (2005, 48) has termed an "observant participant": that is, a researcher who shares aspects of the religious faith of the community she is studying. During my time attending this congregation, my own position as researcher and congregant shifted as I moved from an outsider to this particular church and its denominational tradition to a regular participant in its congregational—and especially its musical—life.

Whether a church worship service is loosely or rigidly structured, it comprises variable elements that the local congregation must choose strategically from a range of possible options. Aspects of music-making—including repertory, style, mode of participation, and performance practice—are vital elements of variation laden with contextually produced meanings, though those meanings may be heavily contested. In his work on American Jewish congregations, Jeffrey Summit (2000) describes the significance of such musical "junctures of choice" within corporate worship:

> One might assume that worship would be a bastion of tradition, an area where practice is firmly established, where all the choices have already been made. In fact, in every community that I examined, musical aspects of the service underwent constant, strategic negotiation, both by leaders and by worshippers . . . These junctures are broad in some worship communities, narrow in others. Yet by examining these choices, and the processes by which they are made, we learn about the locus of authority and power of tradition in each community. (19)

Examining how local church congregations navigate choices between competing musical options for worship provides crucial insights on how they understand and negotiate various sources of religious authority and how music is used to establish, maintain, or challenge ecclesial traditions.

What's more, in the contemporary US Protestant context, musical choices do not merely reflect preexisting values and beliefs of the local community; rather, they help to constitute the church congregations as well. As noted in previous chapters of this book, music does not simply emerge from communal experience but rather is an integral part of *creating* an experience responsible for bringing people together in the first place. Keith Negus describes the process this way: "songs and musical styles do not simply 'reflect,' 'speak to' or 'express' the lives of audience members or musicians. A sense of identity is created out of and across the processes whereby people are connected together through and with music" (133). In other words, musical repertories and the discourses associated with them can constitute a community by drawing people together in a shared musical experience. Music is a crucial element in constituting church congregations because it provides the basis for the powerful worship experiences that shape individuals within it and by attracting people with shared values and common expectations of worship.

Music is one way that church congregations position themselves in time, whether in relationship to a denominational or generalized Christian past, the culture of the present day, or an eschatological future. And music has become an increasingly important way that churches position themselves in space, within the contemporary religious landscape and marketplace. With the continued decline of denominational loyalty in the United States and elsewhere, a congregation's worship style—defined in great part by choice of musical repertory and style—figures prominently in the factors US Christians consider when selecting a local church congregation to attend.[4] Liturgical historian Brian Spinks has described the contemporary scene in Western Christianity as a "worship mall," with a variety of styles "offered by different churches to suit personal taste or spirituality, all enticing in different ways, and in competition with each other" (2010, xxiii). The need for local assemblies to stake out a distinct place within a congregational marketplace has given rise to "niche congregations," defined as those which "reach beyond an immediate neighborhood to create an identity relatively independent of context" (Ammerman 1997, 324). Ammerman adds that "the implications of a mobile, cosmopolitan culture, where congregational choice is the norm, make such specialized religious sorting more and more likely" (324). The designation niche congregation effectively characterizes churches like St. Bartholomew's and can be parsed further as a "liturgical/theological niche congregation," according to Adair Lummis's typology (1998). Lummis defines congregations that make up this niche as "those which offer a different kind of worship service than normally found in churches of the denomination, or are much more theologically conservative or theologically liberal than is denominationally typical." Lummis mentions as a representative example evangelical churches within mainline Protestant denominations, noting the significant role of music and worship style in creating distinctions among these churches and nearby "traditional" churches in the denomination. Exploring how niche church congregations like St. Bartholomew's make decisions about what songs and styles to use in worship—and what meanings they locate within those styles—shows how music locates them within the local religious economy and regional networks.

A GENEALOGY OF WORSHIP: MUSICAL POSITIONING THROUGHOUT ST. BARTHOLOMEW'S HISTORY

Over its history dating back to the 1950s, leaders and congregation members at St. Bartholomew's have used music strategically to position the congregation in relationship to the Episcopal denominational tradition and to evangelical and charismatic church networks. Examining the church's history through the lenses of music and worship highlights internal and external forces and events—including the evangelical worship wars, successive waves of congregational crisis and renewal, and denominational schism—that have influenced the church's music and liturgical structure. Likewise, paying close attention to changes in musical style, organization, and repertory highlights how leadership and lay people have negotiated the varying concerns of charismatic, evangelical, and Episcopal networks and lays the groundwork for understanding the congregation's contemporary context.

St. Bartholomew's began in 1954 as a mission church of a larger Episcopal congregation in West Nashville. Older church members who attended the church as children and youth in the 1950s and 1960s characterized the church's music during this period as more "typically" Episcopal, with hymns out of the denominational hymnal accompanied by organ and choir. Beginning in the early 1970s, St. Bartholomew's became a regional center for the charismatic renewal movement that brought practices such as faith healing, prophecy, and ecstatic speech and singing to many Catholic and mainline Protestant churches.[5] In 1972, several members of St. B's attended the charismatic "Faith Alive" renewal event at an Episcopal church in Houston and then hosted a Faith Alive weekend event at St. B's later that year. An anonymous timeline entitled "The Historical Background of St. Bartholomew's Church" describes the results of St. B's Faith Alive weekend: "Like all 'different' programs, this drew criticism from some, caused confusion in others, was an inspiration to many, and caused a closeness and sense of love among most" (Anonymous, "Historical Background of St. Bartholomew's Church," compiled 1972). After Faith Alive, the congregation's musical styles, practices, and repertoire changed dramatically: pop-rock style contemporary worship songs arrived together with charismatic teachings and ecstatic worship practices.

The initial shifts in musical and worship style toward contemporary worship is attributed to two head ministers: Chuck Murphy, the church's rector from 1972 through 1982, who became a nationally known figure in the charismatic renewal movement, and Ron Jackson, who served from 1982 through 1990. Contemporary worship songs were introduced into weekly worship under Chuck Murphy, a musician himself who performed in contemporary popular styles. Shortly into his tenure, Reverend Jackson fired the congregation's longtime organist and replaced her with a husband-and-wife music ministry team capable of leading both traditional organ hymns and newer praise and worship songs. Under Jackson, in the early 1980s, the church adopted a new two-service format with a Sunday School hour in between. Music at the first service at 8:30 a.m. comprised hymns accompanied by piano and organ, while the 11:00 a.m. service used contemporary songs led by a worship band. In the 1980s and 1990s, an increasing number of congregations implemented the two-service format to mitigate conflicts over music and worship style (York 2003; Nekola 2009); that St. B's two services were established relatively early suggests that the church was at the forefront of evangelical currents. In the late 1980s, a large screen was installed on the right-hand wall at the front of the church for projecting song lyrics during the contemporary service.

Through the 1970s–1980s, St. Bartholomew's demographics shifted as members who did not support the church's new direction left and new charismatic-leaning members replaced them. During this time, congregational singing was rife with demonstrative charismatic practices, including speaking and singing in tongues, prophecy, and spontaneous healing. Widely known as a hub for charismatic teaching and worship, St. Bartholomew's gained a regional and national reputation as being a "Spirit-filled" church (or, for skeptics, a "crazy charismatic" congregation). While remaining within the Episcopal denomination, the congregation distanced itself from other churches in its diocese, aligning itself instead with other area congregations like Belmont Church, a congregation similarly prominent within charismatic renewal circles, and Christ Community Church, a popular evangelical church affiliated with the conservative Presbyterian Church of America.

St. Bartholomew's prominence as a node in charismatic-renewal networks continued into the 1990s. In early 1995, Lakeland, Florida–based Episcopal priest and revivalist Bud Williams came at the invitation of St. B's rector Ian Montgomery and led twice-daily revival services at St. Bartholomew's for three weeks. The charismatic outpouring made front-page news in *The Tennessean* with an article entitled "A Revival? Where? Episcopal Church Hosts Unusual Scene," where an account of attendees shaking, falling on the floor, and breaking into holy laughter was dramatically illustrated by a large photo of a church member lying on the floor while "filled with the Spirit" (Waddle 1995). In the article, Reverend Montgomery noted that, although the revival might cause consternation among other churches in the denomination and region, he was convinced that the revival, part of a worldwide movement within mainly pentecostal-charismatic churches, was truly "a movement of God" involving an outpouring of power not seen since the early church. Under Montgomery's leadership, two different music directors were hired to lead the two services: Eric Wyse, an organist and pianist from an evangelical church background, directed the early traditional service and played organ for select songs in the later service, while Mark McClure, a musician with a charismatic Assembly of God background, was brought on to lead the worship band during the second contemporary service.

Though the two-service format successfully mitigated participants' conflicting style preferences, some felt that St. Bartholomew's had become two separate congregations. The separate-style service format ended abruptly in 2001 after the departure of the worship band leader. To reestablish unity, minister Michael Ellis restructured the two services so that both employed identical music and liturgy. Eric Wyse, who was up until that point the organist and director for the traditional service, served as sole music director of both services from that point until resigning to take up another church post in 2013. Wyse recalled Ellis's tongue-in-cheek comment that "if we do [worship] well, everybody will *not* like something." A handful of disgruntled members left as a result of the change, but Wyse recalled that the majority of the congregation adapted fairly quickly to the new format:

> Within three months, it worked extremely well. People sat by people they'd never sat by before. And . . . some people who liked hymns and [thought they] hated praise and worship found they actually liked some praise and worship, and some people who never wanted to sing anything written by someone who was now dead actually found out they liked hymns. (Eric Wyse, personal interview, October 27, 2006)

To facilitate musical integration, Wyse hired Tom Howard, a pianist, composer, arranger, and session player in Nashville's Christian recording industry, as assistant music director. Together they embarked on a project to make "traditional" and "contemporary" styles less discrete. They bucked several general trends in US congregations during the time period in refusing to sideline the organ, maintaining a choir (though seasonal), and printing song lyrics in the weekly bulletin rather than projecting them onto a central screen.[6] Wyse, Howard, and others in the church's music ministry wrote several new settings for the church's weekly "service music" (i.e., sung settings of liturgical texts like the Lord's Prayer performed in every service) for organ, choir, and worship band. Noting enthusiastic participation in singing contemporary songs but lackluster participation in singing hymns, Wyse and Howard surveyed congregation members and concluded that the difference in participation came from unfamiliarity rather than dislike. A large percentage of the congregation came from evangelical backgrounds and were unfamiliar with Episcopal hymns. Church members could hear contemporary worship songs on recordings or on Christian radio, but did not hear hymns anywhere besides church. Taking a page from contemporary-worship pedagogy, and making use of his position as owner of a small independent record label, Wyse licensed 350 recordings of an organ-led choir singing thirty hymns from the primary Episcopal hymnbook generally known as *The Hymnal* (1982) and gave a CD to every family in the church. The hymns on that recording were introduced in worship over the next two years and became part of the church's core song repertory.

The next major shift that influenced worship practice at St. Bartholomew's was a church split that occurred in 2004. Between one third and one half of the church's members left with St. B's then-interim minister Thomas McKenzie to form Church of the Redeemer, which continues to meet a few miles away from St. Bartholomew's. Redeemer affiliated with the Anglican Mission in America (AMiA) and later the Anglican Church in North America (ACNA), both conservative federations of congregations that split from the ECUSA over the 2003 ordination of Gene Robinson, a partnered gay man, as bishop. In addition to this development within national church politics, congregants and leaders offered many other interpretations of why St. Bartholomew's split, including long-simmering personality conflicts and tensions among ordained and lay leadership. In 2005, the church called a new rector, the Rev. Dr. Jerry Smith, an evangelical-leaning Canadian priest and former seminary professor, who served until taking another appointment in 2016. By mid-2009, St. Bartholomew's had regained the number of members it lost to Church of the Redeemer five years earlier, but the composition of the church had shifted yet again. The new face of the church skewed younger, with young adults in their twenties and thirties and children under ten years old comprising the fastest-growing segments of the church. Many of the congregation members with charismatic backgrounds left to attend Redeemer, while the influx of new members mainly came from non-charismatic evangelical backgrounds, including Baptist, Nazarene, and nondenominational. As a result, charismatic expressions such as speaking in tongues, prophecy, and spontaneous singing or dancing during congregational singing declined noticeably in the years following the church split.

This brief history of worship at St. Bartholomew's Church has highlighted how musical style, repertory, and practices accompanying congregational music-making have shifted along with changes in demographics, leadership, and new influences from a variety of institutions and networks. The next sections turn to more recent ethnographic work to examine the combination of musical styles that comprise the musical "platform" of Sunday morning worship at St. Bartholomew's.

CONSTRUCTING A MUSICAL PLATFORM: LITURGICAL POSITIONING THROUGH SONGS, STYLES, AND PERFORMANCE PRACTICES

Each Sunday, after the final strains of the opening worship song died away, Rev. Jerry Smith welcomed the congregation. He used his opening remarks to frame the service structure to newcomers who had never experienced a highly structured liturgy. Frequently he described the service's structure, taken from the Episcopal *Book of Common Prayer*, as a "platform," a solid foundation and launching point for the activity of worship. The metaphor of the platform can also be interpreted as a public statement that stakes a claim on issues of central importance. Musical styles, songs, and performance practices at St. Bartholomew's serve as a crucial part of the liturgical "platform" in both these senses. Congregational music serves as both an affective jumping-off point for spiritual experience and a form of discourse wherein the community performs its relationship to other congregations, institutions, and networks. The musical elements of St. B's service—including songs, styles and genres, worshipful actions, and their fit into the liturgical structure as a whole—play an essential role in establishing this affective and meaningful platform for worship. The chief elements of the church's worship style are highlighted in the following account written shortly after my first experience participating in St. Bartholomew's worship music ensemble.

August 20, 2006—10:30 a.m. service, St. Bartholomew's Church

I arrive in the balcony Sunday morning a few minutes before the service was to begin. Choosing a seat in one of fifteen chairs placed on three levels of risers, I introduce myself to the middle-aged woman to my right (it happened to be her first Sunday in the loft, too). Three vocalists stand apart from the rest of the singers on the ends of the risers and have been given their own music stands and microphones. They face a half-circle of instrumentalists who include a drummer, acoustic guitarist, and bass guitarist and who are crammed in a small rectangular space bounded by the piano, the organ pipes, the vocalist's platform, and a large narrow window that stands floor to ceiling on the back wall (Figure 3.3). After the service I'm told that Wyse and Howard lead from organ and piano each Sunday, while a rotating roster of congregation members fill the three main instrumental roles (guitar, drums, and bass guitar) and three microphoned vocalists (generally a soprano, an alto, and a tenor). Other instruments including harp, accordion, flute, electric guitar, and cello are sometimes incorporated into the church's worship band.

This morning I expected merely to sit and observe the music-makers. As pianist and assistant music director Tom Howard counts off for the band the entrance to the opening worship song, music director Eric Wyse comes and stands directly in front

Figure 3.3: St. Bartholomew's Church worship band.
©2016 St. Bartholomew's Church. Used by permission.

of me and begins to direct entrances and dynamic levels. By the second song, I re-alize I am sitting right in the middle of the choir loft. With organ pipes immediately behind me and the worship band not ten feet to my right, I am unexpectedly incor-porated into the choir. Over the course of the service, I sight-read several unfamiliar hymns and improvise alto harmonies to worship songs I know well. From my perch in the loft, I can also observe the actions of the congregation members seated below. Though a few more congregation members raise their hands with the contemporary worship songs than with the organ-led hymns, I note that there is still a high degree of continuity in congregational actions regardless of the style of song performed.

Toward the end of the service as congregation members walk to the front to take Communion, the band leads a continuous string of songs, including two contempo-rary worship songs, a short chorus from the ecumenical Taizé community in France, and a hymn well known in Baptist churches that I find later is not included in the Episcopal Hymnal 1982. After all members of the congregation have returned to their seats, the band begins the song "Agnus Dei," a contemporary worship song currently on CCLI's Top 25 list. Its straightforward verse and chorus lyrics were completely unrelated to the Agnus Dei of the Mass Ordinary; rather, they are taken nearly verbatim from verses in the book of Revelation. Each verse is played softly, with a crescendo into the chorus. During the chorus's opening phrase ("Holy, holy / are you Lord God Almighty") the melody soars to its climax and the vocalists break into three-part harmony. After several verse and chorus repetitions, as the worship band enters the chorus again, Eric Wyse takes his seat at the organ, adding the loud strains of the pipe organ to the musical mix. During the final iterations of the chorus, one of the sopranos leading from the microphone begins to sing a descant-like part that fills in the spaces between lyrics. (At the time I think she is improvising; later I discovered she adapted her part from a popular commercial recording of the song.)

After "Agnus Dei," Eric Wyse begins playing the recessional "Singing Songs of Expectation," an up-tempo hymn with a minor-key setting. During the hymn's final stanza that describes the church's unity in its journey toward heaven, many worshipers in the sanctuary below and in the loft raise their hands in praise. After the final strains of the organ cease, a young child's voice rings out clearly in the silence, "Yayyyyyy!" Congregation members chuckle as the service is dismissed, and Wyse grins at me, seeming gratified by the response.

This account highlights the variety of songs and styles that typically comprised the congregational music repertory at St. B's. With repeated visits to the loft as choir vocalist, lead vocalist, and pianist, I came to understand in greater depth the role each of these played within the structure of the worship service. St. Bartholomew's offered two identical Sunday morning services at 8:30 a.m. and 10:30 a.m., each lasting around one and one-half hours. Both services followed the Rite II Eucharistic Liturgy from the Episcopal *Book of Common Prayer* (1979). Table 3.1 shows the liturgical and musical structure of each weekly service.

As this table shows, on any given Sunday, St. B's musicians led the congregation in fifteen to eighteen discrete pieces of music, and all but the offertory were intended for congregational singing. Where different worship songs and styles appeared within the liturgical structure was largely predictable from week to week. Organ-accompanied processional and recessional hymns served as bookends of the service, while contemporary worship songs led by the worship band were placed in a two-to-three-song set after the opening prayer and again during Communion, where greater than half of the congregational songs were drawn from the contemporary worship song repertory. The four pieces interspersed within the Communion liturgy were nearly always accompanied by both organ and band.

Where contemporary worship songs are placed within the service suggests an adaption not only of evangelical and charismatic song repertories, but also of the two-part ritual structure of "praise and worship" (see pp. 8–9 of the introduction). As is expected of opening praise songs within the charismatic musico-ritual structure, the two or three contemporary songs at the beginning of the St. B's service were always musically upbeat with lyrics describing communal actions of praise. Contemporary worship songs sung during Communion embodied many of the defining characteristics of the intimate worship songs that make up the "worship" part of the praise and worship structure: they were generally slower and contemplative, and often centered

Table 3.1. STRUCTURE OF SUNDAY MORNING SERVICES AT
ST. BARTHOLOMEW'S CHURCH

Service Section	Musical Style/Arrangement
Prelude	Organ instrumental
Processional hymn	Hymn accompanied by organ
Welcome/opening prayer	
Worship song set	Two to three songs accompanied by band
Old Testament reading	
Psalm	Call/response between soloist and congregation, accompanied by organ or guitar
New Testament Epistle reading	
Sequence hymn	Changes by season
New Testament Gospel reading	
Sequence hymn (reprise)	Changes by season
Sermon	
Nicene Creed	
Prayers of the People	
Confession of Sin	
Absolution	
The Peace	
The Offertory	Varies each week. The Offertory is sometimes used for teaching the congregation new songs and is the only place in the service for "special music" (non-congregational instrumental or vocal performance) by a soloist or group.
The Presentation hymn	Changes by season
The Eucharistic prayer	
Holy, Holy, Holy (Sanctus)	Newly composed setting accompanied by band and organ
Memorial Acclamation	Newly composed setting accompanied by band and organ
The Lord's Prayer	Newly composed setting accompanied by band and organ
Agnus Dei	Newly composed setting accompanied by band and organ
Communion music	Variable. During Communion, the band leads four to six congregational songs. Usually one half or more of these are contemporary worship songs.
Thanksgiving	
Recessional	Hymn accompanied by organ
Postlude	Either organ solo or worship band reprise of final Communion song

*italics denote musical portions of the service

on personal experience. Several long-time members informed me that the opening praise song set and Communion worship song set were the two points of the service at which charismatic expressions of hand raising, dancing, prophecy, tongues speech, and healing were most likely to occur. Where the liturgical musical structure at St. B's departs from the typical two-part charismatic structure is in the refocusing that happens in the final Communion song and the recessional hymn, which are generally upbeat and triumphant with lyrics focused on mission or justice. Eric Wyse described his vision of the musical structure of the service as an arc that moves from a focus on God's transcendence, characterized by loud proclamations of praise, to softer, more intimate settings that correspond to an emphasis on the individual's personal relationship with God, and then to an outward focus on humanity's participation in God's mission and work in the world.

ST. BARTHOLOMEW'S CHURCH'S MUSICAL "STEW": WORSHIP SONGS AS ACTIVE REPERTORY AND REPERTORY OF ACTION

For an understanding of how and why St. B's music leaders selected songs and styles for use in congregational worship, it is not enough to simply note the church's eclectic stylistic mixture, for not every song in a given style is considered equally suited for use in St. B's worship, and not all styles enjoy equal prominence. This section looks more closely at St. B's songs by using the theoretical frames of "active repertory" and "repertory of action," both of which draw attention to the dynamic set of theological, aesthetic, and ethical associations that adhere to particular songs and styles that preclude or justify their inclusion in worship and help the church to situate itself within various traditions and contemporary trends.

In his research in an Appalachian Baptist congregation, Jeff Todd Titon (1988) compiled a list of the 104 hymns sung in an eight-week period and from that derived a smaller subset of the twenty-one hymns sung two or more times; those selected hymns he called the congregation's "active repertory." The active repertory expresses a set of concerns unique to this congregation that could never have been derived from a study of all the repertory within church's hymnal alone (223–224). Drawing from and expanding Titon's method for establishing the active repertory at St. Bartholomew's, I analyzed a comprehensive list of over 1,500 songs sung during morning worship from July 2006 through June 2009.[7] My analysis revealed that there were two important subsets of the church's active repertoire during this period: the service music (sung settings of the Episcopal liturgy for each week) and the most frequently sung songs that changed from week to week. The four service music settings (the Holy, Holy, Holy [*Sanctus-Benedictus*], the Memorial Acclamation, the Lord's Prayer, and Lamb of God [*Agnus Dei*]), were each composed by past or current members of the worship band and were sung in nearly every service. The organ and worship band always played together in leading the service music for the congregation. Occurring next in frequency was a subset of seventy songs that were most frequently sung during the three-year time period, hereafter referred to as St. B's "Top 70." Each of these songs was sung between eight and sixteen times. Through conversations with Eric Wyse, Tom Howard, and other musicians in St. Bartholomew's music ministry, I assigned genres to each song in the Top 70, shown in Table 3.2.

Of the Top 70 songs, contemporary worship songs make up slightly under half (47 percent) of the song repertoire. The second most common song genre is what church leadership called "modern hymns" (24 percent). The modern hymn is a genre term first applied in the middle of the 2000s to the songs of British evangelical songwriters Keith Getty and Stuart Townend. Getty, a classically trained arranger and film and television music composer, and Townend, a charismatic contemporary worship leader, began composing these congregational songs in an attempt to unite churches torn apart by struggles over musical style and generational divides. Modern hymns use strophic or verse-refrain form and feature rhythmically straightforward, folk-tune-like melodies and simple harmonizations. As such, they are designed to occupy a middle ground between "traditional" hymns and contemporary worship music, to be easily learned by congregations accustomed to one style or the other and to be accompanied equally well by contemporary band instruments or by organ and choir. Comprising 13 percent of St. Bartholomew's active repertory are songs from the ecumenical Taizé community in France (or newly written contemplative pieces written in that style), which are characterized by two-to-four-line choruses intended to be repeated multiple times. The remaining 16 percent of the active repertory is made up of two types of hymns. Following Eric Wyse's nomenclature, I designate "classic

Table 3.2. ST. BARTHOLOMEW'S 70 MOST FREQUENTLY SUNG WORSHIP SONGS BY GENRE (2006–2009)

Congregational Song Genre	Number (/70)	Percentage
Contemporary worship song	33	47%
Modern hymn	17	24%
Taizé (or Taizé-style) chorus	9	13%
Classic hymn	6	9%
Retuned hymn	5	7%

hymns" those which appear with original text and tune out of a hymnal (generally, but not always, the Episcopal *Hymnal 1982*). Retuned hymns are well-known hymn texts with newly composed tunes and often contemporary musical arrangements.

While these congregational song genres may strongly imply specific musical styles, they do not determine them in full. Though contemporary worship songs were always played by the worship band (with organ often joining for the final verse or chorus), the St. B's musical leadership made an effort to challenge the overlap of genre and style for the other song genres. Modern hymns, retuned hymns, and Taizé choruses could be accompanied by worship band, organ, choir or all three; on some songs, the accompaniment changed from performance to performance. For instance, on one Sunday a Taizé chorus might be accompanied by organ, while on another, it might be accompanied by band or sung a cappella.

For a description of how songs within St. B's active repertory help the church position itself, it is instructive to draw from sociologist Mark Chaves's theory of a congregation's worship resources as comprising a "repertory of action," in other words, a "tool kit" for collective action that is drawn upon to solve specific social problems (2004, 130). Though the worship activities Chaves studies go beyond music-making (e.g., speaking in tongues, using incense, preaching a sermon), his model can still be useful in for interpreting musical repertories specifically. Chaves notes that, while an individual congregation may be the arbiter of its worship repertory, it does not choose these elements "at random or in wholly voluntary fashion" (130); rather, social contexts and institutions structure a church's selection. Chaves notes that these choices of elements often cluster together to form distinct constellations, which he frames as worship *styles*. Denominational traditions and church networks, as well as the congregation's own history, are some of the influences on an overall worship style; as such, repertories of action reflect both bottom-up choices made by local actors and the top-down influence of institutions (and industries) with which the church is aligned.

St. B's congregational music is a potent "repertory of action" in Chaves's sense, in that it reflects how the church negotiates local concerns and broader institutional and commercial pressures. With its complex history as an Episcopal parish, a hub for charismatic renewal, and a self-described "evangelical" church, St. Bartholomew's must constantly negotiate a complex set of institutional and network affiliations. The next section shows how worship music is one important means by which leaders at St. Bartholomew's variously align and distance the church from other local congregations and to position it within larger institutional networks, including the Episcopal denomination, the charismatic Christian networks, and American evangelicalism more broadly.

FINDING THE CHURCH'S VOICE: STRATEGIC POSITIONING THROUGH WORSHIP SONG AND STYLE SELECTION

I entered the life of St. Bartholomew's congregation at an ideal time to discuss worship music with leaders and members of the congregations. Conversations about worship were facilitated by an unusual development: in the fall of 2006, readers of the *Nashville Scene*, a popular local arts and entertainment magazine, ranked the church as having the "Best Church Music" in Nashville.[8] In the weeks that followed, knowledge of the award became widespread among members of the congregation. Some were elated, while others were amused or ambivalent that their worship music was included in the same rankings as "Nashville's Best Cheeseburger." Regardless of how it was received, the ranking gave me ample opportunity to engage in conversation about music and worship at St. B's. Over the course of just a few weeks, dozens of congregation members told me what they appreciated (or didn't appreciate) about music at St. B's in relationship to that of other area congregations or their church backgrounds, and in the process I learned about the values and associations they assigned to various songs and styles. I was told that the accolades for best church music generally went to one of several usual suspects in town, generally either megachurches that featured contemporary worship bands comprised of well-known Christian pop musicians, or "high church" congregations with large, semiprofessional choirs. While a few congregants insisted that St. B's could compete head to head with these churches on the basis of musical quality, most others admitted that many other churches in town featured music performed at a higher standard, whether "traditional" music judged by adherence to a classical aesthetic, or "contemporary" music judged by standards of popular music performance. But even St. B's church members who were more critical of its musical quality believed that their church did one thing better than any other church in town: it successfully blended a diverse range of songs and styles into a seamless, inspiring whole. Music at St. B's was described to me as "unique," "different," "refreshing," and "uplifting" because it could not be easily bifurcated into categories of "traditional" or "contemporary." Many interpreted the successful integration of old and new songs and styles as a powerful sign of spiritual unity and inspiration; words like "Spirit-filled," "anointed," or "God-directed" often came up in conversations about St. B's worship music.

Shortly after the *Nashville Scene's* ranking was announced, I had the first of many conversations over coffee with music minister Eric Wyse about worship music at St. Bartholomew's. Eric, a veteran of both music print and recording industries, had served variously as performer, songwriter/arranger, producer, and owner of his own publishing and recording company. His path to music director of an Episcopal congregation had not been straightforward: raised by former Mennonite parents, he grew up in evangelical churches, was educated at a Baptist college, and served as music minister at a large conservative Presbyterian church in Nashville before making the move to St. Bartholomew's. As Eric discussed aspects of the theology and musical aesthetics of worship at St. B's, I was struck by how often he referenced worship songs and styles as markers of positionality. He was acutely conscious of how certain musical songs and styles served to locate St. Bartholomew's in relationship to other area churches, to other Episcopal parishes, and to trends within US evangelicalism more generally. He gave several illustrations to show how he used musical selections to challenge the boundaries between entrenched traditional and contemporary camps, and between mainstream evangelical and traditional Episcopal expressions of worship. He also gave examples of how he shored up the boundaries between St. B's worship and that of other churches by giving examples of songs or performance practices that he deemed inappropriate for corporate worship at St. Bartholomew's despite how popular they had become in other evangelical churches. For Eric, choosing music for congregational worship required carefully balancing several elements felt to be in tension, including tradition and innovation, emotion and intellect, doctrine and experience, and local and global expressions.

In our first coffee meeting, Eric handed me a copy of the Worship Vision Statement, a one-page document several years in the making that guided and explained the musical selection process. In many churches, statements like these are created and then quickly forgotten; however, this document and the ideas it contained were kept in circulation throughout the three years at St. B's. This vision statement was handed out to each new member of the church's band or choir, and ideas contained within it were echoed frequently in my personal conversations with music leaders as well as in public discourse, including remarks made during music rehearsals and in printed articles in the church newsletter. As such, it can be considered a more or less accurate blueprint for worship at St. Bartholomew's during the time period in question. The text is reproduced here.⁹

St. Bartholomew's Church Worship Vision Statement

©2009 St. Bartholomew's Church. Used by permission.

The vision for worship at St. B's is one of worship of the Triune God with all our beings, with all of our emotions, and with all of our intellect: hence we worship joyfully and exuberantly, as well as meditatively and reverently.

Our focus begins with WHO GOD IS:—We worship him and proclaim his goodness, greatness, love, mercy, holiness and all his attributes, asking nothing in return but to enjoy his presence (see BCP *[Book of Common Prayer]* Catechism for a wonderful description), then moves to an expression of praise for WHAT

HE HAS DONE FOR US, and our petitions—WHAT WE NEED. But our primary purpose, starting point, ending point and overall "umbrella" is simply WHO GOD IS, and our response of worship. This is a very God-focused rather than "me"-focused expression.

Our musical offering is a reflection of who we are as believers living in a post-modern world, connected to the ancient historic faith—we draw from various styles and periods of music—from chant, classic hymns, and anthems to fresh new expressions of music from around the world—praise songs, Taizé music from France, Celtic music, music of renewal from the Roman church, and even music from our Sudanese co-worshippers. And just as the architecture of our buildings, while both modern and historic, is designed to be different in style than other buildings in our daily life, our musical expression will sound somewhat different than the pop or classical music we hear all week long. Our expression, as believers directly connected to our creator, should be unique; not foreign from our culture, but set apart.

Our goal is that rather than offering a smorgasbord of sound (take your pick of what you like . . . hymn, pop song, chant, rock anthem), or a blended soup (everything is a blend of somewhat classical, somewhat pop, somewhat Broadway middle-of-the-road offend-no-one music), that we offer musical "stew"—an expression of various styles, all working within a context of taste appropriate for Sunday worship, each with its distinctive flavor, yet a part of the whole in one cohesive "dish." In very simple terms, rather than having a distinct division of "classic hymns" (organ) and "praise band" (rhythm section of piano, bass, drums, guitar), we find ways to create a modern "chamber music" approach of finding the right combination of instruments to best support a given piece of music (combinations such as guitar/flute/percussion, organ/brass/percussion, bass/guitar, violin/accordion/guitar, harp/organ, piano/bass, etc).

Another facet of our worship vision is that the gifts of musical composition within our parish will be encouraged and used so that our expression of praise and adoration is uniquely ours as we offer new music—hymns, modern songs, service music, chants, Psalm settings, etc. The musicality of our composers will help determine the palette from which we illustrate our expression of praise to God. Thus many of the praise songs, anthems, and new settings of hymns, as well as the majority of our service music, have been composed by members of our parish.

For an understanding of how St. Bartholomew's uses music to position itself relative to other churches and evangelical trends, it is instructive to examine how music leaders interpret and seek to realize the musical vision set forth in this statement. The first part of the vision statement sets out theological criteria found in congregational song lyrics. In speaking further with Eric about the focus on the person of God, he expressed his concern that each Sunday's songs, taken together, would encapsulate the "whole story of Scripture." He criticized contemporary worship music for being too thematically narrow to use exclusively, surmising that "if you look through the CCLI top five hundred songs, there are about four themes out of fifty that ought to be explored." This is one of the main reasons, Eric explained, that St. B's worship incorporates retuned and traditional hymns: to fill in the thematic gaps in the contemporary-worship repertory and to tell the whole story of Christianity. Eric also reinforced his priority that most songs would focus on praising God rather than describing personal experience, a "'God-focused' rather than 'me-focused' expression." Eric attempted a careful balance of praise- and experience-focused songs each Sunday and told me that this value informed his avoidance of some of the top worship songs and artists on the CCLI charts.

While the Worship Vision Statement's concerns about song lyrics are framed theologically, concerns about musical style that make up the bulk of the Statement center on the congregation. When he was choosing music, Eric told me that, after theological considerations and singability, his next priority was "keep[ing] firmly in mind that there was something every Sunday for our classic Anglican, our charismatic, and our post-Bible church person in the pews." He took careful note of how congregation members from each of these different backgrounds connected and responded to different songs and styles. In describing the way St. B's juxtaposed the musical elements of various traditions, Eric preferred the term "convergent worship" to the more commonly heard term "blended worship," using a culinary metaphor further to elaborate the difference:

> Most [churches] who do "blended worship," here's what they do: they take all the classic out of classical and they take all the pop out of pop. And it becomes this bland, bad Broadway-ish kind of thing. It's like a blended soup—they took all the vegetables and put them in the blender and pureed it until it is one sound. What I think it should be is like a stew. In a stew you put various ingredients in and they complement each other, but each ingredient retains its distinctive flavor . . . And it's *our own* stew because we put in different elements. We don't blend—we *choose*. We *create* our voice. (Eric Wyse, personal interview, October 27, 2006)

The stew metaphor highlights the preference of complementarity and juxtaposition to homogeneity and blending. And the elements selected contribute to a sense of uniqueness and ownership—through careful selection of the ingredients, the worship "stew" becomes the church's own expression, its own unique congregational "voice." Through its own unique selection of songs and styles, St. B's worship style situates it within broader trends in evangelical and Episcopal worship and, for many worshipers at St. B's, sets it apart in important ways from both.

PROJECTING THE CHURCH'S VOICE
OUTWARD: MUSICAL BINDING AND LOOSING
IN TWO SPECIAL EVENTS

In church worship services, week in and week out, congregations perform their beliefs and values in part through the songs, styles, and repertories they choose for congregational singing. In performing contemporary worship music, St. B's signals its uniqueness within its denomination and aligns with evangelicalism in emphasizing a personal encounter with God during worship. In addition to weekly worship services, other important spaces within the church congregation to consider are occasional or special worship services, particularly those which draw outsiders to the congregation. Attending to these outward-focused events allows the observer to see how the church seeks to project its image outward, in this case through sound. How does the congregation understand itself and want others to understand it? How does it both represent and constitute itself musically during these special opportunities for positioning when the gathered worshipers hail from beyond the local church congregation?

During my time at St. Bartholomew's, there were two special events generally acknowledged as crucial for the outward-facing witness of the congregation. In April 2007, St. B's hosted a worship concert given by rising stars of the evangelical "modern hymn" movement. Less than a year later, in late January 2008, St. Bartholomew's hosted the annual two-day convention of the Diocese of Tennessee, a gathering that brought together clergy and lay leaders from fifty Episcopal churches in central Tennessee. In both of these events, music was used not only to shore up but also to shift St. Bartholomew's position relative to two different congregational networks. The "voice" that St. Bartholomew's chose to project through musical performance in these two events enabled it to pivot in its positioning relative to others and transform relationships in the process.

On April 22, 2007, St. Bartholomew's hosted a worship concert, simply billed as "An Evening of Worship," of congregational songs led by Northern Irish husband and wife singer-songwriting duo Keith and Kristin Getty. The Gettys originated and popularized a genre of songs referenced earlier in this chapter, which have become known as "modern hymns." Modern hymns, which generally comprise strophic texts set to contemporary or middle-of-the-road instrumental arrangements, are designed to serve as a middle ground between "traditional" hymns and "contemporary" worship songs. Modern hymns' forms and lyrical settings tend to resemble that of hymns more closely than pop-song-inspired contemporary worship songs; the lyrics generally fit established poetic meters. Musically, the melodies are pentatonic, rhythmically straightforward, and folk inspired. The songs' arrangements on the Gettys' recordings can be described as adult contemporary pop with Irish inflections, but they can also be performed by organ- and choir-led church ensembles. (One prominent example of the latter is the congregational performance of "In Christ Alone," led by organ and choir at the enthronement service for Anglican Archbishop Justin Welby in Canterbury Cathedral.) Theologically, the songs espouse a broadly evangelical perspective with occasional inflections of conservative Reformed theology; as a result, they have found affinity within theologically conservative Presbyterian and Reformed-leaning Baptist denominations and networks.[10]

The Getty worship concert was part of a tour featuring songs from the duo's forthcoming sophomore recording, *Awaken the Dawn*, and included a mix of congregational singing, a few solos, and discussion of the writing and themes of some of their songs. During the early stage of their touring career, the Gettys did not bring a house band; rather, they relied on the members of the congregations that hosted them for musical accompaniment. The standard St. B's Sunday morning complement of instrumentalists (organ, keyboard, guitar, drums, and bass, plus accordion), along with three microphoned vocalists and a fifteen-member choir, accompanied the songs during the concert that evening, joined by a string quartet mainly comprising Nashville session players. The familiar sound of the ensemble, and of the team leading the music, imprinted the event with the distinctly local flavor that many members of the St. B's congregation appreciated. A printed lyric sheet distributed to concertgoers contained thirteen congregational songs, with ten penned by Keith and/or Kristin Getty and their co-writer Stuart Townend from the late 1990s to 2007. The program began with upbeat praise songs, moved to songs of personal testimony, then offered a reflection on the life of Christ—a song about the nativity was followed by several emphasizing Christ's substitutionary death on the cross, and then two songs about the resurrection. Several of the songs (particularly those five years or older) had already been sung at St. B's, but some were new to the gathered concert congregation. The concert culminated with the Gettys' most well-known song, "In Christ Alone," sung loudly with fervor and inspiring a multitude of raised hands.

The church sanctuary was packed for the concert, and members from several other area congregations across denominations, including Brentwood Baptist and Christ Presbyterian, joined members of the St. B's community. Though modern hymns were intended to form a bridge between traditional and contemporary styles in churches, the Gettys' own discussions of their music frequently played up their songs as a theologically superior alternative to contemporary worship music, aligned in spirit (if not always in sound) with traditional hymns. On this particular April evening, a rival worship concert happening simultaneously gave attendees a clear choice between the two streams: Hillsong United, the youth-oriented worship band from Australia's charismatic contemporary worship juggernaut Hillsong Church, was performing downtown to a packed house in Nashville's historic Ryman Auditorium.

Hosting the Getty concert, then, aligned St. Bartholomew's with the ideal of reconciliation between "traditional" and "contemporary" sides of the evangelical worship wars even as it signaled alignment with a Reformed-leaning evangelical perspective rather than the more experiential, charismatic stream that had characterized the church in previous decades. Analyzing the St. B's active song repertory shows that the concert confirmed and enhanced the musical choices already inaugurated by Wyse during his tenure as music director. Keith Getty was the most frequently sung songwriter in the St. B's active repertory, with the exception of his co-writer Stuart Townend. Together, the Gettys' and Townend's modern hymns comprised eighteen out of the seventy—fully one quarter—of the most frequently sung songs during the three-year period between 2006 and 2009.

Less than a year after the Getty concert, in late January 2008, St. Bartholomew's hosted another event in which music helped to position it within a very different network of churches. Over 200 delegates descended on St. B's for the two-day annual convention of the Episcopal Diocese of Tennessee, the largest of three denominational administrative regions in the state. This convention was a significant event in the life of the church because it was the first diocesan convention held at St. B's in over twenty years. Throughout its history, St. B's had long been a hub for major interdenominational events and charismatic revival services; however, active participation in evangelical and charismatic circles had long estranged it from other churches in its own denomination. And, in the wake of continued controversy over same-sex marriage in the Episcopal Church, traditionally conservative churches like St. Bartholomew's had been estranged from more liberal ones. According to St. B's minister Jerry Smith, two years of intensive relationship building had been required to lay the groundwork for St. B's hosting the convention. In addition to convention meetings and workshops that took place in the educational wing, two services were held in St. Bartholomew's worship space: an opening service on Friday afternoon and a closing service on Saturday morning. For Tennessee's Diocesan conventions, the host church was free to choose elements of worship for the Friday service, while in the Saturday service, all liturgical elements were chosen by the bishop and his staff. At St. B's, both services followed the standard Episcopal prayer-book liturgy, and the Friday service was designed musically to represent a "typical" St. B's Sunday morning worship service. With Wyse on organ and Howard leading the band from the piano, the service included the bookend processional and recessional organ hymns, two Taizé choruses, two Getty songs, the St. B's service music settings, and several of the congregation's most frequently sung contemporary worship songs. The more formal Saturday worship service was led solely by organ and a choir made up of St. B's singers. The bishop chose hymns exclusively from the Episcopal *Hymnal* (1982), and many of them were unfamiliar to the musicians involved in the service.

These two services, identical in spoken liturgy but diverging widely in musical repertoire and style, were intended to communicate several things to the gathered delegates. Eric Wyse told me that Friday's convention music was chosen to represent the congregation's unique identity, to dispel misconceptions other Episcopalians in the diocese harbored toward the church, and to showcase a musical model that other churches in the denomination might find compelling. According to Jerry Smith, the goal for Friday's service was to ensure that the worship music was "really accessible, theologically sound, and [that] it wasn't way out there musically." In his conversations with the music team, Smith advocated moderation when it came to the contemporary music chosen. While choosing to do an unmoderated St. B's-style service first was a potentially divisive move, the Saturday service was intended to demonstrate a reciprocal willingness to accommodate established convention. Reflecting on comments he received after the Saturday service, Wyse mused, "Many of them had no idea that we could sing hymns with descants. We surprised a lot of people who assumed we just had a rock band that made lots of noise." After the convention, some delegates were confirmed in their suspicions at St. B's as a renegade or "odd duck" church in the parish, while others were more open, even intrigued, by what they had experienced. Several delegates approached Wyse, Howard, and other band members afterward asking for musical resources from the first service to take to their home churches. Drawing in the Episcopal conference delegates through musical participation, St. B's had modeled one way to transplant and integrate music from the denomination's evangelical neighbors into worship. Perhaps contemporary worship music did not have to be inimical to Episcopal worship.

Hosting the convention improved overall St. B's relationship with other churches in its denomination and provided a means for spreading its theological, cultural, and musical influence. It was a major step in bringing the congregation and its leadership from the far margins closer to the center of regional denominational life. The 2008 convention was considered such a success that St. B's was called upon to host the convention again only three years later. The event was significant not just for spreading St. Bartholomew's influence, however. In the process, it was part of a series of moves toward what one long-time member described as a "rediscovered Anglicanism," wherein the church moved away from more conservative charismatic and evangelical church circles and into a more moderate position that the leadership felt was in greater alignment with the denominational tradition.

In both the Getty worship concert and denominational-convention worship services, St. B's leaders and musical staff strategically program music to position the church in clear view (and earshot) of the broader, interchurch congregation. Jonathan Dueck (2011) applies the terms binding and loosing from Mennonite ecclesiology to describe similar dynamics of positioning within a cooperative Mennonite service jointly led by three congregations in Edmonton, Canada. Dueck uses the term "loosing" to describe those processes whereby "Mennonite church groups try to differentiate themselves from each other and draw connections to other groups, discourses and ideas" (242). Processes of musical binding involve "constructing a larger, inter-Mennonite group identity within a shared but multiply defined ritual frame of the service . . . which bound its body of songs and participants together" (243). In the Getty concert, St. B's bound itself to a specific sub-segment of North American evangelicalism—with a regional audience comprising more of conservative Presbyterians and Reformed-leaning Southern Baptists than other Episcopalians—while it simultaneously loosed itself from Nashville's contemporary-worship mainstream. When St. B's hosted the Episcopal Diocesan convention, the congregation announced its distinctive, against-the-grain identity as an evangelical Episcopal congregation to its co-denominationalists through the musical choices made in the first worship service, choosing songs and styles completely outside the experience of many attendees. Yet, by choosing the most accessible and least "out there" contemporary worship songs, and by being willing to perform the unfamiliar music that denominational administrators selected for the Saturday service, St. B's leaders and congregants signaled through music a willingness to comply with established diocesan traditions and to accommodate worship practices more familiar to their regional co-denominationalists.

ALTERNATIVE MUSICAL SPACES: MODELING WORSHIP IN YOUTH SERVICES

For many worshipers at St. Bartholomew's, the musical choices made for Sunday morning worship serve as icons of the church congregation's identity and its position relative to other churches within the three distinct worship traditions—charismatic, evangelical, and Episcopal—that it represents. Though the Sunday morning service is perhaps the most visible space of corporate worship of the congregation, it is not the only space where church members worship together and where worship music forms and informs the shaping of community. Worship within yearly retreats for families, men, women, and teenagers has different dynamics, and so have regular meetings of various age-segregated ministries, such as children's chapel, the Sunday night youth meeting, or the mid-week Young Adult Bible study. In his study of a charismatic Anglican church in Oxford, UK, Mark Porter (2017) calls these the "alternative musical spaces" of church life, observing that "more-marginal locations within the life of the church are able to provide different varieties of musical environment from those found in more visible or more closely supervised outlets and provide the opportunity for different negotiations of musical style than those of the main services" (127). Worship practices within the alternative spaces within church congregations often diverge from those of Sunday morning congregational worship, reflecting differing structures of authority, musical histories, and trajectories. This final section considers one such alternative space at St. Bartholomew's: the teenage youth group's weekly Sunday evening service called Liturgy.

April 2, 2007—Youth Group Liturgy Service in St. B's Parish Hall

On Palm Sunday, when I step into the educational building adjacent to the sanctuary, I am a little late for my second visit to the youth group's Sunday evening meeting, known simply as "Liturgy." Having missed the opening prayer from the Episcopal prayer book, I arrive at the beginning of the ice-breaking question and group game, an improvised sketch around alliterated words in which I find myself playing the role of a "scary spider from outer space." After the game, I follow the teenagers into their meeting room and take a seat on the floor to the side of the four large couches that have been arranged in a square in the center of the room. During the time of announcements, St. B's youth minister, Dixon Kinser, passes around a sign-up sheet for students to volunteer to help with various aspects of worship. The sheet delineates several categories: hospitality (making and preparing food), designing and setting up prayer stations, and leading music. Dixon invites anyone who sing or plays guitar, bass, or drums to volunteer, then adds that really any instrument is welcome—including accordion and glockenspiel—to chuckles from the teens. Dixon jokes that "it can be anything—just as long as you close your eyes and raise your hands," pantomiming the motions. Some of the teens smirk or give knowing laughs.

After a twenty-minute discussion of a Bible passage from one of the New Testament epistles comes the time set aside as the "community's response." Lining the walls of the room outside the couches are response "stations" that the leaders have set up beforehand. On the far side of the room from where I am sitting is a Lenten "desert" with a large photo backdrop of a sandy wasteland superimposed with several written meditations. Beside it is a laptop displaying a virtual lava lamp, where students can type their prayers and watch them "bubble up" to God. Dixon tells the group he will be sitting in the hall just outside the room, and throughout the response time, I watch as several tearful students join Dixon for conversation and prayer. I sit for a while in front of a station that features an analog television emitting static and white noise. A large piece of poster board beside the TV states in bold letters that "sin is spiritual tinnitus" and offers a guided reflection for diagnosing and eliminating the sources of spiritual "noise" in one's life. Two iPods to the right of the television station play electronic and ambient music to aid meditation and prayer. I put in the earbuds but can't hear the tracks very well because of the live music directly behind me.

College-aged youth leaders Jeffrey and Julia—both of whom had been members of the St. B's youth group throughout their high school years—sing several worship songs as they play acoustic guitars, joined by the voices of a handful of teenagers seated on the floor. The song lyrics are projected on the opposite wall, and the slide backgrounds have been designed to complement the lyrics. The first song, "Maker of the Stars," has a starry backdrop behind the lyrics, while the second, "Forty Wait," features rainbow-colored hands reaching heavenward. I am not familiar with either song but notice from the copyright information on the bottom of the slides that they have both been written by the same person. After the peace is passed, marking the ending of the service, I ask Jeffrey and Julia about the songs they led that evening. Jeffrey tells me that each song has come from Faith and Devotions of the Satellite Heart, *a worship album by the indie/electronic/alt-rock band* The Violet Burning. *Though Jeffrey is generally reserved, he demonstrates marked enthusiasm about this group and encourages me to check out the music on the band's website.*

Youth services are often more informal and experimental than a church's Sunday morning services, and St. B's Liturgy Service was no different. Here, as in many other youth groups, teens gathered in a less formal setting, engaged in team-building activities, learned and discussed Scripture, received spiritual counsel, and were afforded an opportunity to respond to God's leading. But the role of corporate singing in Liturgy differs markedly both from most evangelical youth group meetings and from St. B's Sunday morning service. Here, music is decentered as the primary means of collective response. I had several conversations with Dixon Kinser, who served as youth minister at St. Bartholomew's from 2003 to 2014 and priest associate in the years following his ordination to the priesthood in 2008, about music and worship. Dixon, a musician himself who had once been a guitar-playing youth worship leader, explained how his own background in evangelical youth ministry drove the search for an alternative model for worship at the Liturgy service:

> I had this crisis moment when I was doing youth ministry and I was leading people in this sort-of charismatic way of being church, where we would have teaching, and small groups, and singing . . . And the connection to God was always in [the singing]. And there was a night that I remember watching the kids, and after having countless conversations with kids in spiritual crisis because they didn't "feel God" anymore, I realized that I was not making disciples of Jesus, I was making *consumers of God*. And [how] do you get beyond that—what is the alternative? . . . In regards to the music, the first thing I started doing was thinking that if the framework for interacting with music that most of us have was a rock concert, or the sort of "performance-driven" methodology, then I needed to subvert that. So the first thing I started doing was adding other elements to the musical time where the music was still central—we still had

a band up front, still had microphones, this whole kind of thing—but there were other things that you could do so we basically would be saying, "You have other options." So I started creating these things called worship stations where I would put together a little area that you could visit, and it would lead you through an experience that would give you a place to interact with God like the music did but also was tied into the theme of the night . . . And I have since realized that if one of the things that encourages this consumer dynamic of music in the worship is having the band in the front, well, then put the band in the back. So we've decentralized our worship space where the band is in the back of the room, and leadership still came from an area up front but the band was in the back. And then I moved even from there where the leadership was no longer from anywhere in the front because the group met in the round . . . That's how I do it now. I never stand to address the community—we stand together to read the Scripture. But if I'm ever teaching or leading conversation, I always sit when I do it so I'm part of the community, I don't stand, and I don't do like we do on Sunday morning, where a special person stands up dressed a special way, faces a way no one else gets to face with a microphone . . . all of a sudden, there's a lot of power and a lot of things communicated in a way that I don't think make us a better kind of people (right?), if the community is really this transformative thing, which I think it is. So I try to subvert it that way. (Dixon Kinser, personal interview, October 18, 2006)

Dixon's comments here highlight several self-consciously alternative aspects of the Liturgy service. In particular are the practices and beliefs associated with what Dixon described later as the "mainstream model" of worship, in which he sees the musically defined "worship experience" as being the center of a destructive spiritual-consumer mentality. When the human-divine relationship is made dependent on feelings produced during collective singing, Dixon worried that the church's role was reduced to that of a "vendor of a spiritual product" rather than the catalyst for a life centered around love and service to God and others. The alternative worship space of Liturgy subverts the power of music by decentering the worship band within both the physical space and liturgical activities. It also challenges conventional modes of authority by minimizing the distance between leader and congregation, and offering the youth many opportunities not just for participation but also for leadership and liturgical design.

While attending the Liturgy services, I had coffee with Jeffrey and Julia, the two college-aged music leaders for the youth. They used the same self-consciously "alternative"/subversive discourse when describing how they chose songs and styles for Liturgy. They told me that in choosing worship songs, they generally avoided those they considered to be, as Jeffrey described it, "mainstream top forty worship pop." (Together they counted on one hand the songs on the CCLI charts that they regularly sang.) Instead, they introduced the teens to songs from more obscure sources, many of which fell not only outside the worship music genre but also outside Christian popular music more generally. Julia noted that they also made a point to incorporate well-known Christian hymns like "Be Thou My Vision," "Come, Thou Fount," and "Amazing Grace." Regardless of which song genre they led, the two leaders described their performance style as "meditative" or "contemplative." Features of this style included pared-down instrumentation (usually acoustic guitar and djembe, occasionally accompanied by one of the teens on violin or flute), with songs generally played at slower tempos with built-in instrumental breaks to allow for times of silent prayer between the song's verses and choruses.

The youth leaders' critiques of evangelical worship are not unique to St. Bartholomew's, nor are many of the alternative worship practices Dixon and the other leaders have introduced. Many of these worship ideas and practices stem from a network of North American (post-)evangelicals known as the "Emerging Church" or the "Emerging Church Movement" that grew out of a sustained critique of certain evangelical practices and tendencies.[11] Dixon attributed several of the practices he introduced at St. B's to his engagement in both Emerging Church circles as well as the "Anglimergent" network of Episcopal youth workers who incorporated these practices. In their account of the history, beliefs, and practices of the Emerging Church Movement (ECM), Gerardo Marti and Gladys Ganiel (2014) describe Emerging worship practices as overt critiques—deconstructions, even—of certain evangelical practices and beliefs about worship. In particular, Emerging worship practices have targeted evangelicalism's de-emphasis on human agency in worship, the devaluing of the sacraments of Communion and baptism, and the orientation of worship services exclusively toward either the most religiously committed individuals or those outside the church. In searching for alternatives, the ECM freely appropriates liturgical practices from Anglican, Catholic, and Orthodox traditions, including the church calendar, iconography, monastic practices, and formal, set prayers, creating a decontextualized pastiche of these "ancient-future" practices. Worship stations allowing for individual choices between a number of reflective activities are a strategy to promote inclusion: "Emerging Christians' liturgies are open, designed to cater to a pluralist congregation that makes everyone—even atheists or unbelievers—feel welcome to participate. Times of 'open response' are a common feature in [ECM] services, a general time in which those present are given options of what they may do as part of the liturgy—including the option to sit in their chair and do nothing" (Marti and Ganiel, 124–125). As one teenage Liturgy participant commented to me, "We're all figuring it out in different ways, but we're doing it together."

On first glance, the Liturgy service might appear as nothing more than an appropriation of standard Emergent worship practices in an Episcopal youth ministry setting. Yet over the history of the Liturgy service, a subtle but steady shift in rationale and practice resulted in realignment with parachurch and denominational networks. The service ended in a different position relative to both the (post-)evangelical Emerging Church network and the Episcopal tradition than where it started. Reflecting on his eleven years of youth ministry at St. B's, Dixon described a change in his thinking and its implications for worship at the Liturgy service:

> Early on, [Liturgy] was basically Bible study, quirky, funky music, and stations. As it progressed, and when I got ordained, I realized that we needed the sacraments. . . . Liturgy was supposed to be a legitimate expression of church— it wasn't supposed to be half-church, or parachurch, or quasi-church. The things that Christians do, we should do all of them here if we're forming kids into an adult faith that will sustain them the rest of their life. The more I framed it this way, the more I realized I needed to graft these kids into the tradition of the Episcopal Church, even though the church itself, St. B's, had struggled so much with that identity because of its evangelical heritage and the church split. . . . [Liturgy] ended up becoming this super-Episcopal—but kind of "alty-funky"—thing, where we doubled-down on prayer book liturgy and the sacraments. . . . Because the sacraments have sustained the church over two thousand years. Worship music, not so much. (Dixon Kinser, personal interview, November 2, 2016)

As part of what Dixon describes as a "doubling down" on the group's denominational heritage, certain Emergent practices were decentered and replaced with liturgical elements from the Anglican tradition. When Liturgy began, it featured Emergent-style response stations every week. Shortly after Dixon's ordination to the priesthood in 2008, he restructured the service on a three-week rotation, featuring stations one week, Eucharist the second week, and the Compline service from the Episcopal prayer book on the third. What started out as a reaction against the prevailing evangelical model of worship and a critique grounded in its deconstruction over time became an effort to reimagine and reintegrate with the Episcopal tradition. In concert with— and perhaps even helping to drive—the trajectory of St. Bartholomew's as a whole, the youth group's Liturgy service became less an evangelical service with liturgical elements and more, as Dixon put it, "an Episcopal church service with guitars."

As an alternative worship space, St. B's youth Liturgy service subverted several different worship practices and ways of thinking about the relationship between music, worship, and congregation simultaneously. Dixon's and the other youth leaders' early reliance on Emergent practices stemmed from a critique of charismatic and evangelical practices coming directly from (post-) evangelicalism itself. Worship practices like stations and self-consciously "alternative" songs and musical styles challenged the evangelical model of the musically centered worship experience. The Liturgy service's decentering of music also set youth worship apart from St. B's Sunday morning worship service, where music remained the main avenue for congregational response and connection with God. (Despite the apparent tension, any critique of the morning service remained unvoiced.) Yet, while the Liturgy service's worship practices and discourses initially aligned it with the post-evangelical Emerging Church network, like St. B's as a whole, it gradually moved into a closer relationship with its own denominational tradition. The ECM decontextualized and appropriated elements from a variety of traditions into an "ancient-future" pastiche; however, in the process, it validated the worship practices of mainline Christian traditions as viable alternatives to the evangelical practices at the center of its critique. Liturgy's increasing incorporation of specifically Episcopal liturgical elements—what Dixon Kinser called the "doubling down" on Anglican tradition—relied, at least in part, on a (post-)evangelical rationale for embracing its denominational tradition. In the Liturgy service, an evangelical act of deconstruction validated the group's reimagining of and realignment with the Episcopal tradition, highlighting well how porous the boundaries between evangelical and mainline Protestant networks and practices can be.

CONCLUSION: CONTEMPORARY WORSHIP MUSIC, RECONSTRUCTION, AND THE *VIA MEDIA*

Liturgical historian Lester Ruth has called the 2010s "an age of reconstruction" within American Protestant churches after the liturgical "civil war" of the 1990s and early 2000s, in which battles were fought in large part on the contested terrain of music (2017a, 2). Ruth questions whether the poles of "traditional" and "contemporary" were ever as dichotomized in practice as they were in discourse, observing that "contemporary worship itself was never a monolithic, static liturgical phenomenon. It arose in different places; it had multiple strands of development and various modes of expression. . . . That variety also means that the contemporary state of liturgical reconstruction is likewise fluid and ongoing" (2017b, 6). Music within the life of St. Bartholomew's Church demonstrates clearly the fluid, ongoing processes of liturgical division and reconstruction that Ruth describes. Through its unique self-positioning as an "evangelical Episcopal" church in the heart of the southern US Bible Belt, St. Bartholomew's experienced inflamed tensions over worship music; greater than a decade of separate services differentiated by musical style resulted. New leadership, feeling that the separate services threatened congregational unity, attempted to reintegrate the congregation, using music as a means of binding the congregation together, as well as binding the congregation as a whole more closely to its denomination. Examining the musical choices made at crucial junctures in the church congregation's history reveal many other acts of musical (re-)positioning over the years, in which St. B's has renegotiated its place within evangelical, charismatic, and Episcopal networks.

Closely examining these critical musical junctures in the life of St. Bartholomew's suggests strongly that church congregations do not simply adopt or reject song repertories wholesale; rather, the process of selecting among competing songs, styles, and performance practices is a crucial way that church congregations navigate their position within broader regional and national networks. And over the life of St. Bartholomew's, more so than any other musical repertory, contemporary worship music has been an integral component of its positioning strategy. The distinct ways the St. B's musical ensemble leads contemporary worship music, the values that inform leaders as they make choices about which songs to adopt or reject, and the additional musical repertories and styles they choose to incorporate into worship show how the repertory of contemporary worship is used as a means of positioning, at times binding and at other times loosing the congregation from other congregations and church networks. Examining how songs and styles changed since the church's founding in the mid-1950s, as well as the subtle shifts that occurred over the three-year contemporary period of study, reveals how the church has positioned itself differently between these poles, edging closer to one or the other pole at times and backing away from the other.

As iconoclastic as St. Bartholomew's may seem, the way the church has used contemporary worship music since the early 2000s ultimately suggests a move toward a moderating, *via media* orientation. The principle of *via media*—the moderate path between two opposite extremes—is often invoked within Anglicanism to describe the Anglican compromise between poles of Catholic and Protestant belief and practice. In the context of the Southern US Bible Belt, however, St. B's *via media* can be interpreted instead as the attempt to forge a middle path between evangelical and Episcopal worship traditions. Congregational music-making plays a crucial role in how St. B's enacts this mediating position. Intentional decisions made about song repertory and style in more recent years reveal an attempt to preserve the delicate balance between competing options as well as a principled refusal to veer toward extremes on either side, even if this positioning has meant being regarded as the denominational "odd duck" or losing potential evangelical-leaning congregants who want the service to conform to their expectations of a worship experience.

The example of St. B's demonstrates that the "church's voice"—a church congregation's unique identity and position relative to other congregations and within networks—is actively constructed and contested through musical practice. What's more, it reveals that the meaning and affect of congregational music genres like contemporary worship music, though conditioned by broadly circulating discourses and practices, are always subject to imaginative reinterpretation within local church contexts to address their own unique circumstances and to realize their vision.

NOTES

1. Omar McRoberts (2003) contrasts "ethnographic portraits" with "ethnographic landscapes" within the field of congregational studies, noting that the strength of the former is painting a detailed picture of one subject and enabling it to be held up to others for comparison. This chapter joins the growing body of congregational portraits within ethnomusicology that examine musical dynamics of particular religious congregations. See Titon 1988; Summit 2000, 2016; J. Dueck 2011, 2017; Engelhardt 2015; B. Johnson 2008, 2015; Justice 2012; and Mall 2015.
2. YOUR LOVE OH LORD. Brad Avery, David Carr, Mac Powell, Mark Lee, Tai Anderson. ©1999 Vandura 2500 Songs (ASCAP) New Spring Publishing Inc. (ASCAP) (adm. atCapitolCMGPublishing.com) All rights reserved. Used by permission.
3. Membership data on religious traditions in the Nashville-Davidson-Murfreesboro-Franklin, Tennessee Metropolitan Statistical Area is available at the Association of Religious Data Archives site at http://www.thearda.com In 2010, twenty-eight Episcopal congregations with a combined membership of approximately 13,000 made up less than 1 percent of total religious adherents in the greater Nashville metro area.
4. A 2001 survey by the Pew Forum on Religion and Public Life states that 28 percent of US adults have changed religious affiliations during their lifetime, and that "if change in affiliation from one type of Protestantism to another is included, 44% of adults have . . . switched religious affiliation" (Lugo et al. 2008, 25). A Barna survey from the same year identifies worship as the most important feature of Christian congregations life for those choosing a community in which to worship (2001).
5. For discussions of charismatic renewal in the Catholic church, see McGuire 1982 and Csordas 2012. Charismatic renewal in the Episcopal Church, USA began nearly a decade prior and strongly influenced renewal in the Catholic church; however, there is a dearth of scholarly sources that chronicle charismatic renewal in the Episcopal Church.
6. According to a comparative analysis of worship trends from the 1998 to 2012 National Congregations Study, the percentage of congregations incorporating choirs dropped from 54 percent to 45 percent; use of organs declined from 53 percent to 42 percent; while use of visual projection in worship increasing from 12 percent to 35 percent (Chaves and Eagle 2015).
7. Raw data was taken from an Excel spreadsheet provided by St. B's former music director Eric Wyse.
8. For the full listing, see "Best of Nashville 2006 Readers' Poll." October 12, 2006. Accessed March 18, 2018. Available athttps://www.nashvillescene.com/home/article/13013869/best-of-nashville-2006-readers-poll.
9. ©2009 St. Bartholomew's Church. Used by permission.
10. In 2013, "In Christ Alone" was the source of a controversy that highlighted theological divisions between Reformed and evangelical groups. The

Presbyterian Church, USA (PCUSA), a mainline, progressive-leaning de-nomination, wanted to include the song in their new hymnal with a slight alteration to the lyrics of the second verse, which describe the theological import of Christ's death on the cross (changing the lyrics from "the wrath of God was satisfied" to "the love of God was magnified"). The Presbyterian committee found the altered version of the lyrics in *Celebrating Grace* (2010), a hymnal compiled by a theologically moderate Baptist committee. When seeking permission to reproduce the version found in the *Celebrating Grace* hymnal, the Presbyterian committee found that this alteration had not been approved by the songwriters. Getty and Townend denied permis-sion to change the lyrics, and as a result, the song was removed from the PCUSA's list of new songs to include in their hymnal. A flood of discourse surrounding the decision ensued, as theological liberals and conservatives used their differences in atonement theology to reify other differences. For progressive and conservative Reformed perspectives on the controversy, respectively, see Mary Louise Bringle's cover story, "Debating Hymns," in the *Christian Century*, https://www.christiancentury.org/article/2013-04/debating-hymns, and Collin Hansen's 2013 article, "Keith Getty on What Makes 'In Christ Alone' Accepted and Contested," on the conservative Reformed Gospel Coalition blog, https://www.thegospelcoalition.org/article/keith-getty-on-what-makes-in-christ-alone-beloved-and-contested.

11. For Emergent Church sources that discuss worship theology and practice, see J. Baker et al. 2004 and Kimball 2004.

CHAPTER 4

✿

Bringing Worship to the Streets

The Praise March as Public Congregation

The final two chapters of *Singing the Congregation* examine modes of congregating that occur when evangelical worship and music "go public"— in other words, when Christians gather for the purpose of worship in a shared public space rather than in spaces that evangelical institutions, movements, or corporations control. The following ethnographic vignette gives an account of how evangelicals bring worship to the streets through the jubilant musical public procession known as a praise march.

Ethnographic Fieldnotes—September 11, 2010, Toronto, Canada

On a Saturday afternoon in early September, I stand on a street corner and watch as several thousand evangelical Christians process through Toronto's downtown district during the annual Jesus in the City Parade. The parade is a mass of swirling colors from marchers' parade T-shirts, biblical costumes, glittering banners, and handmade signs. Many of the signs contain short biblical quotations, while others I recognize as lyrical hooks from popular contemporary worship songs: "How great is our God!" "Jesus, name above all names!" "You're the God of this city!" (Figure 4.1)

The sounds are just as striking: blaring from each of the thirteen musical parade floats are upbeat contemporary worship songs in a wide range of musical styles, from modern rock to Eastern European pop to gospel soca. The smaller floats, in-cluding vans and pickup trucks, play prerecorded song mixes from their speakers, while the larger floats carry eight to fifteen musicians who perform the music live. Participants marching around the floats sing—and often dance—along with the loud, rhythmic music (Figure 4.2). Sometimes when the floats stop at traffic lights, the musical offerings blend, creating a cacophony of praise.

Figure 4.1: Jesus in the City paraders march with signs featuring biblical and worship song quotations on College Street in downtown Toronto. Toronto, Canada: September 2010.
Photo by the author.

Figure 4.2: Jesus in the City paraders and floats pass under a Christian billboard on Yonge Street in downtown Toronto. Toronto, Canada: September 2010.
Photo by the author.

The Jesus in the City Parade, examined later in this chapter, is an evangelical Protestant public religious gathering known as a "praise march." Praise marches are public demonstrations focused on "literally singing God's praises in the public square" (Bartkowski and Regis 2003, 243). Musical performance is not incidental to praise marches; rather, collective singing is the central means of participation. The role of music within praise marches can be likened to what Suzel Reily describes within Brazilian popular Catholic *folias de reis* processions, in which "musical sounds dominate the ritual time-frame; musical performance is conducted by an ensemble with a more or less inclusive participatory orientation, and music is the primary means of integrating the attendants into the ritual drama" (2002, 3). The "praise" in "praise march" refers generally to the collective activity of worship, and it is also shorthand for the musical repertory used in these processions ("praise and worship" music). The collective performance of the contemporary worship song repertory, more than any other single element, serves to mark the activity in which participants are engaged as "worship."

Using the praise march as a lens, this chapter examines the worship-centered gatherings that emerge at public and civic events that I designate "public congregations." Public congregations include elements of each of the three modes of congregating examined in preceding chapters. They comprise self-selected aggregates of entire church congregations, as well as individuals and families who are part of evangelical networks connected to the gathering. As in the conference congregation, the eschatological discourse often features prominently within public congregations as participants seek to bring the "sound of heaven" and to represent the sound of the global evangelical community to their city's public spaces through music and worship. Public congregations also include elements of concert congregations, with pre- and post-parade worship rallies and promotional worship concerts that showcase regionally known worship bands.

Public congregations are sites where evangelicals engage in two social processes simultaneously: they collectively imagine their community while forming intimacies through face-to-face interaction with other participants. In his work on the public musical performances of Canadian First Nations peoples, Byron Dueck (2013) describes public spaces as bridges between these two interrelated social processes of imagination and intimacy. Drawing from B. Anderson's imagined communities (1991) and Warner's notion of publics and counterpublics (2002), Dueck defines the activity of "imagining" as "an orientation to a public of strangers . . . a relationship, facilitated by mass mediation, between people who, though unknown to one another, understand themselves to have something in common" (2013, 5). Intimacy describes "engagements between known and knowable persons, especially those that involve the 'interaction rituals' (see Goffman 1967) of 'face-to-face' social and musical contact" (6). Dueck's observations about public spaces apply aptly to the public modes of congregating examined in this chapter; public congregations like the praise march likewise "exist at the interstices of imagining and intimacy: oriented to publics of strangers, yet simultaneously sites of face-to-face interaction between known and knowable persons" (213).

When evangelicals come together to form public congregations, the dual processes of imagination and intimacy bring the complex processes of boundary creation and maintenance into full relief. In particular are the contradictory impulses to separate from or identify with the broader society. Praise marches have long been characterized by their emphasis on spiritual warfare, a discourse that places evangelicals and other groups on opposing sides of a moral and spiritual battle for societal influence. But at the same time as evangelicals pit themselves against certain groups within their societies, or even society conceived as a whole, they also seek to portray their religious community as a positive influence and welcoming presence. Through public assemblies like the praise march, evangelicals assert their difference from the societal mainstream while trying to present their religious community in a way that establishes intimacy, so that those outside can identify with them. Therefore, studying the ways musical performance and sonic values construct the praise march will help us to understand how evangelicals constitute public congregations as they navigate internal and external social pressures.

As in individual church congregations, the musical choices these public congregational aggregates make—whether related to style, song selection, lyrics, or socio-musical organization—are not incidental to the event as a whole. Rather, music and sound are central considerations that organizers and participants consider in their attempts to achieve the event's goals. Through bringing musical worship to the streets, evangelicals seek to project a united voice into the public sphere in order to influence civic and national discourses, even as their community is shaped in the process through the dialogue. Music-making is a site of social power where evangelicals may assert themselves; however, it is also a source of vulnerability. In public spaces outside the control of congregations, a broader public is free to scrutinize what they see and hear. And sometimes music reveals internal tensions that may not be apparent to the groups seeking to project a united presence. In the praise march, contemporary worship music serves as the stage on which this contested performance plays out.

This chapter demonstrates the vital role that contemporary worship music plays in helping evangelicals represent and embody both a composite city or regional public congregation (what some participants in my study called the "church of Toronto") and the transnational "imagined community" of evangelicals in the public square through the praise march. I begin with an overview of how the praise march developed, illustrating contemporary worship music's enabling role in its conception and transnational spread. I then examine two different iterations of the praise march in the city of

Toronto: the March for Jesus (1992–1999) and the Jesus in the City Parade (1999 onward). These Toronto-based praise marches are particularly significant for two reasons. The first concerns these events' longevity: while organized annual praise marches came to an end in many North American cities in the late 1990s, as of 2017, Toronto had seen twenty-six continuous years of annual praise marches. Secondly, as the most ethnically diverse city in North America, Toronto brings into full relief the challenges that evangelicals face in creating a unified public congregation out of an aggregate of individuals and church congregations that often self-segregate on the basis of race, ethnicity, or national origin.

Participants in these two successive praise marches have used contemporary worship music to achieve similar ends: to display spiritual (and political) power, to negotiate the relationships among their religious and other identities, to rally the evangelical community while emphasizing its diversity, and to promote receptiveness to their message in the hopes of provoking bystanders' curiosity, with the hopes of their eventual conversion. Though both marches employ the same basic musical repertory and many of the same worship practices, two different models of the public congregation emerge, shaped by a differing set of performance and sonic—and, ultimately, ethical—ideals. Exploring how contemporary worship music is used within public congregations like these, therefore, is crucial to understanding not only how twenty-first-century evangelicalism shapes its public image, but also how it defines the boundaries of its community and manages diversity within those boundaries. Further, it shows the degree to which musical engagement with the broader society through public performance influences other evangelical modes of congregating.

THE BEGINNINGS OF PRAISE MARCHING: THE MARCH FOR JESUS'S HISTORY AND INFLUENCE

The term "praise march" was coined by British evangelicals in the mid-1980s in connection to a series of public demonstrations of worship that became known as the March for Jesus (hereafter referred to as "MFJ" or simply "the March"). Initiated by four British leaders representing influential charismatic and evangelical networks, the MFJ developed from local London-area street demonstrations into city-wide and nationwide marches in the late 1980s (Kendrick et al. 1992; Ediger 2004). The March revived and updated Salvation Army musical processions with the pop-rock based contemporary worship music being produced in the United Kingdom and North America. Beginning in the early 1990s, the MFJ served as a model and resource hub for evangelical praise marches worldwide, exporting its songs, ideals, and performance values. The first global MFJ held on June 25, 1994 was reported to have gathered over 12 million Christians across 179 nations in each of the world's twenty-four time zones (*Christianity Today* 1994). According to the organization's statistics, participants in international MFJ events between 1987 and 2000 numbered an estimated 60 million. Though the MFJ dissolved as an organization in 2000, locally organized Marches continue as an annual display of Protestant solidarity in many cities around the world, particularly in Latin America.[1] In the heyday of the MFJ in the early to mid-1990s, over 500 US and Canadian cities, including Austin, Nashville, Pittsburgh, Vancouver, and Winnipeg, held large-scale marches. While North American praise marches became fewer after the MFJ organization dissolved in the year 2000, many cities and towns continue to celebrate an annual "Jesus Day," a public worship event directly descending from the March (Bartkowski and Regis 2003).

In a study of the social and theological milieu out of which the MFJ grew, Gerald Ediger (2004) points to several key elements contributing to the growth of the movement both in the United Kingdom and abroad. A new wave of evangelical activism in the United Kingdom was emerging through the 1980s, as conservative evangelicals were increasing willing to engage social issues (259). Coordinated action was made possible by increasing interdenominational cooperation. Events such as the Spring Harvest Bible Week brought together British evangelicals across established denominations and new church networks. Ediger notes that the United Kingdom's interdenominational evangelical coalition became increasingly "charismaticized" during this period (274), popularizing the charismatic theology of spiritual warfare—a set of ideas that became influential and widespread among evangelical Christians more generally in the late 1980s and 1990s (see Ediger 2000). One of the original goals of the MFJ was "strategic-level spiritual warfare" against worldly principalities and powers, and worship was enlisted as the primary weapon. Some of the first MFJs in the City of London were targeted against the "strongholds" of greed, corruption, and sexual sin understood not only to be represented by, but also to literally reside in, specific geographical places (Kendrick et al. 1991, 18–19).[2] The belief that "intercessory prayer could be enhanced by placing oneself in proximity to the object of such intercession" inspired prayer walks and early praise marches (Ediger 2004, 269). In marching, the central goal was to confront and defeat the powers of evil by proclaiming the rule of Kingdom of God in those places. The rule of the Kingdom was both announced and enacted (if temporarily) through the worshipful proclamation of the gathered assembly—through "lifting up the name of Jesus." The praise march's sung proclamations were not simply words intended to communicate or persuade; rather, they were, in J. L. Austin's terms (1962, 6), "performative utterances," words of power that were agents in accomplishing the action they invoked.

The collective proclamation of the Kingdom within the MFJ took the form of participatory sonic performance, consisting of singing, chanting, and spoken prayer. Graham Kendrick, a songwriter and worship leader well known within interdenominational British evangelical circles, became both the preeminent songwriter and most prominent theologian of the March. Though his writing, speaking, and musical composition, Kendrick articulated a compelling vision of what he termed "public praise" that resonated with church leaders across the broad evangelical and charismatic coalition. In his *Make Way: Public Praise Handbook* (1991), published in the United Kingdom for a British audience, and *Public Praise: Celebrating Jesus on the Streets of the World* (1992), published in the United States for a North American audience, Kendrick articulates the purpose and practice of praise marches for an increasingly international audience.[3] While Kendrick speaks of the importance of the march as "display," "visibility," and "demonstration," he also foregrounds the centrality of sound—particularly musical sound—as the source of the praise march's power. It is worth spending time to closely examine Kendrick's articulation of a sonic theology because the ideas he articulates continue to resonate within praise marches across contexts.

The primary purpose of the praise march, according to Kendrick, is to provide a space for the church to sing praises in the public square, and in the process to display one unified worshiping congregation (1992, 14–15). In the introductory section of *Public Praise*, "What a March Is Not," Kendrick responds to anticipated misunderstandings and perceived criticisms of the March, clarifying its connection to the controversial theology of spiritual warfare. Kendrick writes that "marches are not *presented as* a method of spiritual warfare" (21, italics mine), while maintaining that, regardless of how they are presented to those outside, the Marches serve exactly this purpose because "they have tremendous potential to displace evil spiritual powers" (21).[4] While Kendrick articulates several other purposes and functions of the MFJ, including promoting and displaying Christian unity and providing opportunities for proselyting, spiritual warfare remains central to how he conceives the event's ultimate purpose. The sixth chapter of *Public Praise* ("The Battle for Worship") contains the most developed statement relating music and worship to a cosmic struggle. Here, Kendrick sets out a theology of the role of musical sound and worship in spiritual warfare. He writes that worship is "a heavenly activity exported to earth" (60) and is thus capable of releasing enormous power, whether divine or diabolical. For Kendrick, the struggle between God and Satan ultimately comes down to who is the subject of humanity's worship: therefore, worship is "center stage in the theatre of spiritual warfare" (64). He writes that the "Battle for Worship" is now being waged between those who worship the Christian God and those outside the Christian faith, who, deceived by Lucifer and his fallen angels, worship other things. Paradoxically, the prize of the battle is also its weapon: the battle *for* worship is won *by* worship. Kendrick explains this paradox by reference to the story of Joshua and the battle of Jericho, a biblical account that strongly influenced his thinking about praise marches. For Kendrick, worship is also a sign of the coming, eschatological kingdom: "When [God's] kingdom comes and His will is done on earth as it is in heaven, it will begin with an invasion of worship—heaven's highest activity" (60).

Though Kendrick elsewhere presents worship as a prayerful orientation toward God that should cover all of life, when discussing worship in the context of the March, he frequently conflates worship with music. Worship songs become musico-spiritual weapons: "my conviction is that properly understood and rightly used, our songs can become the spiritual equivalent of rockets exploding with joy in heaven and wreaking havoc in hell" (Kendrick 1991, 12). Music is a powerful agent that, for Kendrick, is linked inextricably to worship:

> In itself [music] is neither good nor evil, but it has power that can be employed for either end . . . Jesus calls us to harmonize with heaven, to move in rhythmic step with His angel armies and drown out the discordant orchestras of hell with ever-increasing crescendos of praise. (1992, 63)

In this statement, Kendrick uses several crucial musical metaphors that are tied to three crucial sonic values of the MFJ: synchronicity ("harmonizing with heaven"), sonic permeation ("drowning out" the orchestras of hell), and uniformity (moving together "in rhythmic step" with systematically organized musical roles). Examining the working out of these sonic values in a specific instance shows that they are simultaneously social values, providing a blueprint for constructing a public congregation that many found compelling. As such, contemporary worship music in the March was more than a symbol, but also an embodied way to perform these values—and a particular mode of congregating—into being.

TORONTO'S MARCH FOR JESUS (1992–1999): HISTORY, STRUCTURE, AND SONIC IDEALS

For seeing how evangelicals used these ideas and sonic values to create a particular kind of public congregation, it is instructive to examine a particular instance of the March. An early and long-standing instance of the Kendrick/Make Way–style praise march in North America was the annual March for Jesus in Toronto.[5] Toronto's MFJ ran for eight years from 1992 though 1999, reaching a peak in the Global MFJ in 1994 with an estimated 25,000 participants.[6] Toronto's MFJ began in 1992 as a result of several converging influences. Kendrick himself was closely tied to the Toronto area, regularly visiting the city to speak and lead singing at charismatic churches and conferences.[7] The Toronto MFJ emerged as a cooperative effort among predominantly evangelical and charismatic congregations, including several large and influential churches such as Queensway Cathedral, The Peoples Church, and what was then known as the Toronto Airport Vineyard Fellowship (the site of the globally renowned "Toronto Blessing" revival during the same period). While evangelical and charismatic churches formed the Toronto March's core constituency, a small number of groups from Establishment denominations, including Anglicans and Catholics, participated as well.

For an understanding of the kind of public congregation that Toronto's MFJ sought to build, it is important to understand the changing role of religion in Canadian public life and discourse.[8] Beginning in the latter quarter of the twentieth century, both Christian affiliation and political authority in Canada experienced a "rapid and consistent" decline, as secularists sought to extricate religion—particularly the "establishment" Christianity of Anglicanism and Catholicism—from the public sphere. Changes in public policy were increasingly guided by the belief that religious divisions threatened the emergent Canadian multicultural ideal (Bramadat and Seljak 2008; Young and DeWiel 2009). As a result of these societal shifts, Canadian evangelicals began to employ a common rhetoric that Bramadat and Seljak call the "discourse of loss" because their "churches can no longer assume that their values and objectives are . . . co-extensive with the values and objectives of the larger society" (2008, 15). The rhetoric of loss was paired with a call for renewed evangelism that was to lead to national revival. In describing the nationalistic discourse within global charismaticism, Simon Coleman observes that charismatic ideology "talks not only of single nations, but also of the existence of a world-wide division of labour between divinely appointment nation-states. The image invoked is that of a kind of spiritual totemism, whereby each country has the God-given vocation to seek both internal revival and external spiritual influence" (2000, 224).

For many, the Toronto March was an opportunity for active self-representation against a backdrop of Canadian secularism—interpreted as societal indifference to or even hostility toward Christian belief—and a way to assert Canada's importance in the evangelical economy of nations. Though the Toronto March followed differing routes over its eight annual iterations, the most common route began and ended in Queen's Park, located immediately behind the Ontario legislature. Marchers made a roughly rectangular route that included the two most important streets in the city, Bloor (east/west) and Yonge (north/south), of crucial symbolic significance. By marching on these two major thoroughfares in the very heart of the city, participants passed by centers of institutional power—including the University of Toronto and provincial government buildings—as well as one of downtown Toronto's vibrant nightlife districts. These choices were not accidental, but conformed to the "strategic level spiritual warfare" tactics—discourses promoted by

Kendrick and other influential leaders that circulated along with the globally exported MFJ.

The pervasive—if controversial—theology of spiritual warfare provided a significant rationale for Toronto's MFJ. As Canadian theologian Gerald Ediger notes, spiritual warfare was "a subject of increasing concern" among evangelical Christians in the 1990s (2000, 125).[9] Toronto March organizers and participants recall that the overarching purpose of spiritual warfare provided a common focus for the event. According one Toronto MFJ board member, "the very essence of March for Jesus . . . was intentional spiritual warfare: taking the presence of God to the streets and blasting out any of the demonic activities of the area."[10] While the spiritual warfare theology may have informed how organizers conceived of the march, he was careful to qualify: "I don't think bystanders would have realized that what it was all about. [Spiritual warfare] was the intent behind it all, but the way it was done on the street was just simply lifting up the name of Jesus" (personal interview, October 6, 2010).

SONIC VALUES OF THE PUBLIC CONGREGATION IN THE TORONTO MARCH FOR JESUS

Bringing worship to the streets of their city not only helped Toronto MFJ participants to performatively reclaim space for Christianity; it also enabled the formation of a unified front—a public congregation woven together from area churches and other local ministries. Like many other praise marches around the world at the time, the Toronto MFJ used the resources that Kendrick and his Make Way Music, the publishing house he formed specifically to provide resources for the MFJ, produced and sought to embody many of the crucial sonic values laid out therein. Through the songs' participants performed and the way its organizers managed sound production, MFJ Toronto participants sought to perform into being a public congregation that adhered closely to Kendrick's model. Through its eight-year history, Toronto's MFJ moved to be progressively more in line with three critical sonic values set out in Kendrick's work: synchronicity, uniformity, and sonic permeation.

Synchronicity

For the UK Marches, Kendrick envisioned music within the praise march as a "glorious synchronization" that reflected the "glorious coalition of heavenly and earthly forces under [Jesus]" (1992, 66). The synchronicity between heaven and earth is imagined through earthly synchronicity: a temporal, sonic alignment between different geographical places celebrating the March. Both the nation and the international Christian community figured prominently in the experience of synchronicity at the MFJ. The MFJs were frequently synchronized at the national level, beginning with the first national March in the United Kingdom in 1989. To enable participants to experience the synchronous connection, organizers drew on various media technologies. In the 1989 UK March, marches in forty-five different regional centers across the United Kingdom and Ireland were connected by a costly and complicated landline linkup "so that together hundreds of thousands of Christians could be praying, praising and proclaiming in unison" (Kendrick et al. 1992, 72). March participants experienced multifaceted synchronicity as they heard themselves singing the same songs at the same time as others in their same march and in other Marches on a national and international scale, all participating with the worship in heaven.

Toronto's MFJ embodied the ideal of synchronicity in many of the same ways as the UK Marches, seeking to form connections with other Canadian Marches for Jesus and other international praise marches. Each year, the Toronto MFJ was scheduled to coincide with other Marches either nationally or globally: the 1992–1994 Marches were timed to occur on the same day as Global Marches in the United Kingdom and Europe. In Toronto's 25,000-participant MFJ in 1994, a live satellite link was established between Toronto and national marches in other large Canadian cities, including Vancouver, Winnipeg, Edmonton, and Ottawa. Musically, as in many other MFJs in North America, Europe, and the United Kingdom, Toronto's marchers sang along with a recorded album produced each year specifically for the event. Six to ten songs were played in a loop for participants to sing along with as they marched. To ensure a synchronized performance of the songs, in the first few years of Toronto's March, organizers set up large, stationary sound systems evenly spaced along the march route to play CD recordings. Despite efforts to start the playback at the same time, the recordings often played slightly out of sync with one another, a distraction to the marchers as they moved out of one sonic territory into another. The organizers looked for ways to make the March music perfectly in sync, and the opportunity came in 1995 when a local radio broadcaster proposed a solution. Toronto's MFJ was able to purchase a one-day license for a radio-frequency band to broadcast the songs for the march. Local Christian radio host Jim Leek recalls the effect:

> . . . [W]hat was accomplished by [the radio broadcast] was having it all synchronized. [Before] marchers were going along in the street singing along, then they would get to the next [sound] system, and it was not quite in sync, so it would throw them off. That's why we wound up doing the broadcast: so all systems were receiving the same music and putting out the same music at the same time. (Jim Leek, personal interview, October 6, 2010)

During the March, Leek coordinated the musical broadcast from the top of Toronto's CN Tower. For the last few years of the March, the sound systems tuned in to the same radio station. Now the music marchers heard along the parade route was in perfect sync.

Uniformity

The Toronto March's use of a consistent set of musical resources provided the means for embodying the value of uniformity. Graham Kendrick had not only articulated a coherent vision for "public praise" but also created practical resources consistent with this vision that provided the musical tools for achieving uniformity. MFJ songs, musical recordings, handbooks, songbooks, and march "scripts" were published through Kendrick's Make Way Music. Between 1986 and 1993, Kendrick produced six albums for use in the March in the United Kingdom; US worship recording labels Integrity and Word Music reproduced and remixed these materials for North American audiences. Published alongside the albums were accompanying songbooks containing chord charts, lead sheet or piano arrangements, and sometimes other instrumental parts. These products were circulated broadly in the United Kingdom, North America, Australia, and mainland Europe by charismatic music and media distribution networks, including Kingsway Music in the United Kingdom and Europe, and Word Music in the United States and Canada, then two of the largest evangelical music publishers in the United Kingdom and United States, respectively. The March created unity between Christians of different denominational and ethnic backgrounds by affording them an opportunity to participate in a unified, uniform performance of common songs.

In addition to his renown as a worship songwriter and spokesman for the MFJ, Graham Kendrick had personal connections with churches and church leaders across North America, and particularly in the Toronto area. While absent physically, Kendrick was present as a virtual, vocal presence on the recordings played as the backing track for the Toronto March. Churches were encouraged to purchase the annual Make Way CD and songbook so that congregation members could learn the music that would be sung on the parade day. In some churches, representatives or volunteers for MFJ set up product tables in churches to sell CDs to individual members before services. The churches that one former participant described as *"really* on board" with the MFJ held special rehearsals of parade songs in the weeks leading up to the event, building anticipation for the march and ensuring that participants knew the songs well.

The MFJ songs provided common musical ground among church congregations across the city and across denominations. Because the songs were all newly written specifically for the March and distributed by a nondenominational parachurch organization, no one individual church could claim them—the songs belonged equally to everyone. And while some of the songs were eventually incorporated into local church worship, they were learned primarily for the collective performance of the Toronto March's public congregation. One participant recalled a small accommodation generally made for the Canadian March album: the requisite song in French. Each year's album was set in a relatively homogeneous style described by local Christian-radio-station music director Jim Leek as the "Integrity worship sound of the 90s." The musical aesthetic of Integrity, one of the largest producers of praise and worship music in the early to mid-1990s, conformed to the soft rock or adult contemporary style of much 1990s worship music. MFJ songs were accompanied by a guitar- or keyboard-led band and featured Kendrick singing with a small vocal ensemble. The albums often incorporated antiphonal responses between groups of male and female singers, generally anonymous semiprofessional singers who sang with minimal elaboration and a bright vocal timbre. Though occasionally there was a song meant to evoke an "ethnic" flavor (for example, hand drums or Caribbean steel pan, to evoke a celebratory air), the March albums' musical style was largely a homogenous light pop.

Charismatic and evangelical churches found Kendrick's songs useful long after the MFJ. The songs' use in MFJ as well as other interdenominational events and conferences, and their production and distribution by major Christian record producers on both sides of the Atlantic, each fed on the others' success. By the mid-1990s, selected songs from the MFJ were being sung widely in churches in the United Kingdom, North America, and Australia. Perhaps the best known of these worship songs is the rousing mid-tempo anthem "Shine, Jesus, Shine," featured on Kendrick's second *Make Way* album and sung in Toronto and across the world during the 1994 Global MFJ. The song's chorus is a prayer for God to illumine the darkness and kindle renewal within both "this land" and "the nations." "Shine, Jesus, Shine" found enduring popularity in local church congregations across the world in the years following the MFJ. According to Christian Copyright Licensing statistics, the song remained one of the twenty-five most frequently sung worship songs in the US and Canada between 1995 and 2004 (CCLI 2008).

Sonic Permeation

"If a march lapses into silence its energy and effectiveness quickly dissipates," Kendrick observes in his *Make Way Handbook* (1991, 29). The *Handbook* goes on to elaborate strategies for sonic permeation, ensuring that music and sound cover all the sonic space available, temporally as well as spatially. For large Marches, the *Handbook* recommends synchronized sound systems that enable the whole march to sing together with no gaps between companies of band-led singers. Sonic permeation without gaps, further, is presented not only as critical for encouraging a unified interpretation of the March by bystanders, but also as necessary for encouraging marchers to sing confidently (33–35).

Participants in Toronto's MFJ were encompassed by a wall of sound from the synchronized sound systems along the March route. The March waged spiritual warfare through the sonically permeating musical volume and texture—attempting to "blast out" evil, as one participant so memorably put it. Parade organizers attempted to evenly blanket the city streets with a non-stop barrage of songs, shouts, and participatory prayers. Each time the cycle of nine recorded marching worship songs ended, they were immediately repeated, providing a homogenous blanket of sound that covered the march route from start to finish.

A PRAISE MARCH FOR THE NEW MILLENNIUM: TORONTO'S JESUS IN THE CITY PARADE

Partly because of waning participation and of exhaustion on the part of parade organizers, Toronto's final MFJ was held in May 1999. In September of the same year, a new city-wide praise march began: called "The Parade of the Centuries" and later renamed the "Jesus in the City Parade," this praise march was initially planned as a one-off biblical pageant in celebration of 2,000 years of Christian history. Through a close ethnographic study[11] of the 2010 parade, I found that, though Jesus in the City parade participants espouse many of the same values and beliefs as those promoted in the MFJ, the Parade's sonic and social ideals suggest a more complex, sometime even conflicting set of orientations to the national public sphere, resulting in a very different model of the public congregation. Contemporary worship music remains the primary participatory music of the Parade; however, the way it is performed and structures the gathering differs significantly. Music-making in the Jesus in the City Parade establishes a contrasting model both for intra-Christian cooperation and Christian communities' engagement with their broader society, thus constructing a very different public congregation.

Toronto's Jesus in the City parade was founded by the late Myrtle Solomon, an Afro-Caribbean immigrant, and her Canadian-born daughter Ayanna Solomon. This first parade in 1999 brought out an estimated 1,500 marchers with five musical floats. Believing they were called by God to continue the parade, the Solomons founded Festival of Praise, a nonprofit organization that organizes multiethnic music-related seminars and special events throughout the year, though its main event is the annual parade. With year-round publicity in local Christian print and broadcast media, the parade has seen a steady addition of new church networks, averaging between 10,000 and 15,000 participants in the late 2000s and early 2010s.

Rather than relying on a unified set of songs broadcast simultaneously, the Jesus in the City Parade is a Carnival-style procession in which church groups and ministries come together to sponsor floats. Each float is decorated with large banners containing Bible verses, Christian slogans, or other symbols, and most carry between eight and twenty instrumentalists and singers who lead worship songs for the marchers closest to the float sing along with. The 2010 Jesus in the City Parade included twenty-four parade groups and thirteen large musical floats on truck and tractor-trailer beds. Table 4.1 illustrates the ethnic diversity—and also the ethnic segregation—of church congregations and networks involved in the parade. Of the thirteen musical floats, seven were sponsored by groups united by ethnolinguistic rather than denominational identity. The five large churches that sponsored their own floats featured musicians from a variety of ethnic backgrounds, though members of Afro-Caribbean heritage often featured prominently.

After an hour-long pre-parade gathering featuring musical worship, preaching, and prayer, the parade itself took approximately two and a half hours, beginning and ending at Queen's Park and wending its way around a roughly rectangular course along several of the major thoroughfares of downtown Toronto (Figure 4.3). In 2010 and in the several years prior, the parade was scheduled to coincide with the Toronto International Film Festival (TIFF), in part to capitalize on the increased number of visitors and residents that flock to the city centre. The parade was preceded and followed by a two-hour-long pre-parade rally and an hour-long post-parade rally in Queen's Park, featuring music and dance performances, congregational singing, inspirational messages, and prayers from designated speakers.

JESUS IN THE CITY: RATIONALE AND EMPHASES

Participants in the 2010 Jesus in the City parade shared many of the same beliefs and values that characterized the MFJ. In particular, the purpose of spiritual warfare, undergirded by the Canadian evangelical discourse of loss, loomed large. Like the MFJ, marching on the streets was understood by many parade leaders as an act of entering into enemy territory in an attempt to claim (or reclaim) the city, region, or nation. The parade route was chosen in part to encompass symbols of power and moral corruption. Yonge Street, the main north/south road through the heart of the city, is long a contested symbol of the city's moral vision (Ruppert 2006). After walking several blocks of Yonge Street, the marchers headed back west along College Street. The procession's final turn north to Queen's Park gave marchers a full view of the front of the Ontario Provincial Legislature.

Table 4.1. 2010 JESUS IN THE CITY PARADE FLOAT SPONSORS

Church or Organization	Denomination(s) or Church Network(s)	Ethnicity
Festival of Praise	Interdenominational	Predominantly Afro-Caribbean
Destiny and Dominion (church)	Independent charismatic church	Multiethnic
Evangel Temple (church)	Independent charismatic church	Multiethnic
East Scarborough Pentecostal Worship Center (church)	Pentecostal Assemblies of God	Multiethnic
Faith Sanctuary (church)	Independent charismatic church	Predominantly black
Catholic Charismatic Renewal Council	Various area Catholic churches	Multiethnic
Combined Korean churches (1)	Interdenominational, many churches (Baptist, Presbyterian, independent)	Korean
Combined Korean churches (2)	Interdenominational, many churches	Korean
Passion-play demonstration	Interdenominational, many churches	Korean
Combined Hungarian churches	Interdenominational, many churches (Baptist, Pentecostal, independent)	Hungarian
Living Water Assembly Chinese churches	Chinese-speaking network of churches	Chinese
Combined Slavic churches	Interdenominational (Baptist, Pentecostal, independent)	Russian, Belarusian, Polish
Riverside Evangelical Missionary Church	Denominational: Evangelical Missionary Church of Canada	Multiethnic

Similarly to the MFJ, the "discourse of loss" is evident in speeches and conversations, along with an express desire that Christians join together to influence society at large. In pre-parade meetings, rallies, and prayer walks, parade organizers have encouraged the use of music as part of "sonic warfare" against targets, including corruption in government, sexual orientations they deem immoral, and social ills such as joblessness, racism, and homelessness. Rosie, the float musical director for Destiny and Dominion Word Ministries, frames her churches participation in this way: "we are not as Christians standing by allowing every other person who has something to say to just go

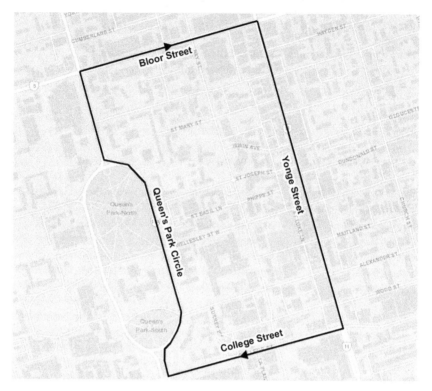

Figure 4.3: Jesus in the City Parade route map.
Created in collaboration with Josh Been.

and say it, [or] just sitting back and doing nothing because we are afraid to stand up for what we believe. We're showing that we're united, we're a strong front" (personal interview, September 2, 2010).

The very first musical performance during the pre-parade rally gave a striking illustration of this confrontational approach, one that Melvin Butler has termed "musicospiritual warfare" (2005, 2008). In his work on Haitian Pentecostal music-making, Butler notes that music is "spiritually amalgamative but socially divisive": "it slices through oppressive spiritual barriers to attack a common 'satanic' enemy, but it also guards the social and theological walls separating them" (2008, 25). The rally began with a choreographed dance number to the urban gospel song "Waging War." The song, popularized by well-known US gospel artist CeCe Winans on her 2008 album *Thy Kingdom Come*, proclaimed the defeat of spiritual enemies and the taking back of territory for the glory of God. As the song opened with a lush string accompaniment and straightforward, march-like rhythm, a dance troupe comprising children and preteens decked in matching camouflage outfits marched in place on the grass in front of the main stage. The dance troupe's leader, a lithe young

Afro-Canadian woman who I later learned is a professional dancer, made interpretive gestures as she lip-synched Winans's solo:

> Anoint my head, anoint my feet
> Send your angels raining down
> Here on the battle ground
> For your glory
> We're taking territory
> Fighting unseen enemies
> Like never before
> We're waging war[12]

As the song increased in volume and moved into the more texturally dense bridge, the solo vocalist sang about "taking territory back" as the lead dancer danced across the field; a gospel chorus, whose response part was underscored by gestures from the troupe, responded with a subdued but insistent chant "we're waging war."

This example shows that "raising a standard" or banner to rally the Christian community and to signal its presence to the broader society was a profoundly musical activity at the Jesus in the City parade. Participants used specific worship songs as expressive weapons and as emblems on this figurative banner—an action participants described as "lifting up the name of Jesus." Parade song choices from across a variety of floats in the parade simultaneously referred to and enabled this act through songs such as "Lord, I Lift Your Name on High," "High and Lifted Up," "Lift His Name," and "We Want to See Jesus Lifted High."[13]

Many songs also invoked the power of God to conquer and subdue enemies. Themes of kingship, authority, power, and dominion abounded in songs like "Our God Reigns," "Jesus, You Reign," "Arise, O God," "Jesus, You Reign on High," "The Whole Earth Is Full of your Glory." While some of these songs treated the dominion of God as a certain present or future reality, others suggested that God's reign could be brought to reality by the performance of human agents. The opening songs chosen for a Korean interchurch band's parade set began with two mid-tempo numbers expressing these themes. According to Junghoo, a singer active in his local church band at the Korean Pentecostal Church of the Resurrection in North Toronto, the songs had been chosen for their power to make known the name of Jesus Christ. The band, comprising five instrumentalists and five singers from a number of North Toronto Korean churches, performed "God of This City," followed by "Jesus, We Enthrone You" with an interpretive dance accompanying it (Figure 4.4).

In "God of This City,"[14] a worship song made popular in the late 2000s by celebrity worship leader Chris Tomlin, the first verse features a series of

Figure 4.4: Singers perform an interpretive dance on a float sponsored by several Korean churches at the 2010 Jesus in the City Parade. Toronto, Canada: September 2010. Photo by the author.

proclamations related to God's dominion, with each phrase set in a low register to the same insistent melodic pattern:

> You're the God of this city
> You're the King of these people
> You're the Lord of this nation
> You are

After a pre-chorus in which intensity begins to build, the chorus melody rises an octave to its climax as the singers proclaim

> Greater things have yet to come
> And greater things are still to be done
> In this city

The second song, "Jesus, We Enthrone You," emphasized the agency of worshipers in constructing a throne through their song.[15] The short repeated chorus began with the prayer "we proclaim You as our King / . . . we raise you up with our praise." The musical performance sonically depicted the lyrical ascent: as the song's melody line spiraled upward, the performance grew in intensity: singers increased their volume and as the instrumental texture and dynamics intensified. Vocalists lifted their hands toward the skies, with upraised faces and closed eyes while reiterating three times the phrase at the end of the chorus, "as we worship, build a throne." Through the act of singing, these parade participants not only recounted but also prayed for empowerment to perform the action described in the lyrics—to bring the reality of heaven's ideal social and religious order into the streets of their city.

SONIC VALUES OF JESUS IN THE CITY

In both the MFJ and the Jesus in the City Parade, spiritual warfare remains a central activity. Both praise marches face the practical issues of deciding how best to represent and manage denominational and ethnic diversity and to present a unified front to the Toronto-area public. However, the sonic shape of the Christian public congregation in the Jesus in the City parade is different in several crucial respects from that of MFJ. The way organizers structure music and sound gives rise to a different set of meanings and results in a different model for the public congregation's relationship to society. The ensuing discussion illustrates how, in the Jesus in the City parade, synchronicity gives way to simultaneity; uniformity to variety; and sonic permeation to sonic unevenness.

Simultaneity

In contrast to the MFJ, in which the sonic value of synchronicity is central, the 2010 Jesus in the City Parade did not emphasize synchronized sound and motion. The MFJ was organized at the national level and took its musical marching orders from the United Kingdom. Jesus in the City, by contrast, grew from local networks rather than national or international ones. The only event it has sought to coordinate with in years past has been the TIFF to capitalize on the increased traffic and visitors to the city.

Toronto's MFJ encouraged a doubly synchronized performance in which all participants in its local march sing the same songs at the same time as others nationally and globally. Jesus in the City's Carnival-style organization encouraged a simultaneous, rather than synchronized, performance of well-known contemporary worship songs. In this simultaneous performance, church networks chose their own songs, which were then led by their own musicians and performed in their own way. In a meeting for local organizers put on by Festival of Praise a month in advance of the parade, the pre- and post-parade rally's sound engineer gave a brief talk about float design and music. Onto a central screen, he projected the organization's minimalist musical advice to church groups sponsoring parade floats:

> We recommend that you select lively upbeat songs with words that send a clear message of Who we are worshipping. Five (5) to seven (7) songs should be enough to repeat throughout the 2-hour route. Whether you are using a live band or CDs make sure your sound equipment, generator and instruments are safely secured on your float.

Festival of Praise organizers attempted to preserve the integrity of the different simultaneous expressions by spacing the parade's largest and loudest musical floats at the widest possible distance from one another. To try to avoid sonic overlap, they filled the space between the large floats with dancers, flag bearers, or smaller groups of singers led only by a leader with a loudspeaker. There were some moments of overlap anyway, with an occasional cacophony of songs in different styles and keys, but these efforts afforded the opportunity for spontaneous synchronization enabled by the shared repertory of contemporary worship songs. Despite the lack of central organization of singing, multiple parade floats performed many of the same popular worship songs, including "Lord, I Lift Your Name on High" (five groups), "Days of Elijah" (four groups), and "Blessed Be Your Name" (four groups). Many groups performed songs from the same celebrity worship leaders and bands, including songs from Sydney, Australia–based Hillsong (six groups), Houston-based celebrity worship leader Israel Houghton (five groups), and Passion's Chris Tomlin (four groups). "Days of Elijah," a widely known praise and worship song that uses prophetic biblical imagery to describe the return of Jesus to earth, was performed by at least four out of the thirteen float bands in the 2010 parade. At one point during the parade, the Catholic Charismatic Renewal Council (CCRC) float band heard the float in front of them, from the predominantly black United Pentecostal church Faith Sanctuary, begin to play the song. CCRC music leader Ray, a twenty-something Canadian of South Asian descent, halted his band in its tracks and led them in an impromptu synchronous rendition of "Days of Elijah" with the other float. This spontaneous, temporary synchronization between predominantly South Asian Catholic and black United Pentecostal church groups was a powerful and memorable experience of unity for Ray and his team. This moment of polyrhythmic synchronization—a temporary coming together of independent rhythms, before they diverge into different patterns in the same overall metric framework—also offers a picture of the way Jesus in the City parade participants performed unity.

Variety

The Jesus in the City parade, rather than insisting on sonic uniformity, encouraged a <u>diverse sound ideal</u>. MFJ participants were asked to sing the same song at the same time in the same way; by contrast, the Jesus in the City Parade music-making was more like a set of variations on a common theme. The difference in the number of songs performed at each march was immense: while MFJ featured eight or nine songs looped until the parade was finished, Jesus in the City's thirteen musical floats featured well over a hundred unique song performances in a variety of styles and languages. In a large gathering that was conspicuously—and audibly—divided along lines of ethnolinguistic background, many musical leaders expressed a felt imperative to create unity through their song choices. However varied the instruments or vocal styles, the thirteen musical floats drew their songs from what was generally perceived as the same repertoire. Participants themselves were aware of the similarity: when I asked participants to comment on the songs they had heard from other groups' parade floats, most underscored their similarity. Andrea, head of the musical selection committee for the Hungarian interchurch float, told me that "pretty much everybody [at the Parade] does the same type of songs" (personal interview, September 17, 2010). Similarly, CCRC band leader Ray recounted that at the 2010 parade "there were a lot of common songs going around. There were different styles, different ways [different groups] played it, but most of the songs we heard were similar" (personal interview, November 17, 2010). In speaking with Andrea, Ray, and nine other parade music directors about their song selection, I constructed a list of 109 songs chosen for performance in individual parade floats. Of the songs on this list, approximately 90 percent fell into the category of contemporary worship songs.[16]

While song choice conveyed a unity of practice across churches and networks, participants felt a simultaneous imperative to represent their diversity. The lead float, with a band comprising mainly members of Caribbean heritage, performed Caribbean soca and calypso, while the Living Water Assembly network of Chinese churches blared Chinese hymns in an orchestral style reminiscent of Chinese Communist patriotic songs. Many of the individual parade floats were committed to stylistic diversity: the CCRC, Evangel Temple, Faith Sanctuary, and Destiny and Dominion Word Ministries all self-identified as "multicultural" ministries and intentionally cultivated diversity in musical style. Because music leaders were practiced at incorporating different musical styles into their Sunday morning worship, they incorporated them into their floats at the parade as well. During the 2010 parade, Destiny and Dominion's band performed a set of over twenty contemporary worship songs set to traditional gospel, urban gospel, adult contemporary, and rock styles.

Sonic Unevenness

In contrast to the MFJ's unbroken wall of sound from its evenly spaced loudspeakers, the Jesus in the City Parade was characterized by a sonic unevenness. The Parade featured intermittent intervals of piercing sound and relative silence, with its individual groups performing at different volume levels. In between the large musical floats were some silent processions (including a dance troupe and tai kwon do studio), as well as a few church groups in which the song leader was equipped with only a handheld megaphone. Sonic unevenness was both a practical result of different groups' resources levels and indicative of disagreements between participating groups about what volume level was appropriate for the parade. Some of the parade groups aimed for sonic penetration: two floats in particular amplified their bands at ear-splitting volumes. Others, however, showed ambivalence about the permeation of public space, often stemming from a desire to appeal to bystanders. More sensitive parade-float sound engineers tweaked the volume throughout the day to conform to the differing acoustical spaces of the city and to avoid bleeding into music of adjacent floats. Two different music leaders explained to me that, when the streets narrowed and were enclosed by tall office buildings, they switched midway through a loud song to a softer song in their set. One leader explained the imperative of being loud enough to hear but not loud enough to offend—to "use your 'inside voice' out in the streets." Dawson, music director on the Evangel Temple float, concurred: "if you see people doing this [putting their hands over their ears], then they're not getting the message" (personal interview, September 9, 2010).

The unevenness in volume stemming from a felt imperative for sonic moderation contrasts not only to the MFJ but to other parades in the city, in which all-encompassing sound at ear-splitting volumes is often understood to be the sonic ideal. Muhammad Huque writes that in Toronto's Caribana and Pride parades, the prevailing aural aesthetic is "the noisier, the better" because the sound is an expression of political power and a means of "drawing attention to transgressive messages" of the parade participants (2009, 147). Jesus in the City music leaders attempt to maintain a sonic balance in part to ensure receptivity to their message. There may be more at work here, however, than simply an evangelistic tactic: for some, it seemed that sonic moderation proceeded from ethical conviction. In commenting on sonic balance, Jason, the float music leader and sound engineer for Faith Sanctuary, explained his sensitivity to amplitude as part of a Christian responsibility to be hospitable to next-door neighbors. In an in-depth conversation after the parade, Jason drew a distinction between public spaces like the streets of downtown Toronto ("their space") and spaces for religious observance within the walls of the church ("our space"): "Let's have them invite us into their space and then let's befriend them in their space and win them into our space" (personal interview, September 21, 2010).

There are vestiges of the warfare rhetoric in Jason's comments: the Jesus in the City parade is framed as a tactic designed to "win" non-Christians to the church. However, there is a subtle rhetorical shift here that is crucial: rather than interpreting the parade's purpose as claiming public space for Christianity, Jason presents the parade as the church being *invited* for neighborly visit into a space over which they do not intend to claim ownership. Participants put their best face forward to encourage interested bystanders to come visit "their" space, the local church communities. Rather than a hostile takeover by a rival army, the parade becomes a ritual enactment designed to give bystanders a glimpse of the kind of life possible in an alternate religious sphere within the increasingly multiethnic, religiously plural Canadian society.

SONIC AND SOCIAL IDEALS OF THE PUBLIC CONGREGATION: A DIVERGENCE OF THE AURAL IMAGINATION

The aims and goals of Toronto's two consecutive praise marches were similar: both the MFJ and Jesus in the City Parades, in filling the public square with what they hoped to be harmonious, compelling sounds, asked bystanders to imagine their society infused with a divine purpose stemming from an evangelical practice of Christianity. Both praise marches illustrate the process that Suzel Reily has termed "enchantment," in which music orchestrates the ritual enactment of a compelling moral vision. In her work on music in Brazilian popular Catholicism, Reily rehabilitates the Weberian idea of enchantment—the seemingly "magical" power of corporate ritual, stemming from its articulation of a shared moral vision, to effect social transformation—from its confinement to the premodern period. Reily argues that enchantment is a process found within religious rituals in the present day—that "enchantment creates a highly charged experiential realm in which devotees gain a momentary glimpse of the harmonious order that could reign in society, provided everyone agreed to adhere to the moral precepts outlined in religious discourse" (2002, 3). Participatory music-making enables "the creation of a morally grounded visionary social world" (4).

While enchantment is integrally tied to moral vision, the means by which enchanting powers are extended can be morally ambiguous: enchantment is generally thought to work by seduction rather than persuasion, the ability to coerce rather than to attract. Praise marchers conceived this way are sonic warriors, asserting their rights to express their religious beliefs and claiming symbolic territory sonically through taking their worship to the streets. However, processes of musical enchantment in both praise marches are marked by a fundamental ambivalence over the source and use of social power. Musical worship is uniquely capable of mediating between these extremes: it can be conceived, on the one hand, as a weapon of sonic warfare that seeks to subdue anyone without earshot. On the other, in using upbeat, contemporary-style music performed in festive, colorful processions, worship in the streets also shows a strong orientation toward persuasion. The militant and separatist spiritual warfare emphasis of both praise marches—"taking territory back," "defeating strongholds" of evil, and "waging war" against the principalities and powers of secular society—is held in tension with the desire to attract and include.

It is clear from the performances within and rhetoric surrounding praise marches that evangelicals wish to see their religious and moral ideals reign in society; however, just as fundamental is their desire that individuals from that society freely choose to convert and join the public congregation in worship. The marches' method of musical enchantment, in this reading, is a beckoning call extending an invitation to anyone within earshot to hear the world through evangelical ears. Whether the marchers see persuasion coming through the veracity of their claims, demonstrations of spiritual power, or supernatural illumination, the domination of spiritual warfare is held in check by democratic orientation to proselytism that holds as inalienable the choice to believe.

In the praise march, the sonic structure, song texts, and styles of worship music are not incidental but rather are central to creating a shared vision and representation of the public congregation. In a gathering like that in Toronto, a gathering marked by considerable diversity, musical choices result from strategic negotiations. Frequently, these sonic ideals are linked to specific social ideals. In the context of Jewish worship, Jeffrey Summit has shown that examining stylistic "junctures of choice . . . and the processes by which they are made, we learn about the locus of authority and the power of tradition in each community. We see which community boundaries are permeable and which are inviolable" (2000, 20).

The musical differences between these two praise marches, then, can indicate where social ideals may differ, leading to two critical differences between the way the two marches seek to constitute the public congregation and relate to the broader society. First, Toronto's MFJ, on the one hand, held the notion of the Christian community as one upheld by a common "script." In *Public Praise* (1992), Kendrick describes how this common script is used to unify the public congregation:

> At the heart of our marches and public praise events have been carefully prepared scripts built around the central truths of the Christian faith, express[ed] through Scripture verses, songs, shouts, and sometimes actual creeds, notably the Apostles' Creed. It is impossible to please everybody and every group all the time. However, believers of diverse traditions and backgrounds have overwhelmingly united on this glorious common ground of truth. (102)

A newly composed body of common songs that emanated from a trusted authority brought performative unity to the gathering. The songs of the

Jesus in the City Parade, by contrast, grew from local church practice, freely converging and diverging, thereby providing a source of unity and diversity. The Parade was, essentially, a collection of different messages riffing off one of the most general—and polyvalent—bases for Christian unity.

A second essential difference in social ideals indexed by sonic ideals concerns the way unity is built and maintained. Meaning is notoriously difficult to control, particularly in public festivities (see Ashkenazi 1987; Regis 1999). The organizers at Toronto's MFJ took a more aggressive approach to shaping the parade's meaning and purpose and making sure participants were on board with it. From printed how-to handbooks and theological rationales, to musical recordings and songbooks, the resources from Make Way music aided MFJ in both self-representation and self-selection. With the readily available and centralized materials, Graham Kendrick noted that "those who cannot assent to the [March's] content tend to opt out ahead of time" (1991, 102). Assenting to a common "content" included not only opting in to a specific set of doctrines, but also involved a tacit agreement about which songs and performance styles best represented the community. By contrast, in the Jesus in the City Parade, the simultaneous performance of variety and the marked ambivalence about the relationship of public congregation to society encouraged a much greater potential divergence in the Parade's "content" as well as its interpretation. The fact that sound ideals are not actively managed creates a space for nonconformity within the ranks and gives bystanders expanded interpretive possibilities. These two Toronto-based praise marches' diverging sonic and musical performance encourages a different relationship to others within the public sphere and, as a result, a different identity as a public congregation.

BEYOND THE WALLS: THE MUSIC OF PUBLIC WORSHIP

In the moment that Joshua worshipped, the outcome of the battle [of Jericho] was decided. Once Joshua had fallen before Jesus, Jericho was certain to fall before Joshua . . . However conscious we may become of a supernatural dimension as we encircle our own Jerichos, we only need to see the captain, worship Him, obey Him and follow Him.
—Graham Kendrick, from *Public Praise* (1992)

The Jesus in the City Parade is about . . . taking worship out from the four walls [of the church] to where we *need* to be . . . to raise up this godly standard and let people know we're here.
—Melanie, personal interview (2011)

The polyvalent metaphor of breaking down walls figures prominently in discourses surrounding praise marches. Kendrick's remark implies that public worship will result in the breaking of God's Kingdom into the stronghold of the world, while Melanie's statement implies that it is worship *itself* that has become an enclosure, something that the church has (wrongfully) contained that needs to break out. Whether the walls are conceived as Jericho's walls—walls around a powerful stronghold that a chosen people have been tasked to break through and conquer—or walls that churches have erected to separate and protect themselves from the outside world, the metaphor reveals a key purpose of the evangelical public congregation: it is ultimately about breaking down the walls that divide evangelicalism from the broader society.

This chapter has shown the layers of complexity added when evangelicals leave the sequestered spheres of church, conference, and concert congregations and bring their musical worship into the space of public performance. Public congregations result when evangelicals attempt to break down these walls through the activity of worship—an activity that, for evangelicals, is structured by specific musical sounds, styles, and repertory. Shared worship music aids not only in building a sense of communal identity among local Christian congregations and organizations, but also in building the public congregation to communicate its vision of a moral order to those on the other side of the walls. Through their worshipful performance, participants within the public congregation seek to sing the presence of God into their city. As they perform congregational songs in the city streets, musical prayers for the God's dominion ("fill this land with the Father's glory") entwine with proclamations of ownership ("You're the God of this city"). The words of the marchers' worship songs become performative utterances, designed to bring into being the reality they describe. By singing "we welcome you here, Lord Jesus," worshipers seek to usher in divine presence; through the ascending melody of "we lift Jesus high," they engage in lifting the Christian savior's name in song for all to hear.

Whether praise march songs are centrally produced or locally chosen, contemporary worship music has been an indispensable resource for evangelicals bringing worship into the public sphere. Further, the Toronto-based praise marches show that this congregational song repertory has proven eminently adaptable: through different performance choices, it has been used to accommodate tensions between competing evangelical theologies, to juxtapose differing social values, and to enable the sonic articulation of divergent social and spiritual visions. Perhaps contemporary worship music is ultimately so useful within the public congregation because it does not uniformly promote one social model: rather, different emphases within the repertory itself can be used to reflect a variety of understandings of the relationship of evangelical communities and their societies.

NOTES

1. In countries outside the United Kingdom during the early 1990s, the MFJ was typically organized at the national level, with national boards set up under the authority of the International Board of the Global March for Jesus based in the United Kingdom. Even after the dissolution of the UK-based International Board in 2000, many of these marches continue. In central and South America, for instance, the MFJ has become institutionalized as a display of Protestant solidarity and power. Brazilian MFJs, generally held near Brazil's public holiday in honor of the Feast of Pentecost, have become the Protestant alternative to Carnival, drawing crowds that number in the hundreds of thousands—and even millions—in several cities each year. See Bartkowski and Regis (2003); Fer (2007); Wightman (2009), and Holvast (2009).

2. Among those who organized and promoted the marches, there were a range of theological perspectives on what worshipful intercession was meant to accomplish. One influential idea was known as "strategic-level spiritual warfare" or "spiritual mapping," which René Holvast defines as "an international Evangelical and Neo-Pentecostal movement that specialized in the use of religious techniques to wage a territorial war against unseen non-human beings" (2009, 1). Lynn Green, one of the founders of the MFJ, describes the importance of this strategy at the beginning of MFJ: "there was a prayer strategy we'd never seen before and we were excited by it. . . . [B]y now we were beginning to think that the principalities, powers, and spiritual strongholds had historical roots, so we looked into different parts of the City of London where we felt there was a stronghold of greed and unrighteous trade" (Kendrick et al. 1991, 17).

3. Kendrick's *Make Way: Public Praise Handbook* (1991), published by Make Way Music and distributed by Kingsway, contained everything MFJ organizers would need: a very brief history and rationale, followed by a range of practical advice on organization, and songs and scripts for performance. *Public Praise* (1992), published by Florida-based charismatic publisher Creation House, gave a history and rationale written for an American and international audience. The book's endorsements on the back cover include C. Peter Wagner, John Wimber, and Tony Campolo, influential US leaders from across the evangelical spectrum.

4. Kendrick and other British evangelicals came under criticism for their strong emphasis upon the theology of spiritual warfare and later sought to downplay the emphasis. See, for instance, an interview with *Cross Rhythms'* Tony Cummings (1992).

5. The MFJ's relative longevity in Toronto may owe to the importance of public festivals and parades in Toronto more generally. These include Caribana, the largest Caribbean Carnival festival outside the Caribbean; the Pride Parade; and the Santa Claus Parade, which are each estimated to draw a million participants or more (Huque 2009).

6. Toronto's March participation was drastically uneven: it began with 2,000 participants in 1992, swelled to 20,000–25,000 in 1994, but came in at under 1,000 in 1995. By the March's end in the late 1990s, it was drawing between 2,000 and 5,000 participants. It stands in contrast to more successful events in Western Canada, particularly Edmonton and Winnipeg, which drew 15,000–35,000 until the March's end in 1999. I encountered the MFJ while I was conducting ethnographic field research for Toronto's Jesus in the City parade. Because none of my contacts or their churches kept primary source materials

from the marches that had occurred some fifteen years prior, the information in this section comes from a combination of oral-history interviews with three former MFJ Board members and archived news reports from the period. I have also drawn from accounts from a few interviewees from the Jesus in the City parade who were involved fifteen years prior with the March. While some of my research consultants saw the newer procession as a legacy of the MFJ, others used it to contrast outreach strategies of the 1990s, or to highlight the changing shape of the Christian community in Toronto.

7. Graham Kendrick, personal conversation, May 21, 2014. Throughout the 1990s, there was a constant flow of ideas, materials, and songs among these charismatic networks in Canada, Southern California (home of the influential Vineyard Fellowship of Churches), and the United Kingdom. These connections were renewed a few years later when a charismatic revival at what was then the Toronto Airport Vineyard Church spread to UK sites such as Holy Trinity Brompton, London. For further detail on how the Toronto Blessing renewed transnational North American and UK charismatic network connections, see Hunt 1997; Percy 1998; and Poloma 2003.

8. The discourse of loss shares many similarities with discourses about religion in the United States—and within global evangelical and fundamentalist Christianity more generally—in the time frame marked by "culture wars." See Brouwer et al. 1996 and Elisha 2010.

9. Ediger (2000) offers a chronology and critical appraisal of the development of the spiritual warfare ideas within evangelicalism through the 1990s. For influential evangelical perspectives on spiritual warfare during the same time period, see also Intercession Working Group of the Lausanne Committee for World Evangelization 1993; C. P. Wagner 1996; and Arnold 1997.

10. Name withheld by request.

11. This project formed the basis for Ingalls 2012b, an examination of the parade through the analytical frame of the politics of voice, and informed Ingalls 2014, a comprehensive overview of global Christian popular music. Field research, beginning in April 2010, consisted of attending parade meetings, accompanying organized prayer walks to prepare participants for the parade, visiting several sponsoring and participating churches, going to performances of the some of the parade bands, and observing the event itself. The formal interviews for this project were designed around the individuals who made organizational decisions or musical choices in the parade. (Shorter interviews with parade participants and informal conversations with parade participants and bystanders supplemented these core interviews.) Two dozen interviews were conducted with eleven out of thirteen music directors for the parade floats. These interviews focused on choices of songs and styles for the parade, the rationales behind these choices, and personal narratives of both musical and non-musical experiences during the 2010 parade and previous parades. I compiled song lists into a master list of a hundred-plus songs sung during the Jesus in the City parade and analyzed them for common themes, songs, and stylistic settings. Over the course of the year of field research, I developed long-term and reciprocal relationships with several parade organizers. On the day of the parade, I served as unofficial photographer, donating my photos of the event to the organization for use in their promotional materials. I continue to keep in contact with parade organizers and attendees via email and on the parade's Facebook site.

12. WAGING WAR. Brannon Tunie, CeCe Winans, Christopher Capehart. ©2008 Little Pooky's Music (Admin. by Pure Psalms Music, Inc.), Pure Psalms Music (Admin. by Pure Psalms Music, Inc.), and Awspire Publishing (Admin. by Third Tier Music, LLC). All rights reserved. Used by permission.

13. "Lord, I Lift Your Name on High" and "Lift His Name" were performed on a float sponsored by several Korean churches. "Lord, I Lift Your Name on High" and "High and Lifted Up" were sung as a medley by the United Pentecostal Faith Sanctuary church's float. The CCRC float also included "Lord, I Lift Your Name on High" and "We Want to See Jesus Lifted High." Numerous conversations with parade music directors and organizers revealed that nearly every group sang at least one song that fit this lyrical theme.

14. GOD OF THIS CITY. Aaron Boyd, Andrew McCann, Ian Jordan, Peter Comfort, Peter Kernoghan, and Richard Bleakley. ©2008 Thankyou Music (PRS) (adm. worldwide at CapitolCMGPublishing.com excluding Europe which is adm. by Integrity Music, part of the David C Cook family. Songs@integritymusic. com) / worshiptogether.com Songs (ASCAP) sixsteps Music (ASCAP) (adm. at CapitolCMGPublishing.com). All rights reserved. Used by permission.

15. JESUS WE ENTHRONE YOU. Paul Kyle. CCLI Song No. 37845. ©1980 Thankyou Music (Admin. by EMI Christian Music Publishing). All rights reserved.

16. The outlying 10 percent included instrumental numbers accompanying a Korean group's passion play, Chinese hymns sung to an orchestral style reminiscent of Chinese Communist patriotic songs, and newly composed Caribbean soca-style praise songs.

CHAPTER 5

⌀⌀⌀

Worship on Screen

Building Networked Congregations through Audiovisual Worship Media

Chapter 4 began to address what happens when contemporary worship music "goes public"—that is, when it is taken out of spaces set aside for religious practice and becomes a public performance. This chapter builds on the foundation established in the previous chapter, examining the new social constellations emerging around contemporary worship music as it weaves in between live performance spaces and public spaces online. Digital audiovisual worship media—whether live-streamed worship services, user-generated YouTube worship videos, or prerecorded audiovisual materials for use in live worship settings—forms the material nodes of new congregational networks. These types of media serve both as extensions of congregations into virtual spaces and as sites enabling new modes of online congregating. This chapter demonstrates that new digital audiovisual technologies and the avenues of online communication along which they travel not only give evangelical worshipers new ways to transmit, share, and discover worship songs; rather, they also strongly condition the practices that evangelicals consider necessary parts of worship. Through audiovisual worship media experienced on small personal screens and large projection screens in church, conference, and concert settings, once-separate aural and visual strands of evangelical devotion are drawn together into a powerful experiential whole. The networked mode of congregating centered around these audiovisual worship experiences challenges the boundaries between public and private worship as it blurs the lines between individual, institutional, and industry authority.

Throughout this chapter, I use the term "networked congregation" to describe the interconnected modes of congregating that digital audiovisual and social media technologies enable.[1] ("Networked congregation" describes a specific instance or gathering, while the related term "congregational network" indicates plural, overlapping networked congregations.) Here I draw inspiration from Heidi Campbell's notion of "networked religion," a term she has coined to explain "how religious experience, belief, and practice are lived out online through dynamic social relations and interaction" (2012, 65). While Campbell's definition focuses primarily on religious expression on the Internet, she notes that scholars cannot easily disentangle online religious practices from the activities in offline contexts on which they are based. Because online and offline spaces are often closely linked, networked religion entails a "complex interplay . . . between the individual and the community, new and old sources of authority, and public and private identities in a networked society" (65). Kiri Miller provides another helpful conceptual model in her work on the musical "communities of practice" that are formed through social media platforms like YouTube. For those with a shared affinity for—or even simply curiosity about—particular music styles or techniques, social media provides not only a new way to consume musical recordings but also "new channels for teaching and learning, for transmitting practical knowledge and drawing together communities of practice," (17) which then translate into offline, face-to-face music-making.

Campbell's observations about networked religious practice and Miller's discussion of online communities of practice centered around music-making can both be readily applied to congregational music-making within digital-age evangelicalism. Contemporary worship music—along with the audio-visual technologies necessary for its successful performance—has been one of the most significant single factors in the rise of evangelical networked congregations and congregational networks. The various forms of digital audiovisual worship media create the nodes of these diffuse congregational networks and serve both as extensions of congregations into the virtual realm and as sites for the creation of new networked congregations. These technologies have enabled networked congregations to expand globally as far as digital technologies and the Internet reach; therefore, like Chapter 4, this chapter's discussion also moves beyond the bounds of the United States. Here I draw from ethnographic research in the United Kingdom and Canada, as well as an online ethnographic study centered on fifty online worship video "fieldsites" (see also Ingalls 2016 and Ingalls, forthcoming) that gathered perspectives of field-research consultants living in the United Kingdom, Iceland, China, Hungary, Germany, and Malaysia whom I met online. Accounts from interlocutors from my online fieldsites are complemented by a close reading of amateur- and professionally produced worship videos, important multimedia nodes for networked congregations. The discussion ends by examining networked congregations on an international scale, analyzing the musical offerings and discourse on the online sites of global worship brands, including Hillsong, based in Sydney, Australia; Passion, based in Atlanta, Georgia; and Jesus Culture/Bethel, based in Redding, California.

Networked congregations are often centered around the "worship experience," an affective time of personal communion with God mediated through contemporary worship music (for further discussion, see Chapter 1, pp. 42–49). Though evangelicals perceive worship experiences to be highly personal, this chapter discusses the extent to which elements of this experience have become standardized and media-dependent. The worship experience draws together once-separate threads of sonic and visual evangelical devotional practice and depends increasingly upon audiovisual screen media to induce it within local contexts; further, the worship experience relies on a combination of live experiences, social media, and professional Internet media to spread it further. The sections of this chapter examine several components of the worship experience and the screen cultures in which it is embedded in order to better understand the new evangelical networked congregations, communities connected through shared affect and affinity. The audiovisual worship experience at the heart of the networked congregation is transforming evangelical sociality and reconfiguring the balance of power between individuals, evangelical institutions, and commercial industries.

WORSHIP EXPERIENCE AND SCREEN CULTURE: THE RISE OF DIGITAL AUDIOVISUAL MEDIA WITHIN EVANGELICAL CONGREGATIONAL SINGING

For an understanding of worship music's role in producing networked congregations, it is necessary first to examine a significant technological development: the pervasive use of audiovisual technologies in worship, particularly digitally projecting song lyrics and still and moving images onto large central screens during congregational singing. The following vignette, by depicting an evening worship service in suburban New Jersey, illustrates the common aspects of the pervasive congregational worship "screen culture."

Morristown, New Jersey, March 2006

At 7:25 p.m., I drive into a Baptist church parking lot in suburban New Jersey for the church's Sunday evening gathering. Earlier in the week, I arranged over email to have a conversation after the service with the worship leader, a friend of a friend whom I haven't yet met in person. Walking into the foyer, I find myself in the middle of a dozen casually dressed twenty-to-thirty-somethings who are milling about and chatting. As I approach the open doors to the sanctuary, a smiling greeter shakes my hand and offers me a flyer for an upcoming event.

I find a seat in the darkened auditorium and look around the room. The two rows of cushioned pews on either side of a central aisle face the stage area. Flanking the stage are two "pits" on either side—one for piano, the other for organ—and a large cross hanging above the organ at the front right. The sanctuary is very dark—though there is a forest of electric chandeliers hanging from the ceiling, each is turned to the dimmest possible setting. A warm orange glow from overhead spotlights bathes the stage, which is ablaze with firelight from candles of all shapes and colors, many on rustic wrought-iron candle trees, others adorning the floor and banister around the organ. A dark-golden curtain divides the stage into front and back halves, and carefully placed potted plants soften the starkness of the curtain. Four worship-band musicians—a keyboardist, guitarist, bass guitarist, and drummer—are onstage conducting sound checks and tuning their instruments. The overhead speakers are piping instrumental music that sounds vaguely Celtic, featuring a string ensemble with synthesizer and earthy-sounding drum timbres.

At the front of the auditorium hangs a large projection screen. Acting as the central reference point of the auditorium from any vantage point, the screen towers above everything else on the stage. Even the cross, hanging ten feet lower at the front right, is dwarfed by the screen. Projected onto the screen is a logo with the evening gathering's name "Liquid" superimposed on a square photograph of a single drop of water falling into a pool and creating rings.

The worship service starts gradually with a lengthy instrumental introduction to the first worship song, during which a message for the gathered worshipers is projected onto the screen: "Silence . . . use this time to prepare for worship." When the musicians begin to sing, the song lyrics are projected onto the screen so that the congregation can sing along. The first song's slides feature the text in the upper right-hand corner, framed by two panels that display photographs of Rio de Janeiro's Christ of the Andes against a striking azure sky. The same image is used as the slide background throughout the second song, though the song lyrics never mention Jesus explicitly. The onscreen image creates a link between the figure of Christ and the lyrical references to "God" and "Lord." The lyrics to the third worship song, "Pure Light," feature a golden-brown background pierced by a brilliant white ray of light. The visual imagery seems clearly intended to complements the song lyrics, which praise Jesus as the Light of the World.

During the Scripture lesson that followed the worship set, the screen never darkens, as a succession of words, images, and schematic drawings are projected to illustrate the speaker's points. After the speaker finishes, the screen is again filled with lyrics to the final song along with a series of new background images that change several times throughout the song. After the final strains of the closing ong die away, the projection on the screen returned to the opening "Liquid" logo, proclaiming once again the identity of this particular worship gathering.

In this church service, the screen occupies a central role in worship: it is a necessary accompaniment for congregational singing, in which a mixture of song lyrics, images, and other texts are projected onto it. In a conversation after the service, the worship leader told me he took great care to choose images he believed complemented and expressed the song lyrics. Indeed, in the course of the service, I noted a place where background images added a new layer of meaning: in the second song, an image of Jesus was projected as a background to song lyrics that never mentioned Jesus by name. And the pre-service message illustrated that the screen can also become an authoritative "voice" in its own right, whether conveying information or delivering instructions to the gathered congregation.

I attended this worship service as an audiovisual technological sea change was occurring in evangelical worship. In the early to mid-2000s, the integration of audiovisual technologies within the service just described represented the technological cutting edge for a mid-sized US congregation; a decade later, this audiovisual setup has become standard. The use of projection technology within evangelical worship has a much longer history; churches, camps, and conferences had been using analog overhead projectors to project song lyrics and other visual materials since the 1960s. In the early 1990s, large and well-resourced gatherings made the move to digital projection. Many local churches felt pressure to adopt not only the music, but also the entire audiovisual technological setup that characterized these large events (see Schultz 2004; Nekola 2009; Mall 2012; Lim and Ruth 2017). Lim and Ruth 2017 notes that the 1990s were the tipping point for the use of electronic technologies within North American Protestant churches, evidenced by "the emergence of trade magazines, conferences, consultants, and church staff" devoted to audiovisual technologies within corporate worship (47). As digital projection technologies became more affordable, more and more churches began to adopt them. In 2002, evangelical media theorist Quentin Schultze wrote that many evangelical churches feel compelled to adopt what he calls "high-tech worship" that "relies extensively on computer-based presentational technologies" (2004, 20).

There is no one comprehensive source that quantifies evangelical use of digital projection onto screens in worship; however, several individual large-scale research surveys together corroborate Schultze's assertion that the digital projection had become the norm by the early 2000s. According to the Barna Research Group's poll of US pastors, the number of churches using computer projection technology in their worship services rose from

39 percent in the year 2000 to 62 percent in the year 2005 (Barna Research Group 2005). According to Christian Copyright Licensing, whose data draws from five years of annual surveys of over 11,000 North American church subscribers, there has been a gradual but steady rise in churches using computer song-lyric projection. In 2007, 78 percent of their subscribing churches used computer projection; by 2011, 84 percent did (CCLI 2012a, 2012b).[2]

Digital projection technology enabled churches to project not only song lyrics, but also other visual media, including backgrounds, images, videos, and other texts for contemplation during worship. Integrating multimedia into church services was justified as necessary to engage the new generation of "digital natives" living in postmodern North American societies for whom digital media technologies were the "indigenous" system of communication (Wilson 1999; Bausch 2002). In *The Wired Church* (1999), one of the first evangelical theological reflections on the use of digital technologies for worship, Len Wilson asserts that the projection screen has become "the stained glass, and the cross, for the electronic media age. . . . Icons were the Bible for the illiterate, and the screen is the Bible for the post-literate" (41).

It did not take long for marketers to seize upon the idea that visual aspects of worship were an untapped spiritual resource. In a three-page advertising spread in a 2007 issue of *Worship Leader* magazine, Church Multimedia frames the spiritual import of its product in these words:

> Worship leaders, pastors, children's ministers, youth pastors, small group leaders and many more have all begun to tap into the spiritual aspect of the visual aesthetic. The response is often a service that carries a tone of excellence and captures a community that is able to give their undivided attention to the teaching of the Word. The visual language is already being spoken in our world; it is now up to leaders to learn how to communicate in that vernacular . . . Read on to discover where to get the tools you need to enhance the visual aesthetic of your service of worship. (2007, 36)

The tools for visual enhancement that followed the advertisement's introduction included LCD projection equipment customized for church use, lyric presentation software, and sing-along worship DVDs for adults' and children's services. These products have now become standard wares in the well-established market for audiovisual equipment and software designed specifically for use in worship services. Along with hardware like digital projectors with retractable screens and now flat panel screens, worship presentation software abounds. The cover story of a 2014 issue of *Christian Computing Magazine's* contains an annual Church Management Software Overview that surveys nineteen different software packages designed for use in congregational worship (Hewitt 2014). These programs can include everything from a bare-bones package of image backgrounds for worship-song slides to expansive worship presentation software packages that include not only a database of song-lyric slides and background visuals, but synced accompaniment soundtracks to which church choirs or congregations can sing along.[3]

Quentin Schultze observed in 2004 that "digital media have created such an explosion in available material, especially images and information of all kinds, that access to texts is no longer linked to any kind of authority" (92). Churches and parachurch ministries have struggled to develop training courses and resources to keep pace with the rapid growth in the audiovisual commodity market. Practical magazines such as *Technologies for Worship, Christian Computing Magazine,* and *Church Production Magazine* arose in the early 2000s to help music directors and ministers merge the technical, aesthetic, and theological aspects of projection technology in their churches.[4] And the omnipresence of digital visual media has led to the rise of a new kind of specialist in churches: the "visual worship" expert, responsible for locating and curating vast libraries of visual materials, designing or downloading song-lyric slides, and attending to presentational media during congregational singing. Many major contemporary-worship music conferences in the United States now feature seminars and sessions on visual media. The National Worship Leader Conference I attended in 2012 offered a visual media track— separate from a more general "tech team" track—as one of fourteen tracks offered. Here, church leaders could attend hour-and-a-half workshops that included organizing and curating visual media for worship, considerations for setting song lyrics, multi-screen and environmental projection, and, for the advanced visual media user, improvisatory "VJ-ing." The year 2013 marked the beginning of an annual worship conference geared toward digital visual artists, known as SALT. This three-day training event and trade show is designed for the professionals and volunteers responsible for presentational media in evangelical churches.

Digital audiovisual technologies for worship are now well established in North American congregations of all sizes, complete with their own product market and recognized experts in an area some are calling "visual worship." As the next section will show, along with evangelical screen culture has come an easily transportable set of audiovisual devotional practices that could be taken up into online spaces and spread even further. These widespread online devotional practices have further entrenched evangelical congregational singing as a site of audiovisual convergence (F. Holt 2011) in which song lyrics, images, and music are combined into a powerful experiential multimedia whole—a state of affairs increasingly capitalized upon by a powerful evangelical media industry. The next two sections of the chapter describe how auditory and visual elements work together within the evangelical worship experience.

WORSHIP ON THE SMALL SCREEN: DIGITAL ICONOGRAPHY AND THE EMERGENCE OF AUDIOVISUAL PIETY

In each of the modes of congregating discussed previously in this book, contemporary worship music is used to facilitate a transformative encounter with God that evangelicals often refer to as the "worship experience." Owing in part to the widespread incorporation of digital presentational technologies and screens within corporate worship, the worship experience has become irreducibly audiovisual, combining two existing strands of evangelical devotional practice: the musical devotional practices that accompany contemporary worship music and the visual piety surrounding the image. An examination of audiovisual tools for worship created and shared online by evangelical amateur video creators reveals how essential the visual dimension has become within the evangelical worship experience.

For a better understanding of what images serve as evangelical "icons" during worship and how they help to produce the worship experience, it is helpful to examine amateur-created evangelical devotional music videos on YouTube, which their creators simply call "worship videos." To make a worship video, video creators overlay commercial audio recordings of their favorite contemporary worship songs with a variety of visual effects, including still photographs, motion imagery, song lyrics, and Bible verses. The visual effects in these videos differ markedly in quality; while some videos feature high resolution photographs, video clips, or texts, others contain visual media that is warped or heavily pixelated. Many of these videos—sometimes in spite of their visual quality—garner hundreds of thousands or millions of views, generate long strings of comments, and motivate thousands of viewers to subscribe to worship-video creators' YouTube channels or to post their own video responses. In their study of communities forming around Christian worship videos on YouTube, Daniel Thornton and Mark Evans (2015) observe that these song videos "have transcended their local church expressions, their denominational origins and even their commercial identities to become facilitators of . . . imagined evangelical community centered around music" (157).[5] Over of the course of examining a selected group of fifty worship videos for popular contemporary worship songs[6] (see Ingalls 2016), I engaged in conversation with over a dozen amateur worship-video creators, a diverse group of evangelical women and men who included a PhD student in ornithology from upstate New York; a self-employed computer repairman in California who was also his local church's webmaster; an Icelandic university student; a Hungarian office worker; a Chinese house church pastor; a middle-aged youth pastor from the Midwestern United States; and a sixty-seven-year-old retiree from rural Texas.

Over the course of multiple conversations over a variety of media, including phone, text, email, Skype, Skype chat, Facebook, and Instant Messenger, I found several things that this diverse cast of evangelical worship-video creators had in common. All worship-video creators I spoke with were explicit that the primary purpose of their videos was to inspire worship, and many added that an important secondary purpose was communicating the faith to non-Christians. Mark from California summed up these dual purposes: "To me the purposes of creating worship videos are to glorify God and also provide a medium for some sort of evangelistic efforts." Some described the act of creating the videos as an act of worship itself. In one conversation over email, Rebecca from Scotland reflected on why she created her first worship video and then articulated what she saw as the purpose of worship videos:

> I chose a song that I loved . . . and I felt that by creating a worship video, it's still worshiping the Lord yet it is also a simple and effective way of sharing the Gospel. To me, a worship video's purpose should be to show to others the love of God, and the love the person who made it has for God. It should be used as *an outer expression of a person's inward faith* [emphasis mine], whether someone makes a video to share on YouTube, for use at their Church service, [or] even for their own personal worship. (email correspondence, March 26, 2012)

In describing the purpose of worship videos, Rebecca employs a theologically significant phrase—"an outward expression of an inward faith"—that evangelicals often use to describe the purpose of Christian baptism. This choice of expression underscores the spiritual seriousness with which video creators regard their creations.

Creators of these worship videos realize that it is worth investing their time and effort in choosing changing image backgrounds, rather than simply placing the songs online with lyrics, because of how images enhance the affective and spiritual experiences of music for worshipers. For worship-video creators, images are an important layer that works together with the digital text and music to point to God's work in the world. James, a rural Texas retiree and prolific worship-video creator, told me that for each of his videos he conducts general Internet image searches and combs through "hundreds of pictures of things that point us to God" (YouTube message, February 11, 2012). Mark, a California-based computer repair technician, described his desire to create a powerful "overall experience" through superimposing a mixture of still images, video clips, and Bible verses in addition to the lyrics. In doing so he hopes to draw viewers in and reinforce the message of the worship songs by appealing to both aural and visual senses: "Worship music, where the message is powerful and easy to understand . . . in collaboration with the images touches on the viewer's senses, which [are] audible and visual as well as allowing them to take in information through reading and processing" (email correspondence,

March 9, 2012). When asked how he chose which images to pair with worship songs, Mark claimed divine inspiration, reflecting that "I have an idea of what to use, but as I'm searching for them, [God] ultimately chooses the right one, uses me, and places it all together." Jónas, a nineteen-year old worship-video creator from Iceland, writes that "it's important that we see pictures that can help us understand the lyrics" (Skype chat, February 13, 2012). Many YouTube worship-video commenters post appreciative comments for a video creator's choice of effective images. These are a few posted in the comments section for Jónas' worship video for the song "Our God":

> LBRalltheway123: the song is amazing and the pictures are gorgeous and makes everything even more amazing!
>
> OksieFoxy: It's amazing—watching pictures of Jesus doing these things and realizing, "It's real! He did this, and He is ready for you to be saved."
>
> Amy Mayfield: Excellent job of matching the photos to the song! I especially like that every time the phrase "our God is stronger" was sung, we saw Jesus on the cross.
>
> Tara Hershey-Lette Hughes: This video is amazing! Love the song, & the pictures make that much greater! God bless whoever made this!
>
> Alena N.: This video is . . . is . . . AMAZING! The song itself is awesome, but the pictures make it so much better![7]

Each of these comments reinforces that viewers find devotional images to be an experientially powerful component of worship videos, enhancing and even shaping how they interpret the worship song. Despite the vast differences in their creators' life situations, geographical locations, and denominational backgrounds, when the fifty worship videos were analyzed together, a constellation of common genre characteristic emerges that provides strong evidence of the extent to which visual dimension has become integral to the evangelical worship experience.

Table 5.1 shows the prevalence of the most commonly used kinds of visual media among the videos in my study. This table shows that song lyrics are one of the most important features of amateur worship videos: nearly three quarters of worship videos in the sample include the full song texts. But even more prevalent than song lyrics are still and moving background images. In my fifty-video sample, the three types of images used most frequently were nature images, depiction of worshipers, and depictions of Jesus. By examining why creators use these common visual categories and how viewers respond to them, we can better understand today's worship videos as extending and expanding on ties to preexisting evangelical visual devotional practices that also used images to enhance the emotional experience of belief.

Table 5.1. VISUAL ELEMENTS WITHIN
THE SAMPLE OF 50 YOUTUBE WORSHIP VIDEOS

Element	Prevalence
Images	88%
Song lyrics	74%
Nature images	64%
Depictions of worshiper(s)	38%
Depictions of Jesus	32%
Scriptural quotations	20%

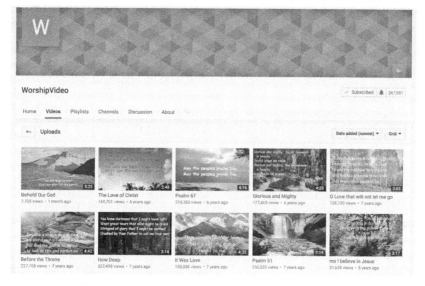

Figure 5.1: "WorshipVideo" upload index (2017).
Screenshot by the author.

By far, the most common type of images used in worship videos are still photographic images of nature, including seascapes, mountaintop vistas, and pristine forests, as well as close-up images of flowers and fauna. In most of song videos, these nature photos have little to do with the song lyrics, as the lyrics to these top-ranking worship songs tend to be fairly abstract. Figure 5.1 is a screenshot taken from the video page for an anonymous video creator whose worship videos have garnered over 269 million views, illustrates the prevalence of nature imagery.

Video creators who relied on nature photos told me they used them to point to aspects of God's beauty and power, using images of the creation to point to a benevolent Creator. They believed that nature images could provide a worshipful atmosphere while not distracting the viewer from the lyrical content or message of the song. Andrew, a creator from China, told me, "I almost exclusively use nature pics. I feel these better show God's creation without distracting too much from the lyrics" (email correspondence, February 27, 2012). Rebecca from Scotland similarly wrote that she chose primarily nature photos because she wanted "simple backdrops to the song lyrics" that did not "distract or detract from them" (email correspondence, March 26, 2012). Mark from California, who saw the purpose of his videos as both inspiring worship among Christians and evangelizing non-Christians, remarked that he believes God uses the biblical messages of the songs "combined with images of his [God's] beautiful creation . . . sometimes [to] open an individual's heart up and make him/her think" (email correspondence, March 9, 2012). He believes worship videos replete with scenes from nature "plant seeds in the hearts of those who do not believe, a little at a time."

Each of these worship-video creators idealized complementation, an interrelationship between musical and visual media described by Nicholas Cook in which forms of media are seen to work on separate levels to achieve a unified effect (Cook 1998a, 103–5). In this case, video creators see nature photos as serving the dominant medium—the sung texts—by working in the background to enhance, not detract from, an atmosphere of worship. Indeed, according to David Morgan, a historian of American visual culture, nature imagery has become a long-standing theme within American religious art because "many wish to regard [immensity] as the imprint of a higher reality" (2007, 232). Further, many nature photos evidence what Morgan calls, referring to the nature photography of Ansel Adams, "the sublime evacuation of human presence from nature" in which the images "register in their size and pristine antiquity some sort of awful gesture, the trace of something before humanity" (232). Nature images are uniquely capable of placating Protestant iconoclastic tendencies, providing a shadow of the sublime and providing visual evidence that stands in for an unrepresentable God.

While nature images may predominate within worship videos, there are two other important categories of images that challenge any easy designation of Protestant iconoclasm.[8] The second most common image type among the selected worship-video sample is a depiction of a single worshiper or groups of worshipers, shown with arms outstretched in prayer. The posture of hands upraised, a common expressive worship practice in evangelical and charismatic congregational singing, has become a more or less universal evangelical symbol for worship (for further discussion, refer to pp. 54–58 of the Introduction). In analyzing music, lyrics, and visual elements together, I found that worship-video creators commonly placed worship depictions at the musical climaxes within the song, especially at the beginning of a song's chorus where the instrumental texture, melodic height, and volume increase. The composite image in Figure 5.2 shows worshiper silhouettes used by three different worship video creators at the beginning of the anthemic chorus of the song "Blessed Be Your Name."

(a)

(b)

Figure 5.2: YouTube worship video images from the chorus of "Blessed Be Your Name," from Charlesc28 (2006), strings n harmony (2007), and RIP KING OF POP (2008). Screenshots by the author.

Worship videos rarely include photorealistic depictions of worshipers. Most often, worshiping bodies are featured as dark silhouettes against the backdrop of a plain color or highly stylized natural setting. Worshiper images often resemble the silhouetted bodies from ads made popular by Apple's iPod advertising campaign beginning in 2005. Justin Burton describes why the dancing silhouettes were key to the overwhelming success of the ad campaign: the dancers were "blank [human]-shaped spaces that could be filled with whatever identity a particular audience most wanted from [the iPod]" (2014, 7).

(c)

(d)

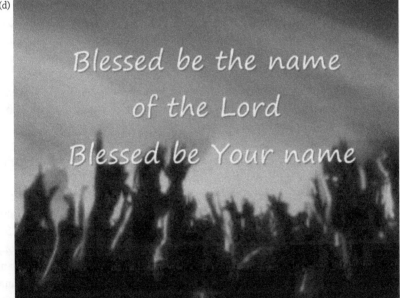

Figure 5.2: Continued.

He continues that this process of identification works two ways: "As [viewers] are invited to imagine themselves in the place of the silhouettes, they are also subsumed in Apple's overarching brand personality. The dancing every/wo/man in the silhouette ads [becomes] a nearly blank space in which any viewer might construct a persona alongside Apple's own brand identity" (7).

Likewise, by modeling the posture of worship at musical climaxes during these videos, the videos' creators show that they have internalized certain expectations of devotional practice and gesture. But they use worshipers not only to represent the act of worship, but also to actively *inspire* the act of worship. By invoking the bodily posture in which the viewer should be receiving the video, the creator inspires some viewers not only identify with or recognize the act, but also experience a bodily response. This dynamic is described by film scholar Vivian Sobchack, who argues that certain religious-themed films encourage the embodied experience of transcendence through "cinematic strategies meant not only to represent but also to present and solicit transcendent or 'spiritual' states of being from the viewer" (2008, 197). Despite the apparent limitations of the film media sensorium, religious moviegoers experience an embodied sense of "transcendence in immanence" that is "formally shaped and experientially heightened" by the sensual enhancement produced by image and sound (197). Similarly, in her study of pentecostal-charismatic video in Ghana, Marleen de Witte has argued that for viewers watching televised charismatic church services in a posture of worship, the visual representation of the worshiping bodies of pastors and congregation members become "'living icons' mediating the power of the Holy Spirit to the spectators by appealing to [viewers'] full sensory being" (2009, 202). Watching the actions of other worshipers "may trigger the viewer's embodied sensory memory of live church events and thereby evoke an experience of spirit presence" (193).

The third type of image used in worship videos mediates divine presence even more directly. Figure 5.3 shows the third type of image used most frequently in worship videos: depictions of Jesus.

The diverse array of Jesus figures in YouTube worship videos includes evangelical popular art from the nineteenth century to the present day, Orthodox and Catholic icons, and stills from films about the life of Jesus such as the International Bible Society's *The Jesus Film* (1979) or Mel Gibson's *The Passion of the Christ* (2004). Common subjects include scenes of the crucifixion, Jesus with the world in his hands, Jesus as King, or Jesus as shepherd. Figure 5.2 shows the range of images of Jesus used in YouTube worship videos of the song "Our God." David Morgan has shown that, though US evangelical Protestant churches may eschew visual aids to devotion in their public worship, individual believers have long used mass-mediated images of Jesus as objects of private devotion. For instance, in examining the historical use and popular understanding of the popular devotional art of Warner Sallman, Morgan asserts that for pious viewers, Warner Sallman's mass-produced representations of Jesus "make visual, and therefore in some sense embody, the personal savior, who 'saves, comforts, and defends' them" (1996, 192). This representational practice corresponds to a key feature of evangelical Christianity: the importance of a personal relationship with God in Jesus Christ. Through images

(a)

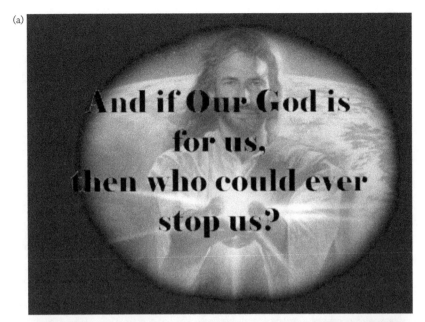

(b)

Figure 5.3: Depictions of Jesus from YouTube worship videos for "Our God," from Always4Jesus7 (2011), juanguaco (2011), rosinkrans17 (2010), and Maltesepilgrim (2010). Screenshots by the author.

of Jesus, "Christ's personal significance for one's life is made visual: the face that one sees belongs to the divinity who cares personally for one's welfare. This visual personification of Christ clearly serves the evangelical imperative for a personal relationship with Jesus. Christ is encountered face-to-face" (1996, 193).

Exploring the resonances and functions of the three most common image types in worship videos suggests some of the ways that images, text, and

(c)

(d)

Figure 5.3: Continued.

music come together to form a potent experiential whole. The nature images in worship videos evoke an atmosphere of worship. Depictions of worshipers model the bodily posture of devotion, giving viewers a template to project past and present experience. And depictions of Jesus remind their viewers of the Divine Subject of worship. As a result, viewers are enabled not only to identify with or recall worship in church settings, but also to experience a real-time physical and emotional response in front of their computer screens. Indeed, among the digital cacophony of trolls, theological debates, shout-outs, and prayer requests, some YouTube users use the comments section for testimonies of how this particular video has invoked a personal experience with the divine. For many worship-video viewers, the video reminds them of powerful "live" worship experiences in the past—for instance, the first time they heard this song in church or at a conference. Some viewers also post narratives of their responses when watching the worship video, ranging from singing along loudly to the video, to being moved to tears by the video, to experiencing chills or goosebumps, or to feeling moved to spontaneously raise their hands in worship in front of their computer screen. These responses indicate that YouTube users who view worship videos whose bodies are inclined in what Sobchack refers to as "mimetic sympathy" with the worshiper icon experience physical reactions associated with expressive worship in congregational settings (Sobchack 2004, 2008). Worship videos model a particular devotional posture and invite their viewers to adopt it. For those YouTube viewers who approach the videos in a posture of worship, it appears that worship videos can produce the "worship experience" that they recognize from congregational worship, mediating a sense of divine presence and evoking the same expressive worshipful responses as affective times of congregational singing.

HEARING *AND* SEEING GOD'S WORDS: KATAPHATIC PRAYER AND THE MULTIMEDIA WORSHIP EXPERIENCE

The previous section illustrated the convergence of visual and aural worship practices to create new audiovisual devotional practices. For a better understanding of how these elements work together to help produce the evangelical worship experience, anthropologist T.M. Luhrmann's observations on evangelical prayer practices provide a useful framework. The assumptions that ground evangelical prayer, according to Luhrmann, are that "God wants to be your friend; you develop that relationship through prayer; prayer is hard work and requires effort and training; and when you develop that relationship, God will answer back, through thoughts and mental images he places in your mind, and through sensations he causes in your body" (2012, 41). In order to experience divine connection, she argues, evangelicals must develop a framework to interpret both the bodily sensations and thoughts (which, she notes, are often treated more like perceptions) that are generated during the time of prayer and "learn to trust that they really are [God-generated]" (41).

Luhrmann describes evangelical prayer as "kataphatic," dominated by a flood of images, words, and sounds. Kataphatic prayer "asks people to dwell lovingly on what is imagined . . . they engage the senses, they evoke vivid memories, and they generate powerful emotions" (162). Interpreting God's voice, then, involves cultivating an inner sense, acquiring the "learned skill of picking from among the many sources of input which ones resonate deeply and attribute them to God" (184). In Luhrmann's view, hearing is the privileged sense in kataphatic devotional practices, and she asserts that evangelical prayer primarily "cultivates the auditory imagination" (184). Evangelical prayer practices centered around contemporary worship music, however, have elevated the visual dimension to a new prominence; here, sound and sight cannot be so easily separated, and visual stimuli can act as powerful interpretants alongside spoken and sung words. Within both individual devotion and private worship centered on music, contemporary evangelical worship has become a site of audiovisual convergence.

Within contemporary worship environments that are highly audiovisual, there are more communicative media forms involved, and therefore many ways to interpret God's voice. I recount one memorable event from field research at a worship conference in the United Kingdom, an occasion that drove home to me just how important the comingling of input from multiple media are in producing spiritual sensations and interpretations:

November 17, 2012—Morning Session at the Mission: Worship Conference, Eastbourne, United Kingdom

During an extended weekend in November 2012, I attended a conference for leaders of contemporary worship music in the southern coastal city of Eastbourne, United Kingdom.[9] I was one of about 1,500 participants gathered in the Congress Theatre, the largest performance venue in the city's modest-sized conference center complex, for a two-and-a-half-hour morning session. To my left sat Sharon, a middle-aged church pianist and singer who chose the songs for the volunteer worship band at her small nondenominational evangelical church in Kent. Before the session began, we introduced ourselves and engaged in small talk for a few minutes, exchanging stories about music at our churches and highlights of the conference so far. The morning session began with a forty-minute worship set led by Brazilian worship leader Nivea Soares, followed by a short message and forty-minute set from US worship leader Paul Baloche.

Immediately after the service ended, I was taken aback when Sharon turned to me and effervesced for several minutes about a powerful spiritual experience she'd had during the opening worship set. Excitedly, she opened her conference program book and pointed to an advertisement page on which she had scrawled numerous words and phrases that had stood out to her during the singing. Most of them, I noticed, were song titles and lyric fragments. Sharon told me that during one particularly powerful worship song led by Nivea Soares, she had closed her eyes and seen swirling blue and green colors forming an orb of light. She said that after she had opened her eyes, she was shocked to see exactly the same colors projected on the screen behind the song lyrics. She interpreted this correspondence between what she had seen with her eyes and with her mind's eye as a message from God. Sharon prayed fervently that God would reveal to her the meaning of these corresponding colors as she sang. Later in the worship set, she was led to an interpretation: the blue and green and the orb-shaped light represented the world. For further proof of divine inspiration, she pointed to the song titles and phrases she had scrawled all over her conference program. Most of them, she told me animatedly, elaborated the same theme: that God was ruler over all the earth. She interpreted this as a message that she needed to hear in the midst of the lack of control she felt sometimes over her daily life and of reports of violence in Britain and elsewhere in the world: that all things were under God's sovereign control and, despite apparent chaos and un-certainty, everything was working according to God's ultimate plan. Through her powerful experience that evening, Sharon was convinced that God had spoken to her and felt she needed to share the message with her congregation. She planned to discuss the theme with her pastor and told me that her revelatory experience would strongly inform what songs she chose for her church when she returned home.

In a densely textured multimedia environment, worshipers like Sharon are given many elements to sift through when seeking to interpret God's speaking to them. Within the densely textured multimedia environment of an audio-visual worship experience, the involvement of a greater variety of communi-cative media offers worshipers many more ways to personally make sense of and interpret God's voice. Digital audiovisual technologies juxtapose sung and projected lyrics, visuals, and music, and these elements can be used individ-ually or in combination as catalysts for spiritual reflection. Deeply felt spir-itual interpretations like Sharon's find coherence in elements that may or may not be designed to be coherent. In designing a powerful worship experience, then, producers must create a multimedia environment that is easy to per-sonalize, enabling individuals to deepen their relationship with God through communicating their love for God and interpreting God speaking to them. Worshipers must be able to interpret the meanings from visual, aural, and tac-tile sources as consistent with shared tenets of evangelical faith and elements of practice. Beyond that, worship producers are free to emphasize their own meanings and to reinforce the signature emphases of the event or even the worship brand as a whole.

In his work on multimedia relationships, Nick Cook (1998a) identified three potential relationships between multiple media in a particular instance: conform-ance, complementation, and contest. Conformance occurs when forms of media correspond directly to one another or when one is subservient to the others. Complementation refers to media forms that serve different roles but reinforce the same overall set of themes or interpretations. And when two or more forms of media are in contest, they "[vie] for the same terrain, each attempting to impose its characteristics on the other" (103). Worship producers try to avoid contest, but instances vary in whether conformance or complementation is valued and promoted. Worship-technology workshops at conferences for worship leaders and literature often seek to teach people the meanings of their technologies and how to harmonize or conform these to a particular set of beliefs. At the beginning of the digital revolution in the mid-2000s, there was a focus on choosing fonts and background images that advanced the meaning of the text. The power of digitally projected words to complement—and, arguably, to nuance, enhance, alter, or subvert—how worshipers interpret sung texts is something that professional creators of visual resources for churches have considered.

Digital words themselves are, like images, capable of serving an iconic function. In an article from a 2004 issue of *Worship Technologies Magazine Online*, church media expert Phil Bates gives examples of how still and moving background images can (and by implication, should) conform with and complement the song lyrics:

> When the lyrics say "You are my Rock," the editor should be prepared with mountains, rock formations or some other representation of something steadfast or permanent. An image of flowers can send a conflicting message and undermine the song's purpose. When the lyrics say "I will rise like an eagle . . ." there should be aerials, or cloud footage on hand. On other phrases that have a more subtle content like "I look up to you. . . ," I often show a camera tiltup to the sun. (Bates 2005)

But Bates's concern with conformance doesn't stop at text. He is also concerned with linking the image to the song's *musical* elements, giving suggestions for backgrounds that match the songs' tempo, texture, and dynamics. Bates goes on to tell his readers how to create conformance between visuals and music:

> Some songs have a large contrast between the verses and the chorus. Songs like All Of My Days and Need You Here by Hillsong get very big during the chorus. To support this change, I often use brighter imagery or abstract imagery with elements that are rising or bursting out from the center like kaleidoscopes. (2005)

Throughout the 2000s, as professionally created worship media became more sophisticated, many worship videos and projection for live worship events stopped relying exclusively on still nature images and began to showcase elaborate, moving texts. While this change may seem to suggest a resurgent iconoclasm, a closer look at these word videos shows that the digital words themselves function much as background images do in creating a platform for affective experience. Like images, these digitally projected, dynamic words afford a new set of possibilities within the evangelical worship experience.

Examining closely a lyric video from a professionally produced worship video well illustrates the ways that digitally projected words are used for aesthetic effects in ways similar to images. In 2002, Integrity Media launched iWorship, a DVD product line juxtaposing professional recordings of popular worship songs with evocative imagery, promising "a total worship experience . . . especially designed to enhance the worshiper's experience through breathtaking visuals."[10] At the beginning, most of the visuals used within iWorship's song videos were nature photos; however, by the late 2000s, some of the videos relied solely on the artistic treatment of the words overtop abstract backgrounds. *iWorship Volume O* (2009) claims to use "the most advanced audiovisual presentation" to "bring worship to life" in settings including both personal and congregational worship. This volume begins with a word video for "Hosanna," a worship song made that was popular by Australia's Hillsong United and that went on to become one of the twenty-five most frequently sung worship songs in the United States from 2011 through 2013. As the song starts, before any words appear on the screen, the worshiper is invited into an immersive three-dimensional visual space. Three juxtaposed, looped layers create the perception of depth in the visual field of the video: there is a top layer of gently rotating scrollwork, a middle-range backdrop of points of light rising slowly like bubbles, and an abstractly patterned background of rust-orange and soft yellow sunset hues coming in and out of focus and providing a visual endpoint. Shifts in the orientation of the scrollwork and abstract background underscore both musical and structural changes; these layers both rotate ninety degrees counterclockwise at the middle of each verse and then right themselves to demarcate the song's chorus.

The verse lyrics are presented in a thin-weighted outline serif font that seems calculated to be unobtrusive; the spaces within the letters reveal the shifting background images behind them, making the lyric's layer blend in with the others within the space. The lyrics appear in chunks of a few words each, and there are generally fewer than five words on the screen at any one time. Differences in the size or placement of the font—sometimes subtle, sometimes more pronounced—give added emphasis to words that one might not expect to be highlighted. The first verse ends with the moving text foregrounding the musically underemphasized word "SING" in large capital letters, while in the second verse, the word "REVIVAL" gets similar treatment. The words of the song's minimalist chorus receive the most elaborate treatment:

Hosanna hosanna
Hosanna in the highest
Hosanna hosanna
Hosanna in the highest[11]

In the video, each iteration of "hosanna" is treated as an independent word image: from the abstract background, the inky black text slowly erupts from the middle of the word outward to its edges, shimmering like ripples in oily water as it expands. Each hosanna rises slowly up the screen as it expands outward and then disappears again as it is replaced by the next word or phrase.

The song's textural and dynamic climax occurs during the instrumental interlude and bridge that follow the second chorus. Here, just as instrumental texture thickens, three more visual layers are added to the abstract background: a moving starfield that gives the viewers the sense that they are traveling quickly, and two different layers of fast-moving clouds that move obliquely to the starfield. In the penultimate chorus, the texture suddenly thins to the solo voice and keyboard and the visual dimensions are stripped down to match. On the final chorus, all of the visual layers present at the beginning return (including one of the bridge's added cloud layers), and the song ends on a more visually and musical dynamic note than it began.

The "Hosanna" lyric video shows how digitally projected words can function much like images, communicating on levels that include but extend beyond semantic meaning. While evangelicals might view this lyric video and others like it as simply "expressing the text," obvious interpretive decisions are interlaced throughout: font size, type, color, shape, and movement are all materials the video creators have chosen, both to convey which words and ideas are significant and to create a general atmosphere for contemplating them. Presentational media forms like those in this lyric video communicate through juxtaposed visual elements even without explicit use of the nature images or icons. The shifting, changing visual patterns accompanying dynamic, moving words provide a wealth of visual materials for a worshiper watching the video in a posture of devotion to interpret as spiritual messages.

FROM CHURCH ONLINE TO VEVO CHURCH: THE AUDIOVISUAL WORSHIP EXPERIENCE AS PORTABLE PRACTICE

Audiovisual worship media builds on the success of worship music recordings and extends their reach and potency. Digital audiovisual technologies have further extended the ability of the individual to choose when and where to worship and have intensified the experience. With the advent of media products like iWorship DVDs, the worship experience can be recreated wherever there is a screen and the capacity for producing—or often simply for reproducing—high-quality pop music. iWorship DVDs, intended for both congregational viewing and home use, were harbingers of the possibilities of audiovisual media in creating continuity between corporate worship and private devotion. Drawing from media theorist Jonathan Steuer (1992) and his work on how virtual reality establishes a sense of presence, Deb Lubken argues that audiovisual resources for private devotional practice like iWorship are more effective at establishing a sense of divine presence because they are more affective: they "engage multiple senses (sensory breadth) through high quality channels (sensory depth) and evoke a greater sense of presence than single channel media or media with poor quality auditory or visual components" (2005, 15).

The Christian media industry promoted audio and video recordings as a personal worship experience that could be had anywhere, at anytime. Anna Nekola (2013) has argued that sound recordings established this foundation. By analyzing advertisements in evangelical magazines and Internet media, Nekola demonstrates how, beginning in the mid-1990s, the US worship music industry began to market musical recordings not just as tools for congregational worship, "but also as products for Christian consumers . . . to relive or even recreate the experience of worship outside of church (117)." Worship music producers promised their products would "transform any profane or secular space into a sacred 'sanctuary' and transform the listener spiritually by transporting him or her into the presence of God" (117). "Not only do these advertisements promise to transform one's everyday life into worship, they also reinforce the discourse that worship is an 'experience' that should 'overwhelm' the listener with feeling" (127–128). The worship experience is an excellent example of what Thomas Csordas calls a "portable practice," that is, a religious practice that travels easily and successfully into new contexts (Csordas 2009, 4–5). Csordas defines portable practices as religious rituals that are easily learned, that are not perceived to be linked to a specific cultural context, and that can be performed without commitment to a particular ideology or set of institutions (4).

The popularity and ease of new interactive social media forms in the first decade of the twenty-first century, forms that involved the democratization both of tools for creating worship videos and enabled new modes of participation in "live" events, blurred this line even further. The pervasive use of digital audiovisual media in worship, as well as the ability of Web 2.0 to provide resources and a platform for experience, enables churches to blur lines between "live" worship and immersive, "virtual" experiences even further. Large ministries and worship brands design creative ways to engage their followers online. By the end of the 2000s, worship conferences like Passion and Hillsong had begun live-streaming some of their events. Hillsong has both a dedicated website channel featuring prerecorded video of its worship events and teaching (http://www.hillsong.com/channel) and a website for live-streamed church services and events (http://www.hillsong.com/watch) (Figure 5.4). The Passion Conference has made extensive use of simulcasting within its annual live events, as well as livestreaming. In January 2018, the three-day Passion Conference, also made available on live stream, drew an estimated

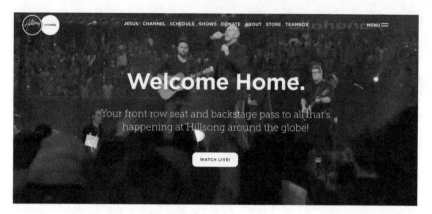

Figure 5.4: Hillsong channel home page (2017).
Screenshot by the author.

32,000 participants to four locations simultaneously (three sports arenas in Atlanta and one in Washington, D.C.), where attendees watched speakers and sang along with worship bands present onstage at their location, as well as the bands live-streamed from the other venues. In these ways, live-streaming technologies blur online and offline online venues and create new ways for individuals to participate with these global brands and produce the desire to join in the live worship experience.

Digital audiovisual media and screen culture of evangelical worship have created a feedback loop between online and offline, private and collective devotional practices. For churches that do not have the financial or human resources (e.g., highly skilled musicians, state-of-the art audio and visual technology, or a large gathering space) to produce the ideal worship experience, there are now audiovisual materials for building worship experiences in their local gatherings, ranging from free promotional materials to paid content. Many of the amateur YouTube worship-video creators I spoke with make their videos in the first instance for use in public worship and post them online as a free resource for other small congregations (see Ingalls 2016 for further discussion). And the Christian media industry now provides free resources like official lyric videos intended for congregational use. Steven Bradley, a friend and research consultant who leads worship at a small Methodist church in a Louisville suburb, coined the memorable description for this phenomenon: "VEVO church."[12]

When Steve and I spoke a few months later about the phenomenon, he told me he had coined the designation VEVO church to describe those churches which rely on prerecorded audiovisual materials to accompany their congregational singing. In his experience traveling in and out of area churches as a piano tuner, he has found that an increasing number of small Baptist and Methodist churches transitioned to using videos available for purchase or downloaded for free off celebrity worship leaders' YouTube VEVO sites to supplement—and in a few instances, to replace entirely—church musicians. In Steve's assessment, the VEVO church phenomenon was not created simply by a lack of musical or personnel resources; it was also a growing sense within these small churches that they could not measure up to the new musical standard. Steve tells about a conversation he'd had recently after his church's evening service with Carl, an older man in the congregation. With nostalgia in his voice, the man recollected gospel singing nights in the rural Methodist church where he grew up. The piano was never tuned, but everyone sang loudly and didn't much care; "of course, we would never be able to get away with that today," he mused. Steve, citing the pervasive use of electronic keyboards and the volume of music available online, agreed with Carl's assessment: "In today's society, doing the best you can [as a small church] just may not be good enough." Steve's observations about VEVO churches suggest the growing pervasiveness and power of several worship music brands. The next section details their interlocked promotional strategies and charts the extent of their influence.

NETWORKED INDIVIDUALS, BRANDED COMMUNITIES: CORPORATE™ WORSHIP IN CONGREGATIONAL NETWORKS

Networked congregations center around the production of audiovisual worship experiences for diffuse evangelical audiences, produced by portable technologies and mediated by screens large and small. Previous discussions in this chapter highlighted the agency of individual evangelical users in selecting and using these resources for their own spiritual and creative ends. While acknowledging the personal agency that these democratized digital technologies enable, however, it is equally important to recognize the increasing power of the Christian commercial music and media industries to structure individual choices and expectations. The tightening control of several influential worship music and media brands was evident to me when, in early 2017, I returned to survey the same field of fifty amateur-created videos on YouTube five years after of my initial study in 2012 (see Ingalls 2016). Going in, I wondered: would a YouTube search still reveal preponderance of amateur worship music videos with high view counts, or would the professionally created "official" videos from well-known worship music brands have supplanted them? My search by song title for worship music videos conducted in 2017 turned up far more official videos than amateur-created ones. The worship music videos from YouTube's early days, those personal expressions of devotion often layered with idiosyncratic interpretations of songs and lyrics, have given way to polished audiovisual products broadcast centrally to promote the events and recordings of international worship brands. In part, the eclipse of amateur worship videos by professional audiovisual media producers is a symptom of a transition in YouTube's platform. José van Dijck (2009) notes that YouTube's user interface has gradually moved from "homecasting" amateur videos to broadcasting professionally generated content. YouTube "prioritizes television features over social networking" (114) as its algorithms increasingly "shepherd" users toward "fewer choices . . . and TV-like channels" (131).

Megachurch music ministries, in collaboration with the Christian media and recording industries, have capitalized on this platform transition, flooding the online marketplace with the products that enable and produce networked congregations. The process is usually cyclical: these worship brands have risen to prominence precisely because they have taken full advantage of social media outlets, thus creating their own dominion that extends across both physical and virtual space. From an institutional perspective, these worship brands can be considered successful congregational networks; in other words, by means of deploying the most current communications media, they have created a large, diffuse network of congregants—whether avid church attenders, annual conference-goers, or occasional concert attendees—who feel connected to others in the network and have become stakeholders in the brand.

To identify how the worship experience has served as the basis for these evangelical media empires arising since the turn of the millennium, this section examines aspects of the online presence of three global brands that are each widely recognized in the contemporary North American context. Passion, Hillsong, and Bethel are three transnational worship brands based in Atlanta, Sydney, and Redding (California), respectively, and can also be understood as gigantic and densely networked congregations. Each of these branded empires combines many if not most of the modes of congregating that this book has discussed. Hillsong and Bethel are multisite churches consisting of multiple local gatherings for worship in different cities, and both put on influential conferences (now with many sessions live-streamed) that draw tens of thousands of attendees from across the world each year. Passion began as a conference—one that, in signature fashion, invites area churches to gather with the conference crowd in large outdoor public space on the final night and form a public congregation—and expanded from there to worship-leader concert tours. In 2009, Passion's founder, Louie Giglio, and celebrity worship leaders started a "local" church congregation in Atlanta, a site that was averaging 2,000 attendees weekly services a mere one year after its founding.[13] All three host large and well-known conferences, and their worship leaders and bands are well-known recording artists who regularly tour nationally and internationally.

Social media has brought about a new era of evangelical broadcasting marked by media convergence and saturation. The ability to broadcast church services is no longer limited to the highest bidder for the limited spectrum of television airwaves; now any church or ministry with a sufficient technological infrastructure can webcast. Individual worshipers can partake of services at the church of their choice in a wide variety of formats, including events streamed in real time, "full service re-airs,"[14] or archived video recordings. And worship media content is available in a variety of sizes to fit all schedules, ranging from individual songs to entire "worship experiences." Each of these networked worship brands makes full use of the various capacities of online media forms to connect with worshipers and promote their brand. In the on-line marketplace, worship music from widely known artists, along with celebrity pastors' sermons, is packaged and sold or used as "free" promotional material for other paid media content.

On its website, the Sydney location of the multi-campus megachurch Hillsong provides free access to a live stream of its Sunday morning services and posts a prerecorded video of the service the following week. While this content is freely available, Hillsong generates revenue from its annual conference and musical recordings from its various ministries geared to different age demographics. Tanya Riches has dubbed Hillsong's standardized music production calendar their "liturgical calendar" (Riches 2010, 146), organized around the twin poles of two annual live musical albums. Other church networks like Bethel monetize their weekly worship experiences in addition to their musical recordings. On the homepage of Bethel Church.tv, the streaming site for the Redding, California–based multisite megachurch, the tagline "fueling personal revival" is superimposed on a series of rotating images, depicting worship (Figure 5.5), preaching, and scenes from church members' daily lives. Serving over one million viewers per month, Bethel offers viewers a range of media packages with four levels of access, from a free subscription to one message per week to an all-access "season pass" that includes weekend services and all Bethel conferences—over twenty-five hours of original content per month (Figure 5.6).[15]

Passion has demonstrated similar ingenuity in using social media to create a devoted congregational network. The year 2010 was pivotal for Passion's audiovisual media marketing; that year, Passion began offering selected audiovisual content for free on its newly inaugurated VEVO channel, live-streaming promotional "taster" events, and packaging its conference media content. By February 2018, Passion's VEVO channel had over 250,000 subscribers, and its ninety-two videos had amassed nearly 100 million views.[16] Like Hillsong and Bethel, Passion has also made use of live-streamed events to give viewers a taste of the Passion "experience." At the invitation of a promotional email, I "attended" one of these online events from my couch on a Monday evening in September 2010. This two-and-a-half-hour live-streamed event gave viewers a taste of the Passion "experience": the evening was structured like a typical session at Passion (a forty-minute opening worship set led by Chris Tomlin

Figure 5.5: Bethel.tv channel home page (2017).
Screenshot by the author.

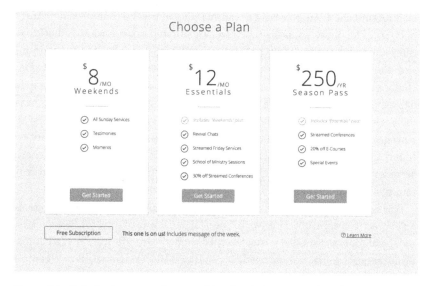

Figure 5.6: Bethel.tv home page bottom with subscription options (2017).
Screenshot by the author.

and band, prayer aloud in small groups, a biblical message delivered by Louie Giglio, and closing song set), though it also included a heavy dose of advertising for upcoming Passion conferences, tours, and recordings.

Also beginning in 2010, the Passion conference began selling Digital All Access passes that progressively release videos of talks and worship-song performances from the conference along with behind-the-scenes stories. I purchased a pass after attending the January 2013 conference (Figure 5.7). Every few days for several weeks, I received an email notification that Passion had released a new talk or song video from the conference. The "grand finale" of the digital content release was the debut of *Let the Future Begin,* the live worship album recorded at the conference, in March 2013.

Passion's Digital All Access passes not only enable worshipers who attended the conference to remember and relive their experience, but they also extend a sense of belonging to former attendees beyond their college years. Passion's online store contains this product review from 2016 All Access Pass purchaser Christopher:

> For those of us who are no longer 20 (or even close), getting the all access pass from the most recent Passion is the next best thing to being young again lol! The messages are shared with all members of my family to watch and of course, the new CD is filled with some of the strongest songs of any Passion release to date. It is beautiful to see Jesus being lifted up by the younger generation and the access pass is always a great value. I do hope Passion continues to do all access passes, so that hopefully my daughter in 2018 will be able to remember her first trip to Passion in this way. Thank you friends at Passion! :)[17]

Significantly, in 2013, Passion's integrated strategy propelled Chris Tomlin's album *God's Great Dance Floor* to the number-one spot on the *Billboard* top 200 charts—only the fourth Christian album ever to attain *Billboard*'s top spot—in the second week of January 2013. Of the 73,000 recordings sold that week, an estimated 40 percent came from prerelease sales at Atlanta's Passion Church and Passion Conference preorders (Caulfield 2013). (One of these prerelease purchases was mine. At the end of the 2013 Passion Conference, when purchasing

Figure 5.7: Passion Digital All Access Pass (2013).
Screenshot by the author.

a Digital All Access Pass, I recall taking advantage of the substantial discount that was extended to conference-goers who preordered the Tomlin album.)

In each of these branded online worship experiences, it is difficult to see where evangelical institutions end and media industries begin. Worship on the small screen allows influential ministries and worship leaders to broadcast their messages and songs far and wide and, in doing so, to build an even larger base of constituents. As Tom Wagner has shown in his work on how music and social media fit into Hillsong's branding practices, this multi-pronged promotional strategy is remarkably effective because it gives individual worshipers' a strong sense of agency even as it uses their active and enthusiastic participation to spread its message and products (T. Wagner 2014a, 2014b). Through Hillsong's "two-way" social media marketing campaigns, participants are "afforded a real, immediate experience of God through its participants' own agency" (2014b, 35). Worship brands like Hillsong and Passion have mobilized social media to create powerful congregational networks in which evangelical worshipers are nodes. These participatory consumers form interconnected links in increasingly diffuse and widespread networks by participating with the brand on social media as well as promoting it in their offline relationships and in the process enlisting others.

CONCLUSION: NETWORKED CONGREGATIONS AND SHIFTING MODES OF EVANGELICAL COMMUNITY AND AUTHORITY

The rise of the networked congregation that promulgates the multimedia worship experience carries several important implications for evangelical sociality, that is, what it means and feels like to be part of a Christian community and what belonging looks and sounds like. Among individual worshipers, networked congregations encourage a sense of belonging that is often diffuse. On the one hand, these developments appear to augment the agency of individual worshipers: the worshiper can choose from a plethora of audiovisual worship materials—from interactive worship music recordings to live-streamed conferences to prerecorded full church services—and engage with them wherever and whenever he or she wishes. These audiovisual media resources have made it easy for individuals to participate in several types of congregations simultaneously where they are connected to a constant stream of musical resources for personal devotion. In this new kind of religious networked sociality, individuals can choose the networks with which they want to be affiliated and their level of commitment to these networks. For instance, one can regularly attend a satellite church of a multisite congregation on Sundays; travel annually to conferences like Passion and maintain a sense of connection throughout the year via live-streamed events, concert tours, and podcasts; view on occasion the weekly gathering of a megachurch like Hillsong or Bethel; and view worship videos on YouTube of amateur worship-video creators as well as "official" videos from powerful worship brands. These various networked congregations can overlap, synergize, or even contradict.

On the other hand, and somewhat paradoxically, the ascendancy of individual choice over congregational networks plays into the hands of large corporations and powerful media industries, concentrating cultural power and financial capital in the hands of a shrinking few, a consolidation that in turn limits the options available on the online marketplace for worship media. In her study of user agency on social media, José van Dijck concludes that "instead of bringing down the reigning professional leagues, [user-generated content] actually boosts the power of media moguls, enhancing their system of star ratings and upward mobility" (2009, 53). In her study of "amateur-to-amateur" (A2A) music pedagogy on YouTube, Kiri Miller similarly observes that "A2A discourse flourishes in connection with practices that involve canons, codified techniques, acknowledged master practitioners, and instruments that shape practitioners' experiences. These established structures give rise to shared knowledge and visceral experiences that in turn build a scaffold for meaningful online discourse" (2012, 218). In other words, online technologies that enable greater individual control of musical learning can destabilize certain hierarchies, remove cultural intermediaries, and provide space for experimentation, all the while reinforcing and extending the domain of the most powerful players in the commercial marketplace.

Because evangelical worshipers who desire powerful worship experiences are armed with increased awareness of the various networked congregations in which these regularly take place, there is pressure on congregations of all sizes to conform to expectations set by a limited set of powerful players in the evangelical media industry. As this chapter demonstrated, expectations of the worship experience produced during times of congregational singing increasingly rely upon high-tech audiovisual technologies that require access to a certain set of resources to execute successfully. Congregational music-making, particularly within smaller congregations, often seems subpar in comparison to the powerful musical experiences on offer at the click of a mouse or swipe of a screen. Where the desire for an audiovisual worship experience is not being or cannot be met in local churches, individuals have an increasing array of options for having this felt need meet elsewhere. They actively seek out worship media—both recorded audiovisual resources and live conferences or concert tours—to get what one young man at a Nashville worship concert described to me as his "worship fix." Others resort to finding a sense of belonging in online congregations built around YouTube videos or live-streamed services from well-known churches. Some affiliate with multiple worship brands—more than once over the course of fieldwork, I heard

omeone knowledgeable about current trends in worship music self-describe
as a "worship junkie."

The language of addiction ("worship fix," "worship junkie") evidences the overwhelming success of the major worship brands in not just responding to felt needs,
but also actively producing desire. In his work on the series of transformations
collectively known as globalization, Michel-Rolph Trouillot writes of the formative role of global-communications media in creating desire across geographical
and cultural space for the same objects (and, by extension, experiences):

> The integration of the market [for cheap consumer goods], the speed of com-
> munications, and the oligopolies in media and entertainment contribute to
> projecting the same image of the good life all over the world. Prompted by global
> media, more human beings than ever before share similar lists of the products
> they need to consume and the objects they need to possess in order to achieve
> individual satisfaction. In that sense we are truly witnessing for the first time,
> especially among the youth, a global production of desire. (2007, 60)

In parallel fashion, successful worship brands, though multi-pronged
networked strategies, have come to define the worship experience—a cor-
nerstone of the "good life" for devoted evangelicals—leaving their audiences
hungry for more. The worship experience, visceral proof of divine connection,
is the lynchpin in the affective economics of the worship media industry. Henry
Jenkins has described the way global brands create and exploit emotional
capital; he uses Saatchi and Saatchi CEO Kevin Roberts's term "lovemark"
to describe the way successful media brands "command the love as well as
the respect of consumers" (Jenkins 2006, 72). Likewise, major players in the
worship media industry have saturated the market through brand extension,
in which experiences are not "contained within a single media platform, but
extend[s] across as many media as possible" (69). The constant connection
that social media allows unites worshipers through a range of experiences
that encompass and infiltrate all five modes of congregating that this book
has discussed. Being part of these networked congregations is changing the
way evangelicals understand and experience congregational worship by combining and conflating different spaces and creating synergy across mediated
and live performances.

As evangelicalism has entered the digital age, its congregational worship
has become a prime example of media convergence as described by Henry
Jenkins: a place "where old and new media collide, where grassroots and
corporate media intersect, where the power of the media producer and
the power of the media consumer interact in unpredictable ways" (2006,
2). Worshipers exhibit similar "migratory behavior" to the late capitalist
consumers that Jenkins describes, "going almost anywhere in search of the

kinds of entertainment experiences"—here we could substitute "worship experiences"—"they want" (2). However democratic these moves may be, the fact remains that the power to define and circulate these affective experiences are being concentrated in the hand of a few global worship music brands, highly successful and pervasive congregational networks that influence the balance of power within and among evangelical individuals, institutions, and commercial industries. The book's conclusion examines further the implications of the creation of a global "mainstream" model of music, worship, and congregating; probes contemporary evangelical reactions to it; and suggests potential future directions that tension between these sources of authority may lead.

NOTES

1. Other writers from Christian and Jewish communities have used this term but with slightly different resonances. To date, it has mainly been used in educational materials written to help existing congregations navigate new digital technologies. Andrea Useem's 2009 booklet *The Networked Congregation: Embracing the Spirit of Experimentation,* published by the Alban Institute provides an accessible overview of technological changes in the 2000s decade (particularly the advent of Web 2.0) in order to help congregations adapt to the new possibilities of digital and social media technologies. Similarly, Barry Camson and Debra Brosan (2013) define Jewish synagogues and groups as "networked congregations" by the extent to which they have adopted networked practices of sociability, such as non-hierarchical and voluntaristic organization, fluid membership, and use of new technologies to advance their goals.
2. According to the 2011 CCLI License Holder Survey, 50 percent of the same churches polled reported that they also used hymnals. This statistic suggests that many churches are supplementing rather than replacing their hymnals wholesale with computer projection (2012b).
3. Popular worship presentation software packages include ProPresenter, EasyWorship, and MediaShout. For an overview of some of these programs, see Lauren Hunter's "Worship Software Guide: Options for Every Church from Small to Mega," accessed July 26, 2016, available at Church Tech Today, http://churchtechtoday.com/2015/10/01/worship-software-guide-options-for-every-church-from-small-to-mega.
4. Many of these magazines are now produced exclusively online, though many back issues of the print articles are available in the online archives. See http://www.twfm.com and https://www.churchproduction.com.
5. In this article, Thornton and Evans 2015 analyze the online discourse surrounding a selected YouTube video sample to describe the characteristics of the Christian community formed around online song videos.
6. In carving out the field for my study, I narrowed my video search to the five most frequently sung worship songs in the United States, according to Christian Copyright Licensing International (CCLI) Top 25 Worship Songs for the August 2011 Royalty Payout Period (CCLI 2011). I then searched for these songs on YouTube, selecting the top ten amateur-created worship videos (filtering the

search results by "most relevant") related to each of the five songs for analysis. These fifty videos became both analytical material and field-research sites: in addition to aural and visual analyses, I conducted interviews with these videos' creators and waded through thousands of public remarks on song comment pages.

7. These remarks are each taken from the comments section of rosinkrans17, "Our God—Chris Tomlin (And if Our God Is for Us)" posted November 17, 2010, accessed April 24, 2017, http://www.youtube.com/watch?v=UdFzB4MQgEA.

8. Though my field interlocutors readily described the reasons they used images from nature, they rarely mentioned or reflected on other types of images so prevalent within worship videos. Their reticence or inability to articulate the purposes of other categories of images suggests an ongoing tension in how evangelicals understand the power and appropriateness of images in worship.

9. This research was conducted immediately before the buyout and eventual dissolution of Eastbourne's Kingsway's Music by US publisher David C. Cook. From the early 1980s to 2014, Eastbourne was the center of commercial evangelical-worship music production in the United Kingdom. Eastbourne hosted the headquarters of Kingsway Music, then the largest UK recording and publishing company (see Ward 2005 for a detailed history of Kingsway and evangelical worship music in the United Kingdom more generally). The Mission: Worship Conference, then the largest UK worship music-related conference, met annually in Eastbourne's convention center complex. It regularly featured celebrity worship leaders from the United Kingdom and United States and sometimes further afield (Brazil, South Africa, New Zealand, etc.).

10. Lubken 2005 provides a content analysis of the first four iWorship DVDs, and Ingalls 2016 discusses how this product line has expanded into products designed for use in congregational settings.

11. HOSANNA (Fraser). Brooke Fraser Ligertwood. ©2007 Hillsong Music Publishing (APRA) (adm. in the US and Canada at CapitolCMGPublishing.com). All rights reserved. Used by permission.

12. VEVO, a joint venture between Google, Universal Music Group, and Sony Music Group (two of the three record company "majors" at the time of this writing), hosts videos and syndicates them to a variety of websites, including YouTube.

13. The Hartford Institute for Religion Research keeps an online Database of Megachurches in the USA. The entry for the Passion City Church in the database, last updated in 2010, asserts that the church had an average weekly attendance of 2,000. Accessed May 2, 2017, http://www.hirr.hartsem.edu/megachurch/database.html.

14. This is the term that Gateway Church, a multi-campus megachurch based in Dallas, TX, gave live-streamed reruns of its worship services, accessed July 2, 2016, http://gatewaypeople.com/watch.

15. The number of subscribers was publicized on a two-minute promotional video describing subscription options, accessed July 18, 2016, can be found on the Bethel Church website https://www.bethel.tv/home.

16. Passion's VEVO channel, accessed May 2, 2017, can be found at https://www.youtube.com/user/PassionVEVO.

17. Christopher's five-star review from February 24, 2016, entitled "ENCOURAGING" and accessed July 17, 2016, can be found on the comment stream, at http://passionresources.com/products/passion-2016-digital-all-access.

CONCLUSION

٭

Worship Music on National and Global Stages

The Mainstream Model and Its Alternatives

*S*inging the Congregation has examined how the collective performance of contemporary worship music shapes the activities that evangelicals define as "worship" and how these musically centered collective performances ("musical modes of congregating") have brought into being a set of distinct social constellations that participants often experience as being integrally connected. Each of the preceding chapters shows that these congregations include and yet extend far beyond the weekly worship gatherings of local churches. While each musical mode of congregating has its own unique set of affordances, shared musical and worship practices help make evangelical participants' religious experience coherent across the different performance spaces. Understanding congregations as social groups that are defined by shared practices rather than fixed structures enables us to gain a more accurate picture of contemporary religious practice and experience. Within the context of broader social change, the incorporation of new media technologies, and shifts in the various discourses that define religious community, contemporary worship music becomes an increasingly significant means whereby evangelicals position themselves, as they draw heavily on it in their efforts to create, maintain, and efface various social boundaries.

Music is a multivalent medium that is a crucial component of evangelical positioning strategies. One of the most significant uses of contemporary worship music described throughout this book is in facilitating a transformative personal encounter between the worshiper and God. This powerful "worship experience" mediates a sense of divine presence as it creates unity among gathered participants and absent others across space and time. The expectation that each gathering for congregational music-making lead to a powerful worship experience has created considerable challenges for religious authorities, whether church leaders, parachurch ministry organizers, or worship musicians, who seek to impart or authorize these experiences. Participants must be on the same page about the meaning of the activity in order for it to be experienced as authentic, and ensuring that musical worship practices are "genuine," spiritually transformative, and theologically accurate means that individual churches, evangelical media institutions, and church networks must often go to great lengths to shape the discourse both within and outside the gathered congregations. In this way, contemporary worship music enables evangelicals to erect and maintain boundaries between the activities of worship and entertainment as it makes audible the contours of their religious community in relationship to the broader society.

Performing worship music together creates and mediates a sense of unity not only among gathered participants, but also among the local congregation and other congregations in its regional church networks, as well as among the local congregation and the evangelical community imagined across time and space. As Chapter 2 demonstrated, musical worship allows participants to efface boundaries between earthly and heavenly community and between members of the evangelical "imagined community" who are separated by geographical distance but brought together through shared media and worship practices. Chapters 3 and 4 show how contemporary worship music enables individual evangelical congregations to negotiate their relationships to other congregations, Christian denominations, and networks. And Chapters 1 and 5 showed how contemporary worship enables evangelicals to combine personal piety and corporate worship, whether through private worship on the small screen of computers and cell phones or the social abrogation involved in treating God as an "Audience of One" in a stadium worship setting. In seeking to create a unified body composed of differentiated parts, evangelicals create the "voice" with which they communicate to one another and to the broader society through their collective musical practices.

Within each of the five musical modes of congregating that this book examines, the practice of music-making can unify and divide. In addition to—and often concurrently with—forming a unified community of worshipers, the collective performance of contemporary worship music allows a range of tensions to surface. Internal differences within the gathered community, particularly across racial, national, and ethnic lines and denominational background, must either be subsumed, acknowledged, or managed. Chapters 2 and 4 compared and contrasted two evangelical conferences and two praise marches, respectively, to highlight how differing groups of evangelicals and evangelical organizations approach the tensions that result from congregations marked by difference. Some gatherings understand differences between evangelicals as something to be encouraged and celebrated, while in others difference is a problem to be managed.

The degree to which participants experience different modes of congregating as related also varies. Participants in worship sometimes experience the different modes of congregating as interfacing seamlessly; at other times, however, worshipers experience them as being in conflict with one another. The online worship music videos discussed in Chapter 5 are prime examples of nodes of congregational connection that function both as resources for and spaces of worship. The videos draw together evangelical individuals who listen to them during their own personal devotions and church congregations that use the videos in their worship services, all the while providing a platform for the Christian media industry to encourage individuals to join concert and conference congregations where they can worship as the "original," authoritative versions of the songs are performed. Some evangelicals regard concert and conference gatherings as primary, rather than secondary, sites of religious experience. Chapters 1 and 5 highlighted several self-described "worship junkies" who regard musical worship in their own local congregations as substandard and anticipate special worship gatherings that are for them "more sacred than church." In the case of St. Bartholomew's Church (Chapter 3), the musical products of the Christian music industry are treated with a heavy dose of suspicion, resulting in both an emphasis on local creation and on alternative sources for congregational music. These conflicts over musical authority do not merely reflect or symbolize conflicts in other spheres (social, political, economic, etc.); rather, music is the terrain on which these contests play out, and one of the most powerful weapons in the arsenal.

MODELING THE WORSHIP MUSIC "MAINSTREAM" ON THE GLOBAL STAGE

One source of conflict to which several chapters of this book attested results from the tendency, driven by commercial interests and theological justifications alike, to normalize one style of congregational music-making and a particular understanding of worship. Privileging one musical style and one theology (or ideology) of worship often serves to bolster the authority of certain modes of congregating. These interrelated musical, theological, and social norms within North American evangelicalism have coalesced into what some have called the worship "mainstream." We might think of the contemporary worship mainstream as a matrix that combines a specific understanding of music, worship, and congregating that is set forth as a model for the way these three activities should relate across geographical and cultural space. This music-worship-congregating matrix is a highly portable set of practices and embodied understandings; as a result, it has been exported widely to where it has conditioned profoundly how Christian congregations elsewhere in the world understand the contours of their community and practice their faith.

For an understanding of the pervasive presence and widespread influence of the mainstream model of music, worship, and congregating, it is helpful to return to yet another version of the worship song "How Great Is Our God" discussed in the book's introduction. In early 2013, the Passion Conference released a new music video of the song that draws on footage from a live performance at the 2012 Passion Conference at Atlanta's Georgia Dome. (An audio recording of this version, subtitled "World Edition," is the opening song on *Chris Tomlin: The Essential Collection* [2011], a greatest-hits album by the brand's central worship leader released two months before the conference.[1]) The official worship music video posted to the Passion Conference's YouTube VEVO channel—which, at the time of this writing, has amassed over 32 million views and 10,000 comments—provides a fascinating glimpse into how this popular worship brand incorporates and represents fellow members of the global worshiping congregation to its North American and global audiences.[2]

In the video performance of this song, Tomlin appears on a stage in front of a youthful crowd filling an enormous stadium, joined by six other singers who sing solos in successive sections of the song. Four solo vocalists perform beside him onstage while two appear via video on the large screens behind the stage and throughout the arena. An African choir of young adults and children files out in the middle of the performance and adds a harmonic accompaniment to the song's bridge and final chorus. The music video is a hybrid of live and prerecorded audio and visual elements. The large screens that serve as a backdrop to the stage in the live performance setting are also active participants in the video: two of the featured vocalists contribute through prerecorded video segments, and a series of constantly changing images flash on three massive screens that span the length of the stage behind the performers. Each of the six featured soloists appears to be a twenty-or-thirty-something male and is dressed in the same trendy mainstream-hipster style. The song begins with a video clip of a South Asian male performer singing a wordless melody with microtonal inflections, surrounded by raggedly dressed children with wide grins in what appears to be an Indian slum. (In describing the litany of different languages used in this version of the song, many of online sources say that this section is "in Hindi.") Tomlin begins the first verse in English, and successive worship leaders take up the song's verses and choruses in their own native languages: Indonesian, Russian, Portuguese, and Spanish, respectively. Tomlin interjects several times in English, and the Indian singer's vocalise recurs in a mid-song instrumental break. For the song's final chorus, the video screens show footage of an East Asian singer standing in front of a modernist structure that looks like a Chinese government building as he sings the song's final chorus in Mandarin.

In the music video on Passion's VEVO site, these influential individuals are treated as relatively anonymous stand-ins for national and cultural difference. Little to no information was given about these worship leaders in the live performance (Busman 2015a), nor does the information provided in the VEVO channel video credit the other singers by name or provide links to their music. In his "about the song" promotional video, Chris Tomlin mentions some of the leaders on a first-name basis (e.g., "my friend Dilip from India") along with the languages they sing but gives no additional information about them.[3] In seeking information about the other worship leaders featured in the performance, thanks largely to fan-provided and crowd-sourced information from social media, I was able to piece together the lineup of worship leaders on the video, discovering that it is a veritable who's who of contemporary-worship recording artists from around the globe. Dilip Kurian, the South Asian vocalist who sings the song's opening vocalise, is a popular youth worship leader in Bangalore who has collaborated with Hillsong. At the time the video premiered, he was in the process of kicking off his career as an aspiring modern-worship recording artist in the United States. Sidney Mohede, who sings the second half of the first verse in Indonesian, leads worship at a nondenominational megachurch that is one of the largest congregations in Jakarta, and has also collaborated on numerous projects with well-known worship bands in the United States and Australia. Singing the first chorus in Russian is Roman Kasevich, youth worship leader for the Kiev branch of global megachurch Hillsong Church and the son of its then-pastors. Fernando Santos Junior, known as Fernandinho, is one of the most well-known charismatic worship leaders in Brazil, with concerts held in some of the country's largest performance venues and album sales in the millions. He performs a verse in Portuguese and is joined on the second chorus of the song by Omar Rodríguez, leader of a worship band at the charismatic Abundant Life Church (*Iglesia Vida Abundante*) in Chihuahua, Mexico. Rodríguez and his team are widely known throughout charismatic and evangelical churches in Mexico for their own modern-worship-style hits and for popularizing Spanish-language versions of popular English-language worship artists and bands, including Tomlin, Hillsong, and Jesus Culture.[4] As these brief biographical snippets make apparent, each of the worship leaders featured represents many of the interconnected modes of congregating—the concert, conference, church, public, and online spaces pervaded by worship "megabrands" on regional, national, and international levels—that have been transplanted or adopted in other places throughout the world.

Joshua Busman, who observed the live performance at Passion 2012 from which the video draws, notes the colonialist undertones of the performance and video which, on the one hand, "draws sharp distinctions between Western and non-Western bodies" while ultimately subsuming these differences through sound (2015a, 197). In the video, the various languages in which the worship song is performed and the nonwhite bodies of worship leaders onstage serve as markers of cultural difference. Pop-rock style contemporary worship music, however, is presented as the one universal musical language sufficient to unite Christians from around the world. Not only are the vocal styles of all the lead singers remarkably similar to one another, so also is the range of performative gestures, including the signature "worship leader grimace," a facial expression intended to evoke intense sincerity, expressive hand gestures like fist pumps to accentuate important lyrics, and the raising of hands and faces toward the sky as if in a state of rapture.

By choosing to showcase these particular worship leaders, the "World Edition" video visually implies that those best equipped to lead the global church in participating in worship are middle-class, twenty-to-forty-year-old men who adhere to the stylistic norms—here "style" includes dress, bodily comportment, vocal, and gestural aspects—of the North American white popular cultural mainstream. A close listening to the video's rendition of "How Great Is Our God" reveals that musical sound parallels visual elements in how racial and cultural difference is imagined, represented, and managed. As I listened carefully to the song's musical arrangement, I found only two musical elements (beyond the language each worship leader sings) that distinguish this recording from other recorded versions of "How Great Is Our God." The first difference is the South Asian vocal and instrumental stylistic inflection in the opening, and the second is the use of African choir vocals in the bridge and final choruses. Both these aspects of sonic difference are strongly reinforced by visual choices made in the video. When the South Asian singer performs the opening vocalise with its South Asian–style pitch bends and slides (echoed later in the song's first verse by the electric guitar), he does not appear onstage with the other leaders, but rather is featured on the video screens surrounded by smiling children in a slum. And the African singers who contribute signature Southern African–style choral harmony to the bridge and final choruses wear brightly colored garments and headgear that mark them out clearly as exotic Others, in sharp visual contrast to the closely matching modern garb of the worship leaders. That these markers of aural alterity—in other words, the sonic aspects that deviate from the dominant pop-rock aesthetic—must be underscored with parallel markers of visual alterity suggests a not-so-subtle policing of genre boundaries. Difference is called out, clearly marked, and segregated; the "exotic" elements are used to add flavor to a familiar recipe while not being allowed to pervade the otherwise coherent and undifferentiated whole of the modern worship performance.

The genre to which "How Great Is Our God: World Edition" video performance makes reference when it calls out difference represents a widespread model of the music-worship-congregation matrix that many evangelical observers have dubbed the worship music "mainstream." During my fieldwork, evangelicals invoked the category of the mainstream—a term generally, but not always, imbued with negative connotations—with increasing frequency to describe commercially popular worship music. (See, for instance, the discussion of mainstreams and alternatives in Chapter 3.) Andrew Mall (2012) notes that, within North American Christian popular music more broadly, the categories of mainstream and underground (what I am referring to as alternative) have long been important heuristics that not only reflect differing sets of priorities, but that also shape cultural production in profound ways. Drawing from Kai Fikentscher's work on the electronic dance music underground, Mall writes that mainstreams are "bounded fields of cultural production that can claim a majority rate of participation—a majority that, for Fikentscher, functions to define a society's 'dominant moral and aesthetic codes'"; thus, they "can also be considered vis-à-vis undergrounds as larger, normative, and oppressive" (33). For anyone attentive to the songs, songwriters, and publishers riding high on the CCLI popularity charts, the mainstream is currently dominated by songwriters from globalizing worship brands like Passion, Hillsong, and Jesus Culture. Worship songs from these church networks and organizations tend to sound fairly homogenous, falling into a predictable pop-rock style while also incorporating new trends in chart-topping pop music. One can hear in recent commercially popular worship albums, for instance, inflections from electronic dance music, bluegrass, and the indie-folk styles of bands like Mumford and Sons (see Busman 2015a, 2015b; Hicks 2015).

SPLINTERING WORLDS OF WORSHIP: MUSIC, POLITICS, AND IDEOLOGY IN THE US CONTEXT

As popular-culture scholars have noted, where there is a recognized mainstream, there is usually an alternative defined in opposition to it. As evangelicals have grown aware that a worship music "mainstream" exists, some have become equally convinced that it is theologically or ethically problematic and must be supplemented or replaced entirely. During my field research in Nashville, Jeremy, a college worship leader in his mid-twenties, remarked to me: "I'm kind of disillusioned about worship music . . . I hope in the right way." Involved in leading contemporary worship music since junior high school, Jeremy explained that he was disillusioned because the lyrics of chart-topping contemporary worship songs no longer reflected his experiences of being a Christian, which were punctuated moments of sadness, uncertainty, and doubt, and added that he found the commercial pop-rock style too "performance-driven." Jeremy clarified that he hoped being disillusioned "in the right way" would not lead to cynicism or paralysis but rather to the constructive creation of an alternative (in Jeremy's case, the alternative was helping to write and perform new, folk-influenced tunes to older evangelical hymn texts).

Since the mid-2000s, cracks in the mainstream music-worship-congregating edifice have appeared, in large part because of disillusionment with the predominant model of evangelical worship like what Jeremy describes, and certain of the beliefs and values this music is understood to represent. Self-conscious alternatives differ from the mainstream not only sonically, but also in how worship is understood and how the religious community is imagined. Several audible alternative movements within evangelical worship have appropriated sonic resources from outside its bounds, including evangelical song repertories from the past or songs and styles from Christian worship traditions outside North American evangelical Protestantism. One widespread alternative evangelical repertory has stemmed from younger musicians like Jeremy reclaiming forgotten hymns in the Protestant canon. The "retuned hymn" or "rehymn" movement, spurred by Gen-X and millennial Reformed evangelicals, set these hymn texts to newly composed, frequently folk-inflected tunes and arrangements (Scheer 2014; Benedict 2012, 2017). Many other alternatives to the mainstream model are touched on throughout this book, including the genre of "modern hymns" that fuse contemporary musical styles with lyrics written in the poetic meters of traditional hymns; the Emergent worship practices that seek to decenter music as the primary form of participation and reclaim elements of historic liturgies from mainline, Catholic, and Orthodox traditions; and the consciously "multiethnic" worship music that calls attention to ways the white evangelical mainstream defines itself as normative (Van Opstal 2016) and seeks to broaden contemporary worship music's sonic palette to include popular music styles beyond pop-rock.[5]

I have suggested elsewhere that contemporary worship music may be on its way to becoming a "splintered art world"[6] in which diverging rationales and motivations separate artists, industry executives, and audiences (Ingalls 2017). It remains to be seen whether or not these competing streams will intermingle, and whether the mainstream as it is currently constituted will be willing to accommodate the diversity of ideas and values represented in these alternatives. In participating in contemporary worship music, evangelicals choose to engage one another in a shared practice that is both profoundly affecting and richly meaningful. This activity, with all its intricacies and internal tensions, produces the evangelical religious community in its many modes of congregating. This book has shown many different orientations that the congregations of various kinds can take in relationship to constructing the mainstream: some parrot the songs they hear coming from powerful worship leaders, churches, or brands; others "talk back" through creative misappropriations or musical interventions; and still others, whether out of conviction or pragmatism, seek to live with the conflicts that typify evangelical

Christian belief and practice, adopting contemporary worship music and all the tensions it brings with it into the heart of their worshiping communities.

Looking to the future of contemporary worship music in North America and the modes of congregating it enables, several questions arise: Will alternate understandings of worship that decenter the consumer-driven "worship experience" gain prominence? What musical modes of congregating will exert the greatest influence on local Christian communities? Will one musical style continue to dominate contemporary worship music, or will other styles be embraced? And, related to what this homogeneous musical style signifies, will the mainstream of contemporary worship music be broadened to reflect the growing diversity of North American Christians who hold evangelical beliefs[7] or will it continue to reflect the beliefs, values, and practices of a North American middle-class white conservative bloc?

The latter question takes on a renewed urgency in the wake of developments on the national political stage in the United States since the 2016 election. Though this book has not focused in detail on the relationship between evangelical worship music and US national politics, it has sought to lay bare the workings of power within and outside evangelical worship in several registers. How authority is generated and operates among worshipers, worship-leading musicians, ecclesial institutions, and commercial industries carries implications for how evangelicals engage the national political sphere. Leaders of insistently "apolitical" worship gatherings may try to avoid becoming embroiled in the national political discussion[8]; however, the choices they must make about musical worship make statements that are inescapably political. Through their choices of style, genre, repertoire, personnel, venue, media, and marketing strategies, they weigh in on political questions including where the ultimate source of authority lies for living the Christian life; who is allowed and encouraged to lead congregational assemblies, and what groups of people should be included in the presumed "we" of the gathered congregation (and, by extension, what groups of people are excluded or marginalized and marked as Other).

In the coming months and years, it will be instructive to see to what degree of ideological and political diversity is tolerated within the various evangelical musical modes of congregating. And it will be important to pay close attention to whether performances of contemporary worship music signal inclusion and the willingness to share authority across lines of difference, or whether contemporary worship music will become a means by which evangelicalism's far-right contingent shores up boundaries along racial, ethnic, gendered, and/or sexual lines. It remains to be seen whether North American evangelical Christianity will be able to maintain a common conversation across the political and ideological fault lines that threaten to cleave it. Evangelicalism may fracture along racial/ethnic and class lines, or along ideological or political ones. Or, perhaps, shared activities such as musical worship might form the glue that continues to hold together constituencies that differ markedly on certain national political issues but agree on key tenets of a shared belief. *Singing the Congregation* has shown many kinds of gatherings in which contemporary worship music makes mundane spaces sacred, transforms a gathering of individuals into a congregation, and brings heaven to earth. Shared musical and worship practices have the potential to bind people into congregational coalitions, however fragile, whose members might otherwise be bitterly divided by political, ideological, or other differences. In an era in which polarized "media bubbles" cause people to inhabit different realities, gathering together for worship might serve to keep the channels of communication open between people of opposing political positions by emphasizing the religious ideas, values, and practices that they have in common; then again, musical modes of congregating may also reinforce the ideological echo chamber that insulates many evangelical individuals and communities from neighboring groups in North American society.

Evangelical Christians of all political persuasions believe music and worship have the power to draw them into an intimate relationship with God and can transform individuals and communities. They do not always agree, however, about what the God they worship is like, how that God believes they should relate to others in their society or outside their religious community, what the relative weight of Divine and human authority is, what values Christian individuals and congregations should hold as most important for shaping their lives with others, and what strategies should be used to enact or spread those values. In examining the various musical modes of congregating centered around contemporary worship music, the chapters of *Singing the Congregation* have shown that it is in part *what* songs are performed, but perhaps more profoundly *how* they are performed, that most clearly expresses evangelical positions on the issues that threaten to divide them. Differences in musical style, performance practice, and musical leadership that play out on the musical stage during worship reveal disagreements within the community that often map onto divergent political leanings. Singing contemporary worship music may bring heaven to earth, but divergent ways of hearing the hereafter profoundly affect the here and now.

RECONCEIVING CONGREGATIONS, REMODELING CONGREGATIONAL MUSIC

Using contemporary worship music to investigate questions of authority and community building has the potential to illumine dynamics not only on the US stage, but also increasingly on the global stage as well. Though this book has focused primarily on evangelical Christians living in North America, exploring the interconnections between participatory music-making, the

ritual act of worship, and the social formation of religious communiti
carries implications for other religious traditions in late modernity, as th__
devotional music spreads into online spaces and is taken up into translocal
gatherings and sacred music concerts, and as these instantiations challenge
the authority of local collectives and hierarchies alike. Understanding the
processes involved in how music makes congregations matters profoundly for
understanding how religious social formations throughout the world constitute and understand their communities of practice.

In describing the multifaceted interplay between music, worship, and
modes of congregating, this book has as one of its chief goals to contribute
to the academic conversation about religious music by remodeling and
reinvigorating the analytic categories of both "congregation" and "congregational music." Congregations are reimagined as fluid, contingent social
constellations—albeit conditioned strongly by ecclesial institutions and commercial media industries—that are actively performed into being through
collective practices—in this case, the musically structured participatory activity known as "worship." Music-making is foundational for contemporary
evangelical modes of congregating and should not be treated as incidental or
peripheral. By implication, scholars of evangelical Christianity—and of other
religious communities for whom sacred sound and music-making is a central
participatory activity—cannot afford to ignore music-making. Music is not
only a window or lens onto other social processes; it also is a social force—a
potent and affective way of performing religious community into being.

For scholars already convinced that music-making is a social activity crucial for shaping communities, it is my hope that they will find the category
of "congregation" as it is reimagined in these pages to serve as a useful analytic term capable of carrying more theoretical weight than it currently does
within academic musical discourse. The congregation is a community of practice that is constituted through the common experiences produced through
ritual activity; it is defined both by its local presence and global aspirations,
by emphases on both imagination and intimacy (B. Dueck 2013), and should
not be reduced or relegated to one pole or the other. "Congregational music-
making" is thus reconceived as a participatory religious musical practice not
intrinsically tied to particular performance spaces or institutions; rather,
through its permeation of individual devotion and various social activities, it
weaves together a religious community inside and outside local gatherings for
worship. Performative choices and strategies are both stylistic and substan-
tive; considerations ranging from what instruments are chosen, who sings or
plays, are crucial means by which music forms congregations and shapes these
collectivities relative to other activities within the same mode of congregating
(e.g., how two worship conferences relate to each other) and relative to other
modes of congregating entirely (how local church worship relates to a worship
concert or online worship resources).

The remodeling of congregational music carries several implications for the study of religious communities' music-making in the twenty-first century. Congregational music should not be reduced to the textual and musical content of hymnals or the musical publications of official church hierarchies. Nor can congregational music be interpreted as a purely "local" expression, isolated from broader discursive networks in which it is embedded. While local gatherings are important and formative communities of practice, the study of their music cannot be limited to local instantiations without consideration of the broader discourse; conversely, in examining mass-mediated congregational genres like contemporary worship music, scholars must not gloss over the agency of local individuals and contexts to shape the music for their own purposes. Rather, future work must find ways to represent the activities of congregational music-making as a densely connected network of interlinked practices. Further work could identify other modes of congregating, theorizing the relative influence of the various modes of congregating within a given local community, translocal body, or movement. It could focus on other kinds of participatory practices that form religious communities, including oral genres like spoken prayer, cantillation, and prophecy, and audiovisual ritual practices dependent on electronic media technologies. It could follow additional movements or "brands" that elide the distinctions between discrete modes of congregating. And it could pursue further the way music and worship practices are used in processes of "binding and loosing" (J. Dueck 2011, 242), variously widening or mending the fault lines between co-religionists on the basis of race, ethnicity, and nationality, denominational tradition or network, or political ideology. One thing is certain: for an understanding of the shifting constellations of religious community, it is crucial to observe and listen closely to collective music-making. Congregational worship music serves as a resounding reflection of practice and as a powerful creative force at the very heart of the beliefs and practices of millions within North American evangelicalism and beyond.

NOTES

1. Following the Passion Conference's first "world tour" in 2009, Chris Tomlin frequently sang the chorus lyrics of his song "How Great Is Our God" in languages of the various places he had visited in his concerts. In one Toronto performance I observed in late 2009, Tomlin sang the chorus in Portuguese, Russian, Indonesian, and French. See Busman (2015a, 196–98) for a brief firsthand account of the performance of World Edition at Passion 2012.
2. "How Great Is Our God (World Edition) [feat. Chris Tomlin]," Passion VEVO, accessed April 15, 2017, https://www.youtube.com/watch?v=vg5qDljEw7Q.

3. Capitol Christian Music Group, "Chris Tomlin Talks About 'How Great Is Our God [World Edition],'" accessed April 16, 2017, https://www.youtube.com/watch?v=MRUBEgdVSzc.

4. The Spanish version of the chorus on Tomlin's album is sung by Marcos Witt, the founder of a Latin American worship music-recording, publishing, and worship-leader-training empire known as CanZion Producciones, with an estimated 27 million albums sold since its founding in the late 1980s (see Sánchez 2008; Gladwin 2015).

5. See Marti 2012 for a sociological account of evangelical multiethnic worship; for a discussion of trends within multiethnic worship from the perspective of an evangelical pastor and worship leader, see Van Opstal 2015). Marti and Ganiel 2014 describes Emerging Church worship practices in detail. Also, see the special issue "Worship in an Age of Reconstruction," 2017, *Liturgy* 32, no. 1, ed. Lester Ruth, for descriptions of several of the more recent alternative trends in evangelical and mainline Protestant worship.

6. I borrow this term from sociologists Jay Howard and John Streck (1999), who use it to describe the world of Contemporary Christian Music in the late 1990s.

7. According to the 2016 report "America's Changing Religious Identity," "young evangelical Protestants are far more racially and ethnically diverse than previous generations . . . half (50%) of evangelical Protestants under the age of 30 are white, compared to more than three-quarters (77%) of evangelical Protestant seniors (age 65 or older)" (Cox and Jones 2017).

8. North American worship leaders and their associated brands generally take care to studiously avoid being seen to take political sides. In an interview with Chris Tomlin during the 2015 presidential primaries, interviewer Chelsea Patterson asks Tomlin to comment on the feeling among many Christians that "America's only hope is electing a Republican president" (Patterson 2015). Tomlin responds, "I think people feel like we're going in a million directions, and spinning out of control. The truth is, there's not a man that's going to lead in a way that three million [*sic*] people agree with. There's not a man who's going to save America through policy. While I think policy is extremely important, it isn't what's going to save America. . . . Awakening doesn't come through politics, but it comes through prayer and the holy spirit, that's what we're trying to do! May people know the love of God, and may it start with us!" Accessed December 27, 2017, http://www.patheos.com/blogs/joyindestructible/2015/08/11/interview-with-chris-tomlin-worship-night-in-america.

REFERENCES

Althouse, Peter, and Michael Wilkinson. 2015. "Musical Bodies in the Charismatic Renewal: The Case of Catch the Fire and Soaking Prayer." In *The Spirit of Praise: Music and Worship in Global Pentecostal-Charismatic Christianity*, edited by Monique M. Ingalls and Amos Yong, 29–44. University Park: Pennsylvania State University Press.

Amit, Vered. 2000. "Introduction: Constructing the Field." In *Constructing the Field: Ethnographic Fieldwork in the Contemporary World*, edited by Vered Amit, 1–18. London and New York: Routledge.

Ammerman, Nancy T. 2011. "Congregations: Local, Social, and Religious." In *The Oxford Handbook of the Sociology of Religion*, edited by Peter B. Clarke, 562–80. Oxford and New York: Oxford University Press.

Ammerman, Nancy Tatom. 1997. *Congregation and Community*. New Brunswick: Rutgers University Press.

———, ed. 1998. *Studying Congregations: A New Handbook*. Nashville: Abingdon.

———. 2005. *Pillars of Faith: American Congregations and Their Partners*. Berkeley: University of California Press.

Anderson, Allan, ed. 2010. *Studying Global Pentecostalism: Theories and Methods*. Berkeley: University of California Press.

Anderson, Benedict R. 1991. *Imagined Communities: Reflections on the Origin and Spread of Nationalism*. London and New York: Verso.

Arnold, Clinton E. 1997. *Three Crucial Questions about Spiritual Warfare*. Grand Rapids, MI: Baker Academic.

Ashkenazi, Michael. 1987. "Cultural Tensions as Factors in the Structure of a Festival Parade." *Asian Folklore Studies* 46, no. 1: 35–54.

Austin, J. L. 1962. *How to Do Things with Words*. William James Lectures 1955. Cambridge, MA: Harvard University Press.

Bailey, Sarah Pulliam. 2017. "'A Spiritual Battle': How Roy Moore Tested White Evangelical Allegiance to the Republican Party." Acts of Faith (blog). *Washington Post*, December 13, 2017. Accessed December 17, 2017. https://www.washingtonpost.com/news/acts-of-faith/wp/2017/12/13/a-spiritual-battle-how-roy-moores-failed-campaign-tested-evangelicals/?utm_term=.62ad1df7835b.

Baker, Jonny, Doug Gay, and Jenny Brown. 2004. *Alternative Worship: Resources from and for the Emerging Church*. Grand Rapids, MI: Baker.

Baker, Paul. 1985. *Contemporary Christian Music: Where It Came From, What It Is, Where It's Going*. Westchester, IL: Crossway.

Balmer, Randall Herbert. 2010. *The Making of Evangelicalism: From Revivalism to Politics and Beyond*. Waco, TX: Baylor University Press.

Banerjee, Neela. 2008. "Taking Their Faith, but Not Their Politics, to the People." *New York Times*, June 1, 2008. http://www.nytimes.com/2008/06/01/us/ 01evangelical.html.

Barna, George. 2001. "Worship Tops the List of Important Church-Based Experiences." Barna Update February 19, 2001. Accessed March 5, 2018. https://www.barna.com/research/ worship-tops-the-list-of-important-church-based-experiences/

Barna Research Group. 2002. "Focus on 'Worship Wars' Hides the Real Issues Regarding Connection to God." Barna.org. https://www.barna.com/research/ focus-on-worship-wars-hides-the-real-issues-regarding-connection-to-god.

Barna Research Group. 2005. "Technology Use Is Growing Rapidly in Churches." Barna.org. http://www.barna.org/barna-update/article/5-barna-update/ 172-technology-use-is-growing-rapidly-in-churches?q=media+technology.

Bartkowski, John P., and Helen A. Regis. 2003. *Charitable Choices: Religion, Race, and Poverty in the Post-Welfare Era.* New York: New York University Press.

Bates, Patricia. 1998. "Christian Artists Branch Out as Market Diversifies." *Billboard*, June 13, 1998, pp. 73–74.

Bates, Phil. 2005. "Technology for Worship Magazine: Bringing Motion Imagery to Worship Part 2." http://tfwm.com/bringing-motion-imagery-to-worship-part-2.

Bausch, Michael G. 2002. *Silver Screen, Sacred Story: Using Multimedia in Worship.* Bethesda, MD: Alban Institute.

Beach, Nancy. 2005. "More to Worship Than Music: Are You Giving Musicians a Voice?" *CT Pastors.* http://www.christianitytoday.com/pastors/2005/fall/ 15.105.html.

Beaujon, Andrew. 2006. *Body Piercing Saved My Life: Inside the Phenomenon of Christian Rock.* Cambridge, MA: Da Capo.

Beaulieu, Anne. 2004. "Mediating Ethnography: Objectivity and the Making of Ethnographies of the Internet." *Social Epistemology* 18, nos. 2–3: 139–63.

Bebbington, David. 1989. *Evangelicalism in Modern Britain: A History from the 1730s to the 1980s.* London and Boston: Unwin Hyman.

Benedict, Bruce. 2012. "Observations on the New Hymns Movement." *Cardiphonia.* January 17, 2012. https://cardiphonia.org/2012/01/17/ observations-on-the-new-hymns-movement.

———. 2017. "Refurbished Hymns in an Age of Vintage Faith: Millennials and the Retuned Hymn Movement." *Liturgy* 32, no. 1: 54–61.

Bergunder, Michael. 2007. *The South Indian Pentecostal Movement in the Twentieth Century.* Grand Rapids, MI: Eerdmans.

———. 2010. "The Cultural Turn." In *Studying Global Pentecostalism: Theories and Methods*, edited by Allan Anderson, 51–73. Anthropology of Christianity 10. Berkeley: University of California Press.

Bhabha, Homi. 1984. "Of Mimicry and Man: The Ambivalence of Colonial Discourse." *October* 28 (Spring): 125–33.

Bielo, James S. 2011. *Emerging Evangelicals: Faith, Modernity, and the Desire for Authenticity.* New York: New York University Press.

Bohlman, Philip V. 1996. "Pilgrimage, Politics, and the Musical Remapping of the New Europe." *Ethnomusicology* 40, no. 3: 375–412.

Bohlman, Phillip V. 2003. "Sacred Popular Music of the Mediterranean and the Journey to Jerusalem." In *Mediterranean Mosaic: Popular Music and Global Sounds*, edited by Goffredo Plastino, 287–306. London: Psychology Press.

Bolter, J. David. 2000. *Writing Space: Computers, Hypertext, and the Remediation of Print.* 2nd ed. Mahwah, NJ: Lawrence Erlbaum.

Botterill, Jacqueline. 2007. "Cowboys, Outlaws and Artists: The Rhetoric of Authenticity and Contemporary Jeans and Sneaker Advertisements." *Journal of Consumer Culture* 7, no. 1: 105–25.

Bramadat, Paul, and David Seljak, eds. 2008. *Christianity and Ethnicity in Canada*. Toronto and Buffalo: University of Toronto Press.

Breimeier, Russ. 2006. "Worship as an Afterthought?" *Christian Music Today*. www. christianitytoday.com/music.

———. 2008. "Modern Worship Is Going Nowhere." *Christian Music Today*. http://www.christianitytoday.com/ct/2008/julyweb-only/modernworship. html?start=1.

Bringle, Mary Louise. 2013. "Debating Hymns." *Christian Century*. https://www. christiancentury.org/article/2013-04/debating-hymns.

Brouwer, Steve, Paul Gifford, and Susan D. Rose. 1996. *Exporting the American Gospel: Global Christian Fundamentalism*. New York: Routledge.

Burnim, Mellonee. 1985. "Culture Bearer and Tradition Bearer: An Ethnomusicologist's Research on Gospel Music." *Ethnomusicology* 29, no. 3: 432–47.

Burton, Justin. 2014. "Dancing Silhouettes: The Mobile Freedom of iPod Commercials." In *The Oxford Handbook of Mobile Music Studies*. Vol. 2. Edited by Sumanth Gopinath and Jason Stanyek, 311–36. Oxford Handbooks. Oxford and New York: Oxford University Press.

Busman, Joshua Kalin. 2015a. "(Re)sounding Passion: Listening to American Evangelical Worship Music, 1997–2015." PhD diss., University of North Carolina at Chapel Hill.

———. 2015b. "'Yet to Come' or 'Still to Be Done'? Evangelical Worship and the Power of 'Prophetic' Songs." In *Congregational Music-Making and Community in a Mediated Age*, edited by Anna Nekola and Tom Wagner, 199–214. Congregational Music Studies. Farnham, UK: Ashgate.

Butler, Mark. 2003. "Taking It Seriously: Intertextuality and Authenticity in Two Covers by the Pet Shop Boys." *Popular Music* 22, no. 1: 1–19.

Butler, Mark J. 2006. *Unlocking the Groove: Rhythm, Meter, and Musical Design in Electronic Dance Music*. Bloomington: Indiana University Press.

Butler, Melvin L. 2002. "'Nou Kwe Nan Sentespri' (We Believe in the Holy Spirit): Music, Ecstasy, and Identity in Haitian Pentecostal Worship." *Black Music Research Journal* 22, no. 1: 85–125.

———. 2005. "Songs of Pentecost: Experiencing Music, Transcendence, and Identity in Jamaica and Haiti." PhD diss., New York University.

———. 2008. "The Weapons of Our Warfare: Music, Positionality, and Transcendence among Haitian Pentecostals." *Caribbean Studies* 36, no. 2: 23–64.

Byars, Ronald P. 2002. *The Future of Protestant Worship: Beyond the Worship Wars*. Louisville, KY: Westminster John Knox.

Campbell, Heidi. 2005. *Exploring Religious Community Online: We Are One in the Network*. Digital Formations 24. New York: P. Lang.

———. 2012. "Understanding the Relationship between Religion Online and Offline in a Networked Society." *Journal of the American Academy of Religion* 80, no. 1: 64–93. https://doi:10.1093/jaarel/lfr074.

Campolo, Tony, and Shane Claiborne. 2016. "The Evangelicalism of Old White Men Is Dead." *New York Times*, November 29, 2016. https://www.nytimes.com/2016/11/29/opinion/the-evangelicalism-of-old-white-men-is-dead.html.

Camson, Barry, and Debra Brosan. 2013. "Observations on Networked Congregations and Communities: The Present and The Future." *Jewish Philanthropy*, July

15, 2013. http://ejewishphilanthropy.com/observations-on-networked-congregations-and-communities-the-present-and-the-future.

Cannell, Fenella, ed. 2006. *The Anthropology of Christianity*. Durham, NC: Duke University Press.

Carl, Florian. 2015. "Music, Ritual and Media in Charismatic Religious Experience in Ghana." In *Congregational Music-Making and Community in a Mediated Age*, edited by Anna E. Nekola and Tom Wagner, 45–60. Congregational Music Studies. Farnham, UK: Ashgate.

Carter, Joe. 2016. "No, the Majority of American Evangelicals Did Not Vote for Trump." *TGC: The Gospel Coalition*. https://www.thegospelcoalition.org/article/no-the-majority-of-american-evangelicals-did-not-vote-for-trump.

Caulfield, Keith. 2013. "Chris Tomlin Scores First No. 1 Album on Billboard 200 Chart." *Billboard*. http://www.billboard.com/biz/articles/news/1490583/chris-tomlin-scores-first-no-1-album-on-billboard-200-chart.

Center for the Study of Global Christianity. 2013. "Christianity in Its Global Context, 1970–2020: Society, Religion, and Mission." http://www.gordonconwell.edu/ockenga/research/documents/ChristianityinitsGlobalContext.pdf.

Chaves, Mark. 2004. *Congregations in America*. Cambridge, MA: Harvard University Press.

Chaves, Mark, and Alison Eagle. 2015. "The National Congregations Study: Religious Congregations in 21st Century America." Accessed May 5, 2017. http://www.soc.duke.edu/natcong/Docs/NCSIII_report_final.pdf.

Christian Copyright Licensing International. 2008. "CCLI Top 25 Songs, Report Period 1007." Accessed February 5, 2009. https://songselect.ccli.com.

———. 2011. "CCLI Top 25 Songs, Report Period 1013." Accessed October 25, 2011. https://songselect.ccli.com.

———. 2012a. "CCLI 2007 License Holder Survey Results." *CCLI.com (CCLI: Did You Know)*. http://www.ccli.com/DidYouKnow.aspx.

———. 2012b. "CCLI 2011 License Holder Survey Results." *CCLI.com*. http://www.ccli.com/DidYouKnow.aspx.

Christianity Today. 1994. "Global Praise Event Draws 12 Million Believers." August 15, 1994. Accessed Feburary 9, 2015. https://www.christianitytoday.com/ct/1994/august15/4t955a.html.

Church Multimedia. 2007. "The Visual Aesthetic." *Worship Leader*, February.

Cohen, Sara. 1997. "Men Making a Scene: Rock Music and the Production of Gender." In *Sexing the Groove: Popular Music and Gender*, edited by Sheila Whiteley, 17–36. London and New York: Routledge.

Cole, Teju. 2012. "The White-Savior Industrial Complex." *Atlantic*, March 21, 2012. Accessed June 12, 2015. http://www.theatlantic.com/international/archive/2012/03/the-white-savior-industrial-complex/254843/?single_page=true.

Coleman, Simon. 2000. *The Globalisation of Charismatic Christianity: Spreading the Gospel of Prosperity*. Cambridge: Cambridge University Press.

———. 2004. "From England's Nazareth to Sweden's Jerusalem: Movement, (Virtual) Landscapes, and Pilgrimage." In *Reframing Pilgrimage: Cultures in Motion*, edited by Simon Coleman and John Eade, 45–68. European Association of Social Anthropologists. London and New York: Routledge.

Coleman, Simon, John Eade, eds. 2004. *Reframing Pilgrimage: Cultures in Motion*. European Association of Social Anthropologists. London and New York: Routledge.

Coleman, Simon, and Rosalind I. J. Hackett. 2015. "Introduction: A New Field?" In *The Anthropology of Global Pentecostalism and Evangelicalism*, edited by

Simon Coleman and Rosalind I. J. Hackett, 1–37. New York: New York University Press.

Conquergood, Dwight. 1986. "Between Experience and Meaning: Performance as a Paradigm for Meaningful Action." In *Renewal and Revision: The Future of Interpretation*, edited by Ted Colson, 26–59. Denton, TX: NB Omega.

Cook, Nicholas. 1998a. *Analysing Musical Multimedia*. Oxford:Oxford University Press.

———. 1998b. *Music: A Very Short Introduction*. Oxford and New York: Oxford University Press.

Cooley, Timothy J., Katherine Meizel, and Nasir Syed. 2008. "Virtual Fieldwork: Three Case Studies." In *Shadows in the Field: New Perspectives for Fieldwork in Ethnomusicology*, edited by Gregory Barz and Timothy J Cooley, 90–107. New York: Oxford University Press.

Cornwall, Judson. 1983. *Let Us Worship: The Believer's Response to God*. South Plainfield, NJ: Bridge.

Cox, Daniel, and Robert P. Jones. 2017. "America's Changing Religious Identity." Public Religion Research Institute Report, September 6, 2017. Accessed December 22, 2017. https://www.prri.org/research/american-religious-landscape-christian-religiously-unaffiliated.

Coyle, Michael, and John Dolan. 1999. "Modeling Authenticity, Authenticating Commercial Models." In *Reading Rock and Roll: Authenticity, Appropriation, Aesthetics*, edited by Kevin J. H. Dettmar and William Richey, 17–35. New York: Columbia University Press.

Crawford, Garry. 2004. *Consuming Sport: Fans, Sport and Culture*. London and New York: Routledge.

Csordas, Thomas J. 2009. "Modalities of Transnational Transcendence." In *Transnational Transcendence: Essays on Religion and Globalization*, edited by Thomas J. Csordas, 1–30. Berkeley: University of California Press.

———. 2012. *Language, Charisma, and Creativity: Ritual Life in the Catholic Charismatic Renewal*. 1st pbk. ed. Contemporary Anthropology of Religion. New York: Palgrave Macmillan.

Cummings, Tony, and Graham Kendrick. 1992. "Graham Kendrick: The Worship Songsmith Talks about the March for Jesus Phenomenon." *Cross Rhythms*. http://www.crossrhythms.co.uk/articles/music/Graham_Kendrick_The_worship_song-smith_talks_about_the_March_For_Jesus_phenomenon/36693/p1.

Cusic, Don. 2002. *The Sound of Light: A History of Gospel and Christian Music*. Milwaukee, WI: Hal Leonard.

———. 2012. *Saved by Song: A History of Gospel and Christian Music*. Oxford, MS: University Press of Mississippi.

David, Rauch. 2002. "Multimedia 101." *Your Church: Prepared for Ministry, Christianity Today Online*. November–December, 2002. Accessed February 11, 2015. http://www.christianitytoday.com/yc/2002/novdec/1.12.html.

Dawn, Marva J. 2015. *How Shall We Worship? Biblical Guidelines for the Worship Wars*. 2nd ed. Eugene, OR: Wipf and Stock.

de la Torre, Miguel. 2017. "The Death of Christianity in the U.S." *Baptist News Global*, November 13, 2017. Accessed November 15, 2017. https://baptistnews.com/article/death-christianity-u-s/#.WkQpVN-nGUn.

Dueck, Byron. 2013. *Musical Intimacies and Indigenous Imaginaries: Aboriginal Music and Dance in Public Performance*. New York: Oxford University Press.

Dueck, Jonathan Mark. 2003. "An Ethnographic Study of the Musical Practices of Three Edmonton Mennonite Churches." PhD diss., University of Alberta.

———. 2011. "Binding and Loosing in Song: Conflict, Identity, and Canadian Mennonite Music." *Ethnomusicology* 55, no. 2: 229–54.

———. 2017. *Congregational Music, Conflict, and Community.* New York: Routledge.

Eade, John, and Michael J. Sallnow. 2013. 2nd ed. *Contesting the Sacred: The Anthropology of Pilgrimage.* Eugene, OR: Wipf and Stock.

Ediger, Gerald. 2004. "The Proto-Genesis of the March for Jesusmovement, 1970–87." *Journal of Pentecostal Theology* 12, no. 2: 247–75.

Ediger, Gerald C. 2000. "Strategic-Level Spiritual Warfare in Historical Retrospect." *Direction* 29, no. 2: 125–41.

Eldridge, John. 2011. "On Authenticity—From the Heart." *Worship Training,* February 7, 2011. Accessed December 15, 2017. https://www.worshiptraining. com/media/from-the-heart/

Elisha, Omri. 2010. "Taking the (Inner) City for God: Ambiguities of Urban Social Engagement among Conservative White Evangelicals." In *The Fundamentalist City? Religiosity and the Remaking of Urban Space,* edited by Nezar AlSayyad and Mejgan Massoumi, 235–56. London and New York: Routledge.

Elsner, John, and Simon Coleman, eds. 2003. *Pilgrim Voices: Narrative and Authorship in Christian Pilgrimage.* New York: Berghahn.

Engelhardt, Jeffers. 2009. "Right Singing in Estonian Orthodox Christianity: A Study of Music, Theology, and Religious Ideology." *Ethnomusicology* 53, no. 1: 32–57.

———. 2015. *Singing the Right Way: Orthodox Christians and Secular Enchantment in Estonia.* Oxford and New York: Oxford University Press.

Eskridge, Larry. 1998. "'One Way': Billy Graham, the Jesus Generation, and the Idea of an Evangelical Youth Culture." *Church History* 67, no. 1: 83–106.

———. 2012. "How Many Evangelicals Are There? Institute for the Study of American Evangelicals. Accessed May 2, 2017. http://www2.wheaton.edu/isae/ defining_evangelicalism.html.

———. 2013. *God's Forever Family: The Jesus People Movement in America.* New York: Oxford University Press.

———. 2014. "Evangelicalism: Defining the Term in Contemporary Times." Institute for the Study of American Evangelicals. Accessed May 2, 2017. http://www2. wheaton.edu/isae/defining_evangelicalism.html.

Evans, Mark. 2006. *Open up the Doors: Music in the Modern Church.* Studies in Popular Music. London: Equinox.

———. 2015. "Hillsong Abroad: Tracing the Songlines of Contemporary Pentecostal Music." In *The Spirit of Praise: Music and Worship in Global Pentecostal-Charismatic Christianity,* edited by Monique M. Ingalls and Amos Yong, 179–96. University Park: Pennsylvania State University Press.

Fer, Yannick. 2007. "Pentecôtisme et modernité urbaine: Entre déterritorialisation des identités et réinvestissement symbolique de l'espace urbain." *Social Compass* 54, no. 2: 201–10.

FitzGerald, Frances. 2017. *The Evangelicals: The Struggle to Shape America.* New York: Simon and Schuster.

Frame, John M. 1997. *Contemporary Worship Music: A Biblical Defense.* Phillipsburg, NJ: Presbyterian and Reformed Press.

Freedman, Samuel G. 2009. "Evangelical, and Young, and Active in New Area." *New York Times,* November 27, 2009. http://www.nytimes.com/2009/11/28/ us/28religion.html.

Frith, Simon. 1996. *Performing Rites: On the Value of Popular Music.* Oxford and New York: Oxford University Press.

———, ed. 2015. *On Record: Rock, Pop and the Written Word*. 2nd ed. London: Routledge.

Frith, Simon, and Angela McRobbie. [1978] 1990. "Rock and Sexuality." In *On Record: Rock, Pop, and the Written Word*, edited by Simon Frith and Andrew Goodwin, 371–89. New York: Pantheon.

Fromm, Charles E. 2006. "Textual Communities and New Song in the Multimedia Age: The Routinization of Charisma in the Jesus Movement." PhD diss., Fuller Theological Seminary.

Galli, Mark. 2011. "The End of Worship Wars." *Christianity Today* "The Trajectory of Worship," edited by Mark Galli, 55, no. 3: 4–5.

Gergen, Kenneth J., and Regine Walter. 1998. "Real/Izing the Relational." *Journal of Social and Personal Relationships* 15, no. 1: 110–26.

Gladwin, Ryan R. 2015. "Charismatic Music and the Pentecostalizatoin of Latin American Evangelicalism." In *The Spirit of Praise: Music and Worship in Global Pentecostal-Charismatic Christianity*, edited by Monique M. Ingalls and Amos Yong, 199–214. University Park: Pennsylvania State University Press.

Goffman, Erving. 1967. *Interaction Ritual: Essays on Face-to-Face Behavior*. Garden City, NY: Anchor Books.

Goldberg, Greg. 2011. "Rethinking the Public/Virtual Sphere: The Problem with Participation." *New Media and Society* 13, no. 5: 739–54.

Good, Kristin R. 2009. *Municipalities and Multiculturalism: The Politics of Immigration in Toronto and Vancouver*. Studies in Comparative Political Economy and Public Policy. Toronto: University of Toronto Press.

Goodman, Steve. 2010. *Sonic Warfare: Sound, Affect, and the Ecology of Fear*. Technologies of Lived Abstraction. Cambridge, MA: MIT Press.

Goodstein, Laurie. 2008. "Obama Made Gains among Younger Evangelical Voters, Data Show." *New York Times*, November 6, 2008. http://www.nytimes.com/2008/11/07/us/politics/07religion.html.

———. 2016. "Donald Trump Reveals Evangelical Rifts That Could Shape Politics for Years." *New York Times*, October 17, 2016. https://www.nytimes.com/2016/10/17/us/donald-trump-evangelicals-republican-vote.html.

Greene, Paul D. 2003. "Ordering a Sacred Terrain: Melodic Pathways of Himalayan Flute Pilgrimage." *Ethnomusicology* 47, no. 2: 205–27.

Gushee, David P. 2008a. "Emerging Evangelical Center May Decide 2008 Election." *American Baptist Press*. Accessed October 1, 2010. http://www.abpnews.com/content/view/3150/121/

Gushee, David P. 2008b. *Future of Faith in American Politics: The Public Witness of the Evangelical Center*. Waco, TX: Baylor University Press.

Haight, Roger D. 2004a. *Christian Community in History*. Vol. 1: *Historical Ecclesiology*. New York: Bloomsbury.

———. 2004b. *Christian Community in History*. Vol. 2: *Comparative Ecclesiology*. New York: Bloomsbury.

Hamilton, Michael S. 1999. "The Triumph of Praise Songs: How Guitars Beat out the Organ in the Worship Wars." *Christianity Today*, July 12, 25–35.

Hannerz, Ulf. 1996. *Transnational Connections: Culture, People, Places*. London and New York: Routledge.

Hansen, Collin. 2013. "Keith Getty on What Makes 'In Christ Alone' Accepted and Contested." Reformed Gospel Coalition. https://www.thegospelcoalition.org/article/keith-getty-on-what-makes-in-christ-alone-beloved-and-contested.

Hartford Institute for Religion Research. 2010. "Database of Megachurches in the U.S." Accessed May 2, 2017. http://www.hirr.hartsem.edu/megachurch/database.html.

Hatch, Nathan O. 1989. *The Democratization of American Christianity*. New Haven, CT: Yale University Press.

Hayles, N. Katharine. 1999. "The Condition of Virtuality." In *The Digital Dialectic: New Essays on New Media*, edited by Peter Lunenfeld, 68–95. Leonardo. Cambridge, MA: MIT Press.

Haynes, Maren. 2017 "'Punk Rock Calvinists Who Hate the Modern Worship Movement': Ritual, Power, and White Masculinity in Mars Hill Church's Worship Music." PhD diss., University of Washington.

Hendershot, Heather. 2004. *Shaking the World for Jesus: Media and Conservative Evangelical Culture*. Chicago: University of Chicago Press.

Hewitt, Steve. 2014. "CCMag's 2014 Church Management Software Overview." *Christian Computing Magazine* 26, no. 10: 4–23.

Hicks, Zac. 2015. "How EDM Is Changing the Form of Song Structure in Pop Music . . . and Maybe Congregational Music." *Zac Hicks // Worship. Church. Theology. Culture* (blog). February 5, 2015. Accessed March 10, 2015. http://www.zachicks.com/how-edm-is-changing-the-form-of-song-structure-in-pop music-and-maybe-congregational music.

Hill, Joshua. 2017. "True Worship Is More Than Singing in Church." *Relevant*. November 30, 2017. Accessed December 12, 2017. https://relevantmagazine.com/god/true-worship-more-singing-church.

Hills, Matthew. 2002. *Fan Cultures*. London: Routledge.

Hillsong Church. 2016. "Hillsong Church Australia Annual Report 2015." Accessed April 26, 2017. http://hillsong.com/policies/annual-report-australia.

Hinson, Glenn. 2000. *Fire in My Bones: Transcendence and the Holy Spirit in African American Gospel*. Philadelphia: University of Pennsylvania Press.

Holt, Douglas B. 2002. "Why Do Brands Cause Trouble? A Dialectical Theory of Consumer Culture and Branding." *Journal of Consumer Research* 29, no. 1: 70–90.

Holt, Fabian. 2011. "Is Music Becoming More Visual? Online Video Content in the Music Industry." *Visual Studies* 26, no. 1: 50–61.

Holvast, René. 2009. *Spiritual Mapping in the United States and Argentina: 1989– 2005 : A Geography of Fear*. Leyden, The Netherlands: Brill.

Howard, Jay R., and John M. Streck. 1999. *Apostles of Rock: The Splintered World of Contemporary Christian Music*. Lexington: University Press of Kentucky.

Howard, Robert Glenn. 2011. *Digital Jesus: The Making of a New Christian Fundamentalist Community on the Internet*. New York: New York University Press.

Hunt, Stephen. 1997. "'Doing the Stuff': The Vineyard Connection." In *Charismatic Christianity: Sociological Perspectives*, edited by Stephen Hunt, Malcolm Hamilton, and Tony Walter, 77–96. Basingstoke, UK: Macmillan.

Huque, Muhammad Enamul. 2009. "Belonging through Participation: An Exploration of the Caribana, Pride, and Santa Claus Parades in Toronto, 1998–2004." PhD diss., University of Toronto.

Hustad, Don. 1993. *Jubilate II: Church Music in Worship and Renewal*. Carol Stream, IL: Hope.

Ingalls, Monique M. 2008. "Awesome in This Place: Sound, Space, and Identity in Contemporary North American Evangelical Worship." PhD, University of Pennsylvania.

———. 2011. "Singing Heaven Down to Earth: Spiritual Journeys, Eschatological Sounds, and Community Formation in Evangelical Conference Worship." *Ethnomusicology* 55, no. 2 (Summer): 255–79.

———. 2012a. "Contemporary Worship Music." In *Continuum Encyclopedia of Popular Music of the World*. Vol. 8, *Genres: North America*, edited by John Shepherd and David Horn, 147–52. London: A and C Black.

———. 2012b. "Singing Praise in the Streets: Performing Canadian Christianity through Public Worship in Toronto's Jesus in the City Parade." *Culture and Religion* 13, no. 3: 337–59.

———. 2014. "International Gospel and Christian Music." In *The Continuum Encyclopedia of Popular Music of the World*. *Vol. 12: International Genres*, edited by John Shepherd and David Horn. A and C Black. http://333sound.com/2014/06/09/epmow-vol-9-gospel-and-christian-popularmusic/.

———. 2015a. "Introduction: Interconnection, Interface, and Identification in Pentecostal-Charismatic Music and Worship." In *The Spirit of Praise: Music and Worship in Global Pentecostal-Charismatic Christianity*, edited by Monique M. Ingalls and Amos Yong, 1–25. University Park: Pennsylvania State University Press.

———. 2015b. "Transnational Connections, Musical Meaning, and the 1990s 'British Invasion' of North American Evangelical Worship Music." *Oxford Handbook of Music and World Christianities*, edited by Jonathan Dueck and Suzel Ana Reily, 425–45. New York: Oxford University Press.

———. 2016. "Worship on the Web." In *Music and the Broadcast Experience: Performance, Production, and Audiences*, edited by Christina Baade and James A. Deaville, 293–308. Oxford University Press.

———. 2017. "Style Matters: Contemporary Worship Music and the Meaning of Popular Musical Borrowings." In "Worship in an Age of Reconstruction," edited by Lester Ruth. *Liturgy* 32, no. 1: 7–15.

———. Forthcoming. "Digital Devotion: Online Multimedia in Ritual and Religious Practice." In *The Cambridge Companion to Music and Digital Culture*, edited by Nicholas Cook, Monique M. Ingalls, and David Trippett. Cambridge: Cambridge University Press.

Ingalls, Monique M., Carolyn Landau, and Thomas Wagner, eds. 2013a. *Christian Congregational Music: Performance, Identity, and Experience*. Farnham, UK: Ashgate.

———. 2013b. "Performing Theology, Forming Identity and Shaping Experience: Christian Congregational Music in Europe and North America." In *Christian Congregational Music: Performance, Identity, and Experience*, edited by Monique M. Ingalls, Carolyn Landau, and Thomas Wagner, 1–15. Farnham, UK: Ashgate.

Ingalls, Monique M., Anna E. Nekola, and Andrew Theodore Mall. 2013. "Christian Popular Music, USA." *The Canterbury Dictionary of Hymnology*, Canterbury, UK: Canterbury University Press. www.hymnology.co.uk.

Ingalls, Monique M., and Amos Yong, eds. 2015. *The Spirit of Praise: Music and Worship in Global Pentecostal-Charismatic Christianity*. University Park: Pennsylvania State University Press.

Intercession Working Group of the Lausanne Committee for World Evangelization. 1993. "Statement on Spiritual Warfare (1993)." Lausanne Movement. July 14, 1993. https://www.lausanne.org/content/statement/statement-on-spiritual-warfare-1993.

InterVarsity Christian Fellowship. 2006. *The Urbana 06 Handbook*. Downers Grove, IL: InterVarsity Press.

———. "Vital Statistics." n.d. Accessed 16 May 2015. http://www.intervarsity.org/about/our/vital-statistics.

Jackson, Anthony, ed. 1987. *Anthropology at Home*. London: Tavistock.

Jackson, Jean. 2016. "Changes in Fieldnotes Practice over the Past Thirty Years in U.S. Anthropology." In *eFieldnotes: The Makings of Anthropology in the Digital World*, edited by Roger Sanjek and Susan W. Tratner, 42–64. Philadelphia: University of Pennsylvania Press.

Jenkins, Henry. 2006. *Convergence Culture: Where Old and New Media Collide*. New York: New York University Press.

Jethani, Skye. 2013. *Divine Commodity: Discovering a Faith beyond Consumer Christianity*. Grand Rapids, MI: Zondervan.

Johnson, Birgitta Joelisa. 2008. "'Oh, for a Thousand Tongues to Sing': Music and Worship in African American Megachurches of Los Angeles, California." PhD. diss., University of California, Los Angeles.

Johnson, Birgitta J. 2011. "Back to the Heart of Worship: Praise and Worship Music in a Los Angeles African-American Megachurch." *Black Music Research Journal* 31, no. 1: 105–29.

———. 2015. "'This Is Not the Warm-Up Act!' How Praise and Worship Reflects Expanding Musical Traditions and Theology in a Bapticostal Charismatic African American Megachurch." In *The Spirit of Praise: Music and Worship in Global Pentecostal-Charismatic Christianity*, edited by Monique M. Ingalls and Amos Yong, 117–32. University Park: Pennsylvania State University Press.

Johnson, E. Patrick. 2005. "Performing Blackness Down Under: Gospel Music in Australia." In *Black Cultural Traffic: Crossroads in Global Performance and Popular Culture*, edited by Harry Justin Elam, 59–82. Ann Arbor: University of Michigan Press.

Joyce, Michael. 1995. *Of Two Minds: Hypertext Pedagogy and Poetics*. Studies in Literature and Science. Ann Arbor: University of Michigan Press.

Justice, Deborah. 2015. "When Church and Cinema Combine: Blurring Boundaries through Media-Savvy Evangelicalism." *Journal of Religion, Media and Digital Culture* 3, no. 1: 84–119.

Justice, Deborah R. 2012. "Sonic Change, Social Change, Sacred Change: Music and the Reconfiguration of American Christianity." PhD diss., Indiana University.

Kärki, Kimi. 2005. "'Matter of Fact It's All Dark': Audiovisual Stadium Rock Aesthetics in Pink Floyd's *The Dark Side of the Moon Tour*, 1973." In *Speak to Me: The Legacy of Pink Floyd's* The Dark Side of the Moon, edited by Russell Reising, 27–42. Farnham, UK: Ashgate.

Keller, Timothy. 2017. "Can Evangelicalism Survive Donald Trump and Roy Moore?" 2017. *New Yorker News Desk*, December 19, 2017. Accessed December 21, 2017. https://www.newyorker.com/news/news-desk/can-evangelicalism-survive-donald-trump-and-roy-moore?mbid=social_facebook.

Kendrick, Graham. 1991. *Make Way Public Praise*. Eastbourne, UK: Kingsway Music.

———. 1992. *Public Praise: Celebrating Jesus on the Streets of the World*. Altamonte Springs, FL: Creation House.

Kendrick, Graham, Gerald Coates, Roger Forster, and Lynn Green. 1992. *March for Jesus: The How and Why of Public Praise; The Official Story*. Eastbourne, UK: Kingsway.

Kimball, Dan. 2004. *Emerging Worship: Creating Worship Gatherings for New Generations*.Grand Rapids, MI: Zondervan.

Klaver, Miranda. 2015. "Worship Music as Aesthetic Domain of Meaning and Bonding: The Glocal Context of a Dutch Pentecostal Church." In *The Spirit of Praise: Music and Worship in Global Pentecostal-Charismatic Christianity*, edited by Monique M. Ingalls and Amos Yong, 97–113. University Park: Pennsylvania State University Press.

Klomp, Mirella. Forthcoming. "Ecclesioscapes: Interpreting Gatherings around Christian Music in and outside the Church through the Dutch Case of the 'Sing Along *Matthäuspassion*.'" In *Studying Congregational Music: Key Issues, Methods, and Theoretical Perspectives*, edited by Andrew Mall, Jeffers Engelhardt, and Monique M. Ingalls. London: Routledge.

Klomp, Mirella, and Marcel Barnard. 2017. "Sacro-soundscapes: Contemporary Ritual Performances of Sacred Music: The Case of 'The Passion' in the Netherlands." *International Journal of Practical Theology* 21, no. 2: 1–19.

Krattenmaker, Tom. 2017. "A Suggestion for Younger Evangelicals: Lose the Label." *Religion News Service*, November 13, 2017. Accessed November 15, 2017. http://religionnews.com/2017/11/13/a-suggestion-for-younger-evangelicals-lose-the-label.

Kurtzleben, Danielle. 2015. "Are You An Evangelical? Are You Sure?" National Public Radio, December 19, 2015. Accessed December 15, 2017. https://www.npr.org/2015/12/19/458058251/are-you-an-evangelical-are-you-sure.

Labberton, Mark, ed. 2018. *Still Evangelical? Insiders Reconsider Political, Social, and Theological Meaning*. Downer's Grove, IL: InterVarsity Press.

Labberton, Mark, and Richard Mouw. 2016 "Post-Election Evangelical: A Statement from Mark Labberton and Richard Mouw." Fuller Studio. November 14, 2016. Accessed April 24, 2017. https://fullerstudio.fuller.edu/post-election-evangelical-statement-mark-labberton-richard-mouw/.

Lange, Patricia G. 2007. "Publicly Private and Privately Public: Social Networking on YouTube." *Journal of Computer-Mediated Communication* 13, no. 1: 361–80.

Lanham, Richard A. 1999. *The Electronic Word: Democracy, Technology, and the Arts*. 2nd ed. Chicago: University of Chicago Press.

Lawther, Sarah. 2009. "What Is 'On?': An Exploration of Iconographical Representation of Traditional Religious Organizations on the Homepages of Their Websites." In *Exploring Religion and the Sacred in a Media Age*, edited by Christopher Deacy and Elisabeth Arweck, 219–235. Farnham, UK and Burlington, VT: Ashgate.

Levinas, Emmanuel. 1998. *Entre Nous: On Thinking-of-the-Other*. New York: Columbia University Press.

Lewis, David, and Darren Bridger. 2001. *The Soul of the New Consumer: Authenticity; What We Buy and Why in the New Economy*. London: Nicholas Brealey.

Liesch, Barry Wayne. 2001. *The New Worship: Straight Talk on Music and the Church*. Expanded ed. Grand Rapids, MI: Baker.

Lim, Swee Hong, and Lester Ruth. 2017. *Lovin' on Jesus: A Concise History of Contemporary Worship*. Nashville: Abingdon.

Lubken, Deborah. 2005. "iPresence: Experiencing the Mediated Presence of God." Annual Conference of the Society for the Scientific Study of Religion. Rochester, NY.

Lucado, Andrea. 2015. "Do You Worship Your Worship Experience?" *Relevant*, April 3, 2015. Accessed June 28, 2016. http://archives.relevantmagazine.com/god/church/do-you-worship-your-worship-experience.

Lugo, Louis, and Pew Research Group. 2008. "U.S. Religious Landscape Study." Pew Research Center's Religion and Public Life Project. Washington, DC. http://www.pewforum.org/religious-landscape-study.

Luhrmann, T. M. 2012. *When God Talks Back: Understanding the American Evangelical Relationship with God*. New York: Alfred A. Knopf.

Lummis, Adair. 1998. "Judicatory Niches and Negotiations." In *Association for the Sociology of Religion*. San Francisco, CA. http://hirr.hartsem.edu/denom/judicatories_Lummis1.html.

Lysloff, Rene T. A. 2003. "Musical Community on the Internet: An On-Line Ethnography." *Cultural Anthropology* 18, no. 2: 233–63.

Magowan, Fiona. 2007. "Globalisation and Indigenous Christianity: Translocal Sentiments in Australian Aboriginal Christian Songs." *Identities* 14, no. 4: 459–83. https://doi:10.1080/10702890701578472.

Mall, Andrew. 2015. "'We Can Be Renewed': Resistance and Worship at the Anchor Fellowship." In *The Spirit of Praise: Music and Worship in Global Pentecostal-Charismatic Christianity*, edited by Monique M. Ingalls and Amos Yong, 163–78. University Park: Pennsylvania State University Press.

Mall, Andrew Theodore. 2012. "'The Stars Are Underground': Undergrounds, Mainstreams, and Christian Popular Music." PhD diss., University of Chicago.

Margry, P. J. 2008. *Shrines and Pilgrimage in the Modern World: New Itineraries into the Sacred*. Amsterdam: Amsterdam University Press.

Marti, Gerardo. 2012. *Worship across the Racial Divide: Religious Music and the Multiracial Congregation*. New York and Oxford: Oxford University Press.

Marti, Gerardo, and Gladys Ganiel. 2014. *The Deconstructed Church: Understanding Emerging Christianity*. New York: Oxford University Press.

McGuire, Meredith B. 1982. *Pentecostal Catholics: Power, Charisma, and Order in a Religious Movement*. Philadelphia: Temple University Press.

McLoughlin, William Gerald. 1980. *Revivals, Awakenings, and Reform: An Essay on Religion and Social Change in America, 1607–1977*, revised ed. Chicago: University of Chicago Press.

McRoberts, Omar M. 2003. *Streets of Glory: Church and Community in a Black Urban Neighborhood*. Chicago: University of Chicago Press.

Merritt, Jonathan. 2015. "Defining 'Evangelical.'" *The Atlantic*, December 7, 2015. Accessed December 15, 2017. https://www.theatlantic.com/politics/archive/2015/12/evangelical-christian/418236/

Meyer, Birgit, ed. 2009a. *Aesthetic Formations: Media, Religion, and the Senses*. Religion/Culture/Critique. New York: Palgrave Macmillan.

———. 2009b. "Introduction: From Imagined Communities to Aesthetic Formations: Religious Mediations, Sensational Forms, and Style of Binding." In *Aesthetic Formations: Media, Religion, and the Senses*, edited by Birgit Meyer, 1–28. New York: Palgrave Macmillan.

Miller, Darin. 2006. "Urbana 06 Breaks Registration Record." *Urbana Today*, December 28, 2006.

Miller, Kiri. 2012. *Playing Along: Digital Games, YouTube, and Virtual Performance*. New York: Oxford University Press.

Miller, Steve. 1993. *The Contemporary Christian Music Debate*. Wheaton, IL: Tyndale House.

Moore, Allan. 2002. "Authenticity as Authentication." *Popular Music* 21, no. 2: 209–23.

Moore, Jason, and Len Wilson. 2006. *Design Matters: Creating Powerful Images for Worship*. Nashville: Abingdon.

Moore, Marissa Anne Glynias. 2018a. "Voicing the World: Global Song in American Christian Worship." PhD dissertation, Yale University.

Moore, Marissa Glynias. 2018b. "Sounding the Congregational Voice." *Yale Journal of Music and Religion* 4, no. 1, Article 3. https://doi.org/10.17132/2377-231X.1093.

Morgan, David. 1996. "'Would Jesus Have Sat for a Portrait?' The Likeness of Christ in the Popular Reception of Sallman's Art." In *Icons of American Protestantism: The Art of Warner Sallman*, edited by David Morgan, 181–206. New Haven, CT: Yale University Press.

———. 1998. *Visual Piety: A History and Theory of Popular Religious Images*. Berkeley: University of California Press.

———. 2007. *The Lure of Images: A History of Religion and Visual Media in America*. Religion, Media, and Culture Series. London and New York: Routledge.

Morgenthaler, Sally. 1998. "Out of the Box: Authentic Worship in a Postmodern Culture." *Worship Leader*, July.

Moring, Mark. 2001. "I Could Sing of Your Love Forever." *Campus Life*, January: 20–14.

Muchow, Rick. 2006. "Heard and Not Seen." *Leadership Journal* 27(1): 15-16.

Muller, Carol Ann. 1999. *Rituals of Fertility and the Sacrifice of Desire: Nazarite Women's Performance in South Africa*. Chicago, Ill.: University of Chicago Press.

Myrick, Nathan. 2017. "Relational Power, Music, and Identity: The Emotional Efficacy of Congregational Song." *Yale Journal of Music and Religion* 3, no. 1: Article 5. https://doi.org/10.17132/2377-231X.1060.

Negus, Keith. 1997. *Popular Music in Theory: An Introduction*. Hanover, NH: University Press of New England.

Nekola, Anna E. 2009. "Between This World and the Next: The Musical 'Worship Wars' and Evangelical Ideology in the United States, 1960–2005." PhD diss., University of Wisconsin–Madison.

———. 2011. "US Evangelicals and the Redefinition of Worship Music." In *Mediating Faiths: Religion and Socio-Cultural Change in the Twenty-First Century*, edited by Michael Bailey and Guy Redden, 131–45. Farnham, UK and Burlington, VT: Ashgate.

———. 2013. "'I'll Take You There': The Promise of Transformation in the Marketing of Worship Media in US Christian Music Magazines." In *Christian Congregational Music: Performance, Identity, and Experience*, edited by Monique M. Ingalls, Carolyn Landau, and Thomas Wagner, 117–136. Farnham, UK: Ashgate.

———. 2015. "Worship Media as Media Form and Mediated Practice: Theorizing the Intersections of Media, Music and Lived Religion." In *Congregational Music-Making and Community in a Mediated Age*, edited by Anna E. Nekola and Tom Wagner, 1–21. Congregational Music Studies. Farnham, UK: Ashgate.

Nekola, Anna E., and Tom Wagner, eds. 2015. *Congregational Music-Making and Community in a Mediated Age*. Farnham, UK: Ashgate.

Nieman, James, and Roger Haight. 2012. "On the Dynamic Relation between Ecclesiology and Congregational Studies." In *Explorations in Ecclesiology and Ethnography*, edited by Christian Scharen, 9–33. Grand Rapids, MI: Eerdmans.

O'Leary, Stephen D. 1996. "Cyberspace as Sacred Space: Communicating Religion on Computer Networks." *Journal of the American Academy of Religion* 64, no. 4: 781–808.

Patterson, Chelsea. 2015. "Interview with Chris Tomlin: Worship Night in America." *Patheos*, August 11, 2015. Accessed December 27, 2017. http://www.patheos.com/blogs/joyindestructible/2015/08/11/interview-with-chris-tomlin-worship-night-in-america.

Percy, Martyn. 1996. *Words, Wonders and Power: Understanding Contemporary Christian Fundamentalism and Revivalism.* London: S.P.C.K.

———. 1998. "The Morphology of Pilgrimage in the 'Toronto Blessing.'" *Religion* 28, no. 3: 281–88.

Peters, Ted. 1994. "Worship Wars: Battling on Four Fronts." *Dialog* 33, no. 3: 166–72.

Pew Research Center. 2016. "Evangelicals Rally to Trump, Religious 'Nones' Back Clinton." Pew Research Center's Religion and Public Life Project. July 13, 2016. http://www.pewforum.org/2016/07/13/evangelicals-rally-to-trump-religious-nones-back-clinton.

Pine, B. Joseph, and James H. Gilmore. 1999. *The Experience Economy: Work Is Theatre and Every Business a Stage.* Boston: Harvard Business School Press.

Poloma, Margaret M. 2003. *Main Street Mystics: The Toronto Blessing and Reviving Pentecostalism.* Walnut Creek, CA: AltaMira.

Porter, Mark. 2014. "The Developing Field of Christian Congregational Music Studies." *Ecclesial Practices* 1, no. 2: 149–66.

Porter, Mark James. 2017. *Contemporary Worship Music and Everyday Musical Lives.* Ashgate Congregational Music Studies. New York and Abingdon, UK: Routledge.

Price, Deborah Evans. 1999a. "'Praise and Worship' Music Extending Its Retail, Radio Reach." In *Billboard* 49, nos. 3–6: 110.

———. 1999b. "Shake-Ups Hit Christian Labels." In *Billboard* 13, no. 1: 111.

———. 2003. "Praise and Worship Genre Blessed with Global Growth." In *Billboard* 7, no. 36: 115.

———. 2004a. "Praise and Worship: A Primer." In *Billboard* 17, no. 36: 116.

———. 2004b. "Praise and Worship: Compilations on the Rise." In *Billboard* 17, no. 36: 116.

———. 2008. "Praised Be! Worship Music Jumps from the Church to the Charts." *Billboard* 120, no. 41: 27–30.

Rabey, Steve. 1991. "Maranatha! Comes of Age." *Christianity Today* 35, no. 5: 44–47.

Rachele, Warren. 2008. "A Growing Ensemble: Worship Presentation Software Continues to Evolve." In *Building Blocks of an A/V Ministry*. Digital download. Accessed February 15, 2015. https://www.bclstore.com/products/building-blocks-of-an-a-v-ministry.

Rausch, David. 2002. "Multimedia 101." *Your Church: Prepared for Ministry*. http://www.christianitytoday.com/yc/2002/novdec/1.12.html.

Reagan, Wen. 2015. "A Beautiful Noise: A History of Contemporary Worship Music in Modern America." PhD diss., Duke University.

Redman, Robb. 2002. *The Great Worship Awakening: Singing a New Song in the Postmodern Church.* San Francisco: Jossey-Bass.

———. 2004. "Worship Wars or Worship Awakening?" Special issue, "Worship Wars," edited by Frank Senn, *Liturgy* 19, no. 4: 39–44.

Regis, Helen A. 1999. "Second Lines, Minstrelsy, and the Contested Landscapes of New Orleans Afro-Creole Festivals." *Cultural Anthropology* 14, no. 4: 472–504.

Reily, Suzel Ana. 2002. *Voices of the Magi: Enchanted Journeys in Southeast Brazil.* Chicago: University of Chicago Press.

Riccitelli, James Michael. 1997. *Sing a New Song: When Music Divides the Church*. Blissfield, MI: H and E Berk.

Riches, Tanya. 2010. "The Evolving Theological Emphasis of Hillsong Worship (1996–2007)." *Australasian Pentecostal Studies* 13, no. 87–133.

Riches, Tanya, and Tom Wagner. 2012. "The Evolution of Hillsong Music: From Australian Pentecostal Congregation into Global Brand." *Australian Journal of Communication* 39, no. 1: 17–36.

Robertson, Campbell. 2018. "A Quiet Exodus: Why Black Worshipers Are Leaving White Evangelical Churches." *The New York Times*, March 10, 2018, p. A1. Accessed March 11, 2018. https://www.nytimes.com/2018/03/09/us/blacks-evangelical-churches.html.

Rommen, Timothy. 2007. *"Mek Some Noise": Gospel Music and the Ethics of Style in Trinidad*. Berkeley: University of California Press.

Rosaldo, Renato. 1993. *Culture and Truth: The Remaking of Social Analysis*. Boston: Beacon.

Ruppert, Evelyn S. 2006. *The Moral Economy of Cities: Shaping Good Citizens*. Toronto: University of Toronto Press.

Ruth, Lester. 2017a. "The Eruption of Worship Wars: The Coming of Conflict." *Liturgy* 32, no. 1: 3–6.

———. 2017b. "Worship in an Age of Reconstruction: Introduction." *Liturgy* 32, no. 1: 1–2.

Ryan, Paul. 2010. "Authentic Worship in a Feel-Good Culture." *Reformed Worship* 96 (June 2010): 46.

Sample, Tex. 2005. *Powerful Persuasion: Multimedia Witness in Christian Worship*. Nashville: Abingdon Press.

Sánchez, Gherman. 2008. "Historia de CanZion." Online video recording at Instituto CanZion: Director de Alabanza.com. http://www.directordealabanza.com/index.php?option=com_content&view=article&id=207%3Ahistoria-de-canzion&catid=30%3Avideos&Itemid=17.

Scheer, Greg. 2014. "Retune My Heart to Sing Thy Grace: How Old Hymn Texts Found a New Home among Evangelicals." *Hymn* 65, no. 4: 19–27.

Schmalzbauer, John. 2007. "Campus Ministry: A Statistical Portrayal." Social Sciences Research Council Essay Forum on the Religious Engagements of American Undergraduates. http://religion.ssrc.org/reforum.

Schultze, Quentin J. 2004. *High-Tech Worship? Using Presentational Technologies Wisely*. Grand Rapids, MI: Baker.

Senn, Frank C., ed. 2004. *Liturgy* 19(4): *Special Issue: The Worship Wars*. The Liturgical Conference: Taylor and Francis.

Shelemay, Kay Kaufman. 2011. "Musical Communities: Rethinking the Collective in Music." *Journal of the American Musicological Society* 64, no. 2: 349–390, 483.

Shelley, Marshall. 1999. "From the Editor." *Leadership Journal* 20, no. 2: 1–4.

Shuker, Roy. 2005. *Popular Music: The Key Concepts*. 2nd ed. London and New York: Routledge.

Skanse, Richard. 2006. "Corporate and Mainstream: Rock Is Dead, Long Live Rock!" In *The Greenwood Encyclopedia of Rock History*, edited by Lisa M. Scrivani-Tidd, Rhonda Markowitz, Chris Smith, MaryAnn Janosik, and Bob Gulla, 49–86. Westport, CT: Greenwood.

Smietana, Bob. 2016. "2016 Election Exposes Evangelical Divides." *LifeWay Research Newsroom*. October 14, 2016. Accessed April 22, 2017. http://blog.lifeway.com/newsroom/2016/10/14/2016-election-exposes-evangelical-divides.

Smith, Christian. 2002. *Christian America? What Evangelicals Really Want*. Berkeley and London: University of California Press.

Smith Pollard, Deborah 2008. *When the Church Becomes Your Party: Contemporary Gospel Music*. African American Life Series. Detroit: Wayne State University Press.

———. 2013. "'Praise Is What We Do': The Rise of Praise and Worship Music in the Black Church in the U.S." In *Christian Congregational Music: Performance, Identity, and Experience*, edited by Monique M. Ingalls, Carolyn Landau, and Thomas Wagner, 33–48. Farnham, UK: Ashgate.

Sobchack, Vivian. 2004. *Carnal Thoughts: Embodiment and Moving Image Culture*. Berkeley: University of California Press.

———. 2008. "Embodying Transcendence: On the Literal, the Material, and the Cinematic Sublime." *Material Religion* 4, no. 2: 194–203.

Sorge, Bob. 1987. *Exploring Worship: A Practical Guide to Praise and Worship*. Canandaigua, NY: Oasis House.

Spinks, Bryan D. 2010. *The Worship Mall: Contemporary Responses to Contemporary Culture*. New York: Church Publishing.

Stackhouse, John G., Jr. 1990. "The Protestant Experience in Canada since 1945." In *The Canadian Protestant Experience, 1760 to 1990*, edited by George A. Rawlyk, 198–252. Burlington, Canada: Welch.

Steuer, Jonathan. 1992. "Defining Virtual Reality: Dimensions Determining Telepresence." *Journal of Communication* 42, no. 4: 73–93.

Stevenson, Jill. 2013. *Sensational Devotion: Evangelical Performance in Twenty-First-Century America*. Ann Arbor: University of Michigan Press.

Stock, Jonathan P. J., and Chou Chiener. 2008. "Fieldwork at Home: European and Asian Perspectives." In *Shadows in the Field: New Perspectives for Fieldwork in Ethnomusicology*, edited by Gregory Barz and Timothy J. Cooley, 108–24. New York: Oxford University Press.

Stoddard, Robert H., and E. Alan Morinis. 1997. *Sacred Places, Sacred Spaces: The Geography of Pilgrimages*. Baton Rouge: Louisiana State University Press.

Stowe, David W. 2002. "'An Inestimable Blessing': The American Gospel Invasion of 1873." *ATQ* 16, no. 3: 189–212.

Stowe, David W. 2013. *No Sympathy for the Devil: Christian Pop Music and the Transformation of American Evangelicalism*. Chapel Hill: University of North Carolina Press.

Summit, Jeffrey A. 2000. *The Lord's Song in a Strange Land: Music and Identity in Contemporary Jewish Worship*. New York: Oxford University Press.

———. 2016. *Singing God's Words: The Performance of Biblical Chant in Contemporary Judaism*. New York: Oxford University Press.

Swatos, William H., and Luigi Tomasi. 2002. *From Medieval Pilgrimage to Religious Tourism: The Social and Cultural Economics of Piety*. Westport, CT: Praeger.

Thornton, Daniel. 2015. "Exploring the Contemporary Congregational Song Genre: Texts, Practice, and Industry." PhD diss., Macquarie University.

Thornton, Daniel, and Mark Evans. 2015. "YouTube: A New Mediator of Christian Community." In *Congregational Music-Making and Community in a Mediated Age*, edited by Anna E. Nekola and Tom Wagner, 141–60. Congregational Music Studies. Farnham, UK: Ashgate.

Thornton, Sarah. 1996. *Club Cultures: Music, Media and Subcultural Capital*. New York: Wiley and Sons.

Titon, Jeff Todd. 1988. *Powerhouse for God: Speech, Chant, and Song in an Appalachian Baptist Church*. Austin: University of Texas Press.

Tomlin, Chris. 2004. *The Way I Was Made: Words and Music for an Unusual Life*. Sisters, Oregon: Multnomah Press.

Towns, Elmer L. 1997 *Putting an End to Worship Wars*. Lynchburg, VA: Liberty University Press.

Trilling, Lionel. 1972. *Sincerity and Authenticity*. Cambridge, MA: Harvard University Press.

Trouillot, Michel-Rolph. 2007. *Global Transformations: Anthropology and the Modern World*. New York: Palgrave Macmillan.

Turino, Thomas. 2008. *Music as Social Life: The Politics of Participation*. Chicago: University of Chicago Press.

Turner, Victor W., and Edith L. B Turner. 1996. *Image and Pilgrimage in Christian Culture: Anthropological Perspectives*. New York: Columbia University Press.

Useem, Andrea. 2009. "The Networked Congregation: Embracing the Spirit of Experimentation." Alban Institute. http://www.congregationalresources.org/Networked/About.asp.

van Dijck, José. 2009. "Users like You? Theorizing Agency in User-Generated Content." *Media, Culture and Society* 31, no. 1: 41–58. https://doi:10.1177/0163443708098245.

Van Opstal, Sandra Maria. 2016. *The Next Worship: Glorifying God in a Diverse World*. Downers Grove, IL: InterVarsity.

Waddle, Ray. 1995. "A Revival? Where? Episcopal Church Hosts Unusual Scene." *Tennessean*, February 7, 1995, pp. 1A and 2A, col. 1.

Wagner, C. Peter. 1996. *Confronting the Powers: How the New Testament Church Experienced the Power of Strategic Level*. Ventura, CA: Regal.

Wagner, Tom. 2014a. "Branding, Music, and Religion: Standardization and Adaptation in the Experience of the 'Hillsong Sound.'" In *Religion as Brands: New Perspectives on the Marketization of Religion and Spirituality*, edited by Jean-Claude Usunier and Jörg Stolz, 59–73. Farnham, UK and Burlington, VT: Ashgate.

———. 2014b. "Music, Branding and the Hegemonic Prosumption of Values of an Evangelical Growth Church." In *Religion in Times of Crisis*, edited by Gladys Ganiel, Heidemarie Winkel, and Christophe Monnot, 11–32. Leiden: Brill.

———. 2015. "Music as Mediated Object, Music as Medium: Towards a Media Ecological View of Congregational Music." In *Congregational Music-Making and Community in a Mediated Age*, edited by Anna E. Nekola and Tom Wagner, 25–44. Congregational Music Studies. Farnham, UK: Ashgate.

———. 2017. "Christianity, Worship, and Popular Music." In *The Bloomsbury Handbook of Religion and Popular Music*, edited by Christopher Partridge and Marcus Moberg, 90–100. London: Bloomsbury.

Walser, Robert. 1993. *Running with the Devil: Power, Gender, and Madness in Heavy Metal Music*. Music/Culture. Hanover, NH: University Press of New England.

Ward, Pete. 2002. *Liquid Church*. Milton Keynes, UK: Paternoster.

———. 2005. *Selling Worship*. Milton Keynes, UK: Paternoster.

———. 2015. "Blueprint Ecclesiology and the Lived: Normativity as a Perilous Faithfulness." *Ecclesial Practices* 2, no. 1: 74–90.

Warner, Michael. 2002. *Publics and Counterpublics*. New York and Cambridge, MA: Zone.

Warner, R. Stephen. 1994. "The Place of the Congregation in the American Religious Configuration" in *New Perspectives in the Study of Congregations*, volume II of

American Congregations, edited by James P. Wind and James W. Lewis, 54–99. Chicago: University of Chicago Press.

"The Wars of Worship." 2002. *Baylor Magazine*, September–October 2002. July 17, 2002. http://www.baylor.edu/alumni/magazine/0102/news. php?action=story&story=7322.

Webb, Michael. 2015. "Every Creative Aspect Breaking Out!: Pentecostal-Charismatic Worship, Oro Gospel Music, and a Millenialist Aesthetic in Papua New Guinea." In *The Spirit of Praise: Music and Worship in Global Pentecostal-Charismatic Christianity*, edited by Monique M. Ingalls and Amos Yong, 78–96. University Park: Pennsylvania State University Press.

Webber, Robert. 2000. "Authentic Worship in a Changing World: What Happens Next?" *Theology Matters* 6, no. 5. Accessed March 29, 2015. http://www. theologymatters.com/SepOct002.PDF.

Wegner, Phillip E. 2002. *Imaginary Communities: Utopia, the Nation, and the Spatial Histories of Modernity*. Berkeley: University of California Press.

Wehner, Peter. 2017. "Why I Can No Longer Call Myself an Evangelical Republican." *New York Times Sunday Review*, December 9, 2017. Accessed December 12, 2017. https://www.nytimes.com/2017/12/09/opinion/sunday/wehner-evangelical-republicans.html?_r=0.

Wiersbe, Warren W. 2000. *Real Worship: Playground, Battleground, or Holy Ground?* Grand Rapids, MI: Baker.

Wightman, Jill M. 2009. "Healing the Nation: Pentecostal Identity and Social Change in Bolivia." In *Conversion of a Continent Contemporary Religious Change in Latin America*, edited by Timothy Steigenga and Edward L Cleary, 239–55. New Brunswick, NJ: Rutgers University Press.

Wilson, Len. 1999. *The Wired Church*. Nashville: Abingdon.

Wilson, Len, and Jason Moore. 2008. *The Wired Church 2.0*. Nashville: Abingdon.

Witte, Marleen de. 2009. "Modes of Binding, Moments of Bonding: Mediating Divine Touch in Ghanaian Pentecostalism and Traditionalism." In *Aesthetic Formations: Media, Religion, and the Senses*, edited by Birgit Meyer, 183–205. New York: Palgrave Macmillan.

Witvliet, John. 1999. "The Blessing and Bane of the North American Evangelical Megachurch: Implications for Twenty-First Century Congregational Song." *Hymn* 50, no. 1: 6–12.

Wong, Connie Oi Yan. 2006. "Singing the Gospel Chinese Style: 'Praise and Worship' Music in the Asian Pacific." PhD diss., University of California, Los Angeles.

Wood, Abigail. 2008. "E-Fieldwork: A Paradigm for the Twenty-First Century?" In *The New (Ethno)musicologies*, edited by Henry Stobart, 170–87. Lanham, MD: Scarecrow.

Woods, Robert, and Brian Walrath, eds. 2007. *The Message in the Music: Studying Contemporary Praise and Worship*. Nashville: Abingdon.

Wuthnow, Robert. 1989. *The Restructuring of American Religion: Society and Faith since World War II*. Princeton, NJ and Oxford: Princeton University Press.

Wuthnow, Robert. 1994. *Producing the Sacred*. Urbana, Ill.: University of Illinois Press.

York, Terry W. 2003. *America's Worship Wars*. Peabody, MA: Hendrickson.

———. 2014. "Multicultural Congregations and Worship: A Literature Review," *Journal of Family and Community Ministries* 27, no. 1. Accessed February 24, 2015. http://www.familyandcommunityministries.org/journal/article. php?articleid=53.

Young, John F., and Boris DeWiel. 2009. *Faith in Democracy? Religion and Politics in Canada*. Newcastle upon Tyne, UK: Cambridge Scholars.

Young, Shawn David. 2015. *Gray Sabbath: Jesus People USA, Evangelical Left, and the Evolution of Christian Rock*. New York: Columbia University Press.

Zauzmer, Julie. 2016. "Hopeful and Relieved, Conservative White Evangelicals See Trump's Win as Their Own." *Washington Post*, November 11, 2016. https://www.washingtonpost.com/news/acts-of-faith/wp/2016/11/15/hopeful-and-relieved-evangelicals-see-trumps-win-as-their-own.

Zauzmer, Julie, and Sarah Pulliam Bailey. 2017. "After Trump and Moore, Some Evangelicals Are Finding Their Own Label Too Toxic to Use." *Local Headlines: Washington Post Online*, December 14, 2017. Accessed December 17, 2017. https://www.washingtonpost.com/local/social-issues/after-trump-and-moore-some-evangelicals-are-finding-their-own-label-too-toxic-to-use/2017/12/14/b034034c-e020-11e7-89e8-edec16379010_story.html?utm_term=.2df1713f1332.

INDEX

CPSIA information can be obtained
at www.ICGtesting.com
Printed in the USA
BVHW032310030319
541669BV00002B/4/P